DEVELOPING AND LEADING THE SALES ORGANIZATION

THAD B. GREEN

QUORUM BOOKS
Westport, Connecticut • London

Library of Congress Cataloging-in-Publication Data

Green, Thad B.
    Developing and leading the sales organization / Thad B. Green.
      p. cm.
    Includes bibliographical references and index.
    ISBN 1–56720–004–4 (alk. paper)
    1. Sales management. 2. Motivation (Psychology) 3. Sales
personnel. I. Title.
HF5438.4.G72   1998
658.8′1—dc21   97–22745

British Library Cataloguing in Publication Data is available.

Copyright © 1998 by Thad B. Green

All rights reserved. No portion of this book may be reproduced, by any process or technique, without the express written consent of the publisher.

Library of Congress Catalog Card Number: 97–22745
ISBN: 1–56720–004–4

First published in 1998

Quorum Books, 88 Post Road West, Westport, CT 06881
An imprint of Greenwood Publishing Group, Inc.

Printed in the United States of America

The paper used in this book complies with the Permanent Paper Standard issued by the National Information Standards Organization (Z39.48–1984).

10 9 8 7 6 5 4 3 2 1

Contents

	Preface	vii
1.	The Motivation to Buy	1
2.	Motivating People to Buy	13
3.	Selling to Style Is Motivating	25
4.	Prospecting That Motivates	41
5.	Preparing to Motivate	71
6.	Selling That Motivates	105
7.	Closings That Motivate	129
8.	Motivating to Buy Again	159
9.	Self-Management Is Motivating	179
10.	Making Goals Motivating	197
11.	The Motivation to Sell	219
	Index	241

Preface

Sales executives are faced with an enormously complicated job. It can be filled with feelings of both hope and hopelessness. At a distance it looks like a thankless job and an up-close view shows that it indeed can be. On some days it even sounds like a job better suited for someone, anyone, else. The magnitude of the job and the pressure that surrounds it can easily cause sales executives to wish they could just get a better handle on how to develop and lead the sales force more effectively and meet and exceed quota with greater predictability and ease.

Most sales executives observe an interesting and invariably damaging transition in their careers as they move up the ranks from salesperson to sales manager and eventually to the position of sales executive. As they advance they discover that the need to "see the forest for the trees" becomes greater and greater. Fortunately most sales executives make a smooth shift to this way of thinking. Unfortunately, however, they lose their gasp on, and leave behind, the ability to clearly "see the trees." Rather than gaining a new perspective, they tend to trade in the old one for a new one when in fact both are essential to effectively manage a sales organization.

This book is designed to show sales executives how they can continue to "see the forest," and view it more effectively, while at the same time give them a sense for how to "see the trees," to know which trees to focus on and what to do with those that are calling for their attention. Sales executives will find that by touching and feeling the trees they will regain a perspective that will strengthen their decisions and lead to better sales results.

I have tried and tested almost every suggestion in this book over the past five years in a variety of sales organizations across America including many sales organizations within AT&T. Some of the people who made this possible for me include Bill Barkley, Ray Butkus, and Dick Fuller. There are special memories of the hard work and good times with many talented people including Sandra Bond, Le Ann Coe, Ian Cunningham, Pat Gorman, Doris Jean Head, Carol Heller, Lucy Kratovil, and Jane Sanders.

And a special thanks goes to Stacy Green Sindle for her trojan effort on the production side of this book. I also want to thank Shannon Green, Eslie Green, and Jay Knippen for reviewing the book; Kurt Sutton for teaching me about behavior style and how to apply it to the sales process; and Leif Roland for teaching me the principles of NLP that are sprinkled through out the book.

DEVELOPING AND LEADING THE SALES ORGANIZATION

CHAPTER 1

The Motivation to Buy

Sales executives are finding it increasingly difficult to meet their numbers. They see this difficulty in quota attainment. They hear about it from top management. They may even feel it in their compensation. Sales executives are looking around and asking themselves if there is a better way to get a firm grasp on the situation. If approaches currently being used are not focused enough, if they are not exactly the right fit, if results are not meeting expectations, now may be the time to do something different.

Much of the difficulty sales executives face stems from factors over which they have little control. Some of the pressing issues are external, such as changing markets; increased competition; and short supply of experienced, professional salespeople. Others factors clearly are internal, including production and shipping problems, resources for advertising and training, quality customer service, and antiquated support systems. Yet sales executives have a good sense that many factors are within their control. This sounds like a situation that calls for sales executives to take action right away.

In view of this, sales executives may want to focus on improving their sales organization by turning to areas that meet two criteria: (1) areas over which they have significant control and (2) areas that offer plenty of improvement opportunity. Two areas that fit both criteria are: (1) the way the sales forces sells and (2) the way the sales force is managed and motivated to sell. This is exciting since these are hands-on areas where enormous positive impact is possible.

This book discusses a definitive way for sales executives to achieve organizational improvement. The approach simply calls for sales executives to fine tune the way they go about managing, leading, motivating, and training the sales force. Sales executives will conclude that the approach is easy to use, and, more important, that it looks, sounds, and feels right. As a result, many of them may want to listen up and give serious consideration to this approach.

The focus of this book is on showing sales executives how to improve the sales organization by equipping the sales force to apply principles of motivation to the selling process (Chapters 1 through 8). The message is loud and clear. When selling is viewed as motivating people to buy, and when the sales organization learns to sell this way, sales results improve dramatically. This is what any sales executive wants to hear. Equally important are the benefits that can be secured when sales executives also convey this perspective to their managers, particularly sales managers, and encourage and enable them to apply the same principles of motivation when managing, leading, and motivating the sales force (Chapters 9 through 11). In the pages that follow, sales executives will see an exciting approach that sounds right and feels good, and, more important, gives results. This creates the desire to learn more about motivation and selling.

VIEWING SELLING AS THE MOTIVATION TO BUY

The framework for viewing selling as the motivation to buy is derived from the theoretical work on motivation in the workplace during the 1960s by Victor Vroom of Yale University.[1] Vroom's theoretical model, called the expectancy theory of motivation, has been simplified for clarity and an application model has been developed to give it practical value.[2] It is this application model, labeled The Belief System of Motivation and Performance™, that is used as the theoretical and practical foundation for Belief System Selling™.

The Belief System of Motivation and Performance™ clearly points out that people have beliefs about their work that form the basis for their motivation to work. So it is with buyers, too, as they have beliefs about buying that form the basis for their motivation to buy. It is important for salespeople to (1) be aware that beliefs influence buying behavior, (2) identify and clearly see buyer beliefs that can work against them, and (3) call on all of the resources available to them to change those beliefs so they can make the sale.

Beliefs and the Motivation to Buy

Sales executives are aware that buyers hold beliefs that sometimes work in their favor, and sometimes don't. That is, the beliefs may motivate buyers to buy or not to buy, to buy from one organization or another. Sales executives can't help wondering how many of these beliefs get surfaced by their salespeople and how many don't. Once known, the beliefs can be adeptly handled by skilled salespersons. The problem occurs when the beliefs are never heard and never addressed.

Take the case of Mary, a quiet, soft-spoken, very bright manager who did not feel comfortable confronting others. She was the technical communications manager for a large company and was responsible for deciding whether to renew a multimillion-dollar contract with the current telecommunications provider or switch to another one. Mary had observed and felt the impact of not having reliable service and she stressed this in her request for proposals (RFPs). The second concern she focused on was having a provider who would handle downtime problems quickly. She received three elaborate proposals and looked over each one thoroughly before deciding to move her business from Company A to Company B. Six months later, after facing several downtime problems with the new provider, Mary felt that she should have gone with Company C. She talked to the salesperson whose proposal she had rejected and mentioned that his reliability data seemed too good to be true. She also remarked that her decision was swayed by a negative comment she heard from her counterpart in another firm. Mary discussed with the salesperson her reluctance to confront him about the data and rumors. The bottom line is that she was not motivated to buy from Company C because she did not *believe* she would get the kind of reliable service she needed.

Sales executives can observe at least two interesting points about beliefs from this story. First, it does not matter whether the buyer's beliefs are well founded or not; buyers are motivated to buy based on what they *believe* to be true. Second, beliefs that hold back a buyer's motivation to buy are not likely to be addressed when they are unknown to the salesperson.

Sales organizations are more effective when sales executives are outspoken about preparing the sales force to find out what buyers *believe*, what they believe they will *get and want*, what they believe they will *get but not want* (Mary believed she would get unreliable service), and what they believe they will *not get but want*. Preparing the sales force also means stressing the importance that salespeople recognize the behavioral tendencies of their buyers (Mary doesn't like conflict), use that information to predict behavior (Mary will not be confrontive and ask challenging questions), and act accordingly so that damaging beliefs will be heard and handled.

Shared versus Silent Beliefs

Research shows that some people generally are reluctant to talk about beliefs on which their motivation is based and most people feel hesitant to discuss at least some of their beliefs, even when encouraged to do so.[3] As you will see later, it is easy to predict which buyers are most likely to withhold their beliefs. And intuitively we know that some beliefs are more likely to be voiced than others.

Interviews with a sample of buyers confirmed that they are more likely to talk about their beliefs during a sales call when the beliefs revolve around the product or service being sold rather than the people involved. Here are examples of beliefs that buyers say they feel comfortable sharing with salespeople.

- "I don't believe we will get the results we want."
- "I don't think the customer service will be adequate."
- "I don't believe the product quality will meet our standards."
- "I think the maintenance cost will be too expensive."
- "I believe they are giving a better price to our competition."

Buyers indicated they were reluctant to share beliefs during sales calls when the beliefs involved *feelings* about themselves or others. The following are examples of beliefs that buyers say they feel uncomfortable sharing with salespeople.

- "I believe my boss will be upset with me if I buy from you."
- "I think it will be too risky for me personally to change suppliers."
- "I think it will be a painful buying process."
- "I believe I will get a lot of runaround if we have problems."
- "I don't believe I can trust the salesperson."
- "I don't think the salesperson understands my business."
- "I don't believe I will get what is promised."

While some beliefs are more likely to be shared than others, sales executives are aware that even those most likely to be mentioned are not always revealed. Buyers simply do not tell all, not unless skillful salespeople are persistent in uncovering the beliefs. Maybe now is the time to prepare salespeople to surface the beliefs that are working against the motivation to buy.

Improvement Opportunity

Sales executives can imagine that most sales organizations have a preponderance of salespeople who are not consciously aware that buyers are silently holding beliefs that have a negative impact on their motivation to buy. Even when salespeople are aware, they likely are not tuned in to the full range of beliefs. This may mean the sales force is not actively looking for important buyer beliefs and therefore may not have a firm grip on handling those beliefs. If this is true, salespeople are not being as effective as they could be in motivating buyers to buy. The result is that sales organizations are not performing to their potential. Sales executives see this and want to take advantage of this organizational improvement opportunity.

APPLYING PRINCIPLES OF MOTIVATION TO SELLING

The more sales executives understand about the motivation to buy, the better they can equip the sales force and lead the sales organization to greater heights. Why are some people motivated to buy while others are not? Why are some motivated to buy from competitors who clearly do not offer greater value? What conditions must exist for people to be motivated to buy from your organization? Knowing the answer to these and related questions about the motivation to buy is essential for any sales organization to reach its full potential.

Belief System Selling™

The sales model that gives the most complete and most accurate picture of the motivation to buy is Belief System Selling™. The model is based on a chain of events that occur when people—anyone, including buyers—do something, *anything*. The person puts out a certain amount of effort, which results in some level of performance, which leads to certain outcomes, which yield some level of satisfaction, as shown in the following figure. Understanding this chain of events as it applies to buyers provides a new and valuable perspective on how to sell.

The *effort* buyers put out includes things like determining product specifications, identifying sources of funds, reviewing product literature, meeting with salespersons, evaluating available products and services, getting approval to buy, preparing RFPs, reviewing proposals, and making a wide variety of tentative decisions about what to buy, how much, when, preferred delivery dates, and so on. Salespeople see some buyers expend a lot of effort in reaching buying decisions while others appear to put out very little.

Performance in the case of a buyer simply means buying. The *buying* includes finalizing all decisions required to actually make the purchase, then handling those decisions in accordance with the organization's purchasing system and the buyer's personal preferences.

EFFORT ▶ PERFORMANCE ▶ OUTCOMES ▶ SATISFACTION
(*buying*)

The effectiveness of the buyer's performance is judged by the quality of the buying decisions. Some buyers perform well. Others don't. But all buyers are performing in the sense that they are buying.

Buyers see two categories of *outcomes* resulting from their performance, namely organizational and personal outcomes. Once a buying decision is made, outcomes to the organization include: (1) things directly related to the product or service like delivery, quality, performance (does it do what it is supposed to do), and servicing; and (2) things that result from having the product or service like increased sales, higher productivity, and reduced costs.

Personal outcomes to the buyer include: (1) the usual things like promotions, raises, bonuses, praise, recognition, and other similar rewards; and (2) other things like people noticing the improvements resulting from the product or service, everybody talking about how happy they are with the product or service, or evidence of a more relaxed atmosphere now that things are more stable and predictable with the new product or service.

The buyer feels some amount of *satisfaction*, or dissatisfaction, from the outcomes that result from the buying decision. For example, the buyer would be satisfied if a service that was purchased (like sales training) increased sales as expected, but would be dissatisfied if a purchased product (such as manufacturing equipment) did not reduce production cost as anticipated. Other examples include the buyer who would be dissatisfied if the product purchased (say a computer) caused more change and uncertainty than expected and desired, or the buyer who did not get the bottom-line improvement anticipated from the strategic planning services she purchased.

So, how does this effort-performance (buying)-outcomes-satisfaction chain of events influence the motivation to buy? The influence shows up in the *beliefs* that buyers have about the relationship between effort and performance, performance and outcomes, and outcomes and satisfaction. There are three beliefs. Here they are.

The Effort-Performance Belief (B-1)

First, all buyers have a belief about effort leading to performance. Notice, as mentioned earlier, that for the buyer, performance is defined as buying, whereas effort refers to doing those things that lead to the buying decision. Specifically, then, buyers have a belief about whether or not they can actually buy, or whether they can exert the necessary influence to get someone else to buy what they want.

This effort-performance belief flows from three things: need, money, and authority or influence. When buyers have the need, money, and authority or influence, they will believe they can buy. Why? Because they can. If they have the need, but not the money and authority, they still may believe their effort will lead to performance (buying) if they believe they have enough influence over someone with the money and authority to buy.

A person's belief about whether or not he or she can actually make the buying decision, or influence the way it is made, is the first of three beliefs that help explain the motivation to buy. This first belief, called B-1, refers to the buyer's belief about the relationship between effort and performance, as shown in the following diagram. This belief will be treated in depth in the discussion on prospecting and qualifying buyers in Chapter 4.

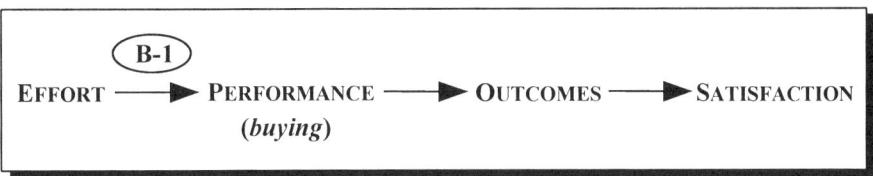

The Performance-Outcomes Belief (B-2)

The second belief all buyers have is the belief about performance (buying) leading to outcomes. This is the belief about whether or not buying the product or service will lead to certain outcomes. For example, if the buyer sees the salesperson as dishonest, she may believe that the outcomes promised will not be forthcoming. This holds back her motivation to buy. On the other hand, she may believe a competing salesperson who provides extensive product documentation about promised outcomes. This will push her motivation to buy a step closer to the competition.

This second belief, called B-2, deals with the buyer's belief about whether or not performance (buying) will lead to certain outcomes, like reducing cost, improving customer service, increasing productivity, and so on. Be aware that B-2 has nothing to do with the desirability of the outcomes, only with the buyer's belief about whether or not buying leads to the outcomes. That is, B-2 is the belief about the relationship between performance (buying) and outcomes, as shown in the following diagram.

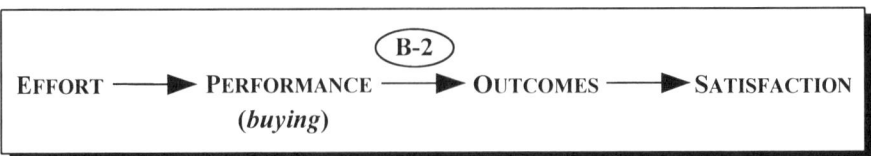

The Outcomes-Satisfaction Belief (B-3)

The third belief all buyers have is the belief about outcomes leading to satisfaction. This is the belief about whether or not the outcomes, if received, will be satisfying. Sometimes, for example, the anticipated outcome of the buying decision is a substantial reduction in cost. Buyers typically feel considerable satisfaction from such an outcome. When outcomes are expected to be satisfying, the motivation to buy is pushed up a notch. The buyer, however, may believe other outcomes will be dissatisfying. For example, the outcome of some purchases can be a negative reaction by employees. Not wanting to face this, the motivation to buy may be pulled down.

This third belief, called B-3, deals with the belief about whether or not outcomes will be satisfying. In other words, buyers say to themselves, "If I buy this, I will get certain things (outcomes). Now which ones do I believe will end up being satisfying to me and which ones will be dissatisfying?" That is, B-3 is the belief about the relationship between outcomes and satisfaction, as shown in the following diagram.

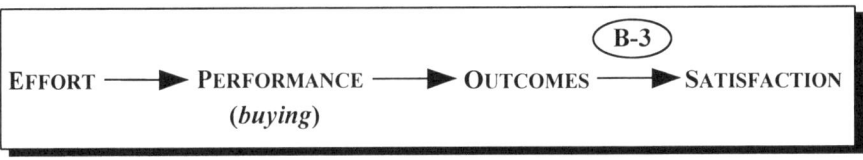

These three beliefs can be summarized with the kind of questions buyers often ask themselves when going through the buying process. Here they are, first in the shorter versions, then in expanded form.

QUESTIONS BUYERS ASK THEMSELVES

B-1	B-2	B-3
"Can I buy this?"	"Will I get them?"	"Do I want them?"
"Can I buy this product or service?"	"Will I get the promised outcomes?"	"Do I want the outcomes?"
"Can I buy this, given the need, money, and authority or influence I have?"	"Will I get the outcomes that are supposed to come with this product (or service)?"	"Do I want the outcomes associated with this product (or service)?"

Here is the big question: How do these three beliefs, namely B-1, B-2, and B-3, influence the motivation to buy? The answer is this. B-1, B-2, and B-3 represent three conditions which must be met for a buyer to buy. Buyers will not buy unless they: (1) believe their effort will lead to performance (buying); (2) believe performance (buying) will lead to certain outcomes; and (3) believe the outcomes will lead to satisfaction. Here are some examples that allow sales executives to see the hard and solid reasons all three of these conditions must be met.

Let's say the prospect has the need for the product or service, it offers everything the buyer is looking for, and the price is fair. Next, let's say there is a money-back guarantee if everything promised is not realized. The buyer says to herself, "This product is priced right and it offers everything we could ever ask for (B-3). I feel certain we will realize all of the expected benefits (B-2). The only problem is that I am not the decision maker, and have no influence over him (a B-1 problem)."

Is this person motivated to buy? No. Even though two of the three conditions are met (B-2 and B-3), she is not motivated to buy because she doesn't believe her effort will result in a buying decision (B-1). She would have the same belief if she were the decision maker but did not have the money to buy ("I can't afford it"). She will not be motivated to buy as long as she believes, "I can't buy." This is a B-1 problem.

Now, let's suppose she has the need, decision-making authority, and the money to buy. Again, let's say the things the salesperson promises of the product or service are clearly what she wants. Finally, let's assume she has bought from this salesperson in the past, but many of his promises have been false claims, and now she has doubts when he tells her what the product or service will do. So, she says to herself. "I have the need, money, and authority to buy (B-1). We want and need everything this product seems to offer (B-3). But I'm really skeptical about getting all that has been promised (B-2)."

Is this person motivated to buy? No. Not as long as she has doubts about getting the promised outcomes (B-2). Even though two of the three conditions are met (B-1 and B-3), she will not be motivated to buy as long as she doesn't believe performance (buying) will lead to outcomes (B-2). She will not be motivated to buy as long as she believes "I will not get the promised outcomes (B-2)." This is a B-2 problem.

Suppose again that she has the need, money, and authority to buy. And let's say she believes the salesperson when he tells her all of the benefits that accompany the product or service, including lower operating cost through staff reductions. She says to herself, "I know we need this and I can buy it if I want to (B-1). I've looked at this product closely and feel certain it will do what it's supposed to do (B-2). But this is not a pretty picture. I don't want everything I'd get (B-3). Reducing cost sounds great, but I'm the one who'll have to decide which two people have to go and I'm the one who will have to tell them. That does not feel good. I'm also the one who'll get blamed for breaking up a great team, the one who'll have to deal with resistance and resentment from everybody else, and the one who may not be able to get things running smoothly again. The price may be right for the equipment and it certainly will do the job, but the human cost is pretty high. I don't like the way this whole things looks and feels."

Is this person motivated to buy? No. Too many of these outcomes are personally dissatisfying to her (B-3). Even though two of the three conditions are met (B-1 and B-2), she will not be motivated to buy as long as she believes the negative outcomes involving the human element outweigh the positive outcomes associated with reducing cost. This dulls her motivation to buy. In her mind, when all outcomes are considered, the bad outweighs the good. She believes the outcomes will lead to too much dissatisfaction. She will not be motivated to buy as long as she concludes, "Overall the outcomes will be dissatisfying." This is a B-3 problem.

What does all of this mean? Three things. First, sales executives are aware that these three beliefs are very real. Buyers hear these beliefs as they talk to themselves, they see how the beliefs influence their behavior, and they feel the pronounced impact of these beliefs on their motivation to buy. Second, sales executives see that it is only when all three conditions (strong B-1, strong B-2, and strong B-3) are met that buyers are motivated to buy. It's that simple. If any one of the three conditions is not met, buyers will not be motivated to buy. It's an all-or-nothing situation with every buyer. Third, sales executives plainly see that knowing what motivates people to buy provides a greater opportunity to make the sale. This opportunity comes from knowing how to look for and effectively handle beliefs (B-1, B-2, and B-3) that buyers hold which have an impact on their motivation to buy.

Sales executives clearly can grasp the notion of viewing selling as the motivation to buy. It is a perspective that offers a rush of momentum in organizational improvement efforts. It provides a bright future when sales executives step forward and prepare the sales force to motivate people to buy.

NOTES

1. Victor H. Vroom, *Work and Motivation* (New York: John Wiley & Sons, 1964).

2. Thad B. Green, *Performance and Motivation Strategies for Today's Workforce: A Guide to Expectancy Theory Applications* (Westport, Connecticut: Quorum Books, 1992).

3. Thad Green and Merwyn Hayes, *The Belief System: The Secret to Motivation and Improved Performance* (Winston-Salem, North Carolina: Beechwood Press, 1993); and Thad Green and Bill Barkley, *Manage to the Individual: If You Want to Know How, ASK!* (Atlanta, Georgia: The Belief System Institute, 1995).

CHAPTER 2

Motivating People to Buy

Sales executives can see why Belief System Selling™ quickly and easily provides the sales force with the tools needed to motivate people to buy. Acquiring these tools is not difficult because salespeople are not asked to set aside the way they are selling now and replace it with something new. Instead they simply need to get a sense of how to incorporate some of the basic principles of motivation into whatever selling process they currently are using.

Specifically, sales executives must nudge the sales force into a firm appreciation of two sets of skills, namely diagnostic skills and solution skills. Salespeople need to see how diagnostic skills are used to identify beliefs that buyers hold that may be interfering with the motivation to buy. (These beliefs are categorized and labeled B-1, B-2, and B-3, as discussed in Chapter 1.) Sales executives also must come through loud and clear about the use of solution skills for successfully addressing beliefs that are holding back buyers and keeping them from being motivated to buy. Let's take a look at these two sets of skills and get a good feel for how to use them. The next step is for sales executives to pass these skills along to the entire sales force.

DIAGNOSING BUYER BELIEFS

Sales executives want to get their salespeople to listen up and get a firm grasp on two diagnostic skills. One is obtaining B-1, B-2, and B-3 information from buyers, the other is interpreting this information and determining the B-1, B-2, and B-3 levels of buyers.[1] These two skills, as sales executives can clearly see, will go a long way toward preparing the sales force to uncover information that will greatly increase their ability to make the sale.

How does the salesperson get enough information to paint an accurate picture of the buyer's B-1, B-2, and B-3? The best way is to apply the principle, "If you want to know, ask." This means asking buyers the right questions, listening to what they say, and getting in touch with the beliefs they are holding. A suggested list of questions follows. Each question has been tried and tested. They all work. Salespeople simply need to select one or two from each category, make a few changes, if necessary, in the wording so the questions look, sound, and feel right, then start using them!

Obtaining B-1, B-2, and B-3 Information

Remembering that B-1 is the belief that buyers have about whether or not effort will lead to performance (buying), B-1 questions must focus on three things. First, does the person have the need to buy? Second, is money available to buy? Third, does the person have the authority to buy, or does the person have influence with the decision maker, if it is someone else? Sales executives may be wondering if it would pay off to teach and motivate the sales force to gather this information. The answer may be best found by imagining what happens when salespeople do *not* obtain all of this information. Here are some B-1 questions that provide a clear picture and a good feel for how salespeople can get the B-1 information they need from buyers.

B-1 QUESTIONS

REGARDING "NEED TO BUY"

- "Do you have a need for this?"

- "Would this help meet your objectives?"

- "Is this a solution to the problem?"

B-1 QUESTIONS
(CONTINUED)

REGARDING "MONEY TO BUY"

- "Do you have a budget for this?"

- "Is enough money available to buy this product?"

- "How much money do you have allocated for this?"

REGARDING "AUTHORITY TO BUY"

- "Are you the decision maker?"

- "Do you have to get approval on your decision?"

- "Who else would have to be in this meeting to make a decision?"

REGARDING "INFLUENCE TO BUY"

- "Who is the decision maker on this?"

- "What is your relationship with the decision maker?"

- "Can you get a decision on this?"

Remember that B-2 is the belief buyers have about whether or not performance (buying) will lead to the outcomes promised or implied. This means that salespeople must ask B-2 questions to determine if buyers (1) clearly *understand* the outcomes they have been told they will get and not get if they buy and (2) firmly *believe* what they have been told. Obviously it is important for buyers to see what they will get, and not get, if they buy. Most salespeople focus on clearly communicating this and typically have a pretty good handle on how to do it effectively. However, salespeople must learn to recognize when buyers do not *believe* everything they are being promised because these beliefs have a way of turning into lost sales. Here are some questions that allow salespeople to tune in to what buyers are thinking and believing, thereby obtaining the B-2 information they need to make the sale.

B-2 Questions

- "What all do you think will happen if you buy this product?"

- "Do you believe the results will be as I've described them to you?"

- "Do you have any reservations about any of the promises I've made?"

- "Are you as confident as I am that things will turn out the way we have discussed?"

The emphasis with B-3 questions is on satisfaction. Remember that B-3 is the buyer's belief about whether or not outcomes will lead to satisfaction. In other words, if the buyer received the outcomes promised or implied with the purchase of the product or service, would the outcomes be satisfying or dissatisfying? Knowing this is particularly important because it takes the guesswork off the shoulders of the salesperson. Here are some questions buyers like to hear that will generate the B-3 information salespeople need to get a glimpse of how buyers feel about the outcomes that accompany buying the product or service.

B-3 Questions

- "What are you looking for in a product (service) like this?"

- "What do you want the product (service) to do for you?"

- "Can you see anything negative with this product (service)?"

- "Is there anything else we need to discuss?"

Listen up here, sales executives! The three most important questions salespeople can ask will follow shortly. Each of the three generates a perspective on both B-2 and B-3. If a buyer is a qualified prospect (having the need, money, and authority or influence to buy), these three questions will reveal the information, all of the information, salespeople need to make the sale. These are without a doubt the most important questions any salesperson can ask. Here are the big three questions and they should always be asked with every buyer, yes, with every buyer.[2]

Motivating People to Buy

B-2 AND B-3 QUESTIONS

- "If you buy this product (service), what do you believe you will *get and want*?"

- "If you buy this product (service), what do you believe you will *get and not want*?"

- "If you buy this product (service), what do you believe you will *not get but want*?"

Interpreting B-1, B-2, and B-3 Information

Sales executives can imagine the importance of asking questions, getting answers, and then getting a good sense for the information received. How is the information interpreted? This usually is the easy part, especially when sales executives make a point to prepare their salespeople to use Belief System Selling and think in terms of *beliefs* buyers have that determine their willingness or reluctance to buy. Let's take a look at some typical buyer responses and see how to interpret them.

How is B-1 information interpreted? Remember, B-1 is the belief about effort leading to performance (buying), that is, the belief about being able to buy the product or service. Using a rating scale makes the interpretation of this belief easier to grasp. For B-1, a 10 means the buyer definitely believes "I can buy it" and a 0 means "I can't buy it." Points in between show varying degrees of this belief.

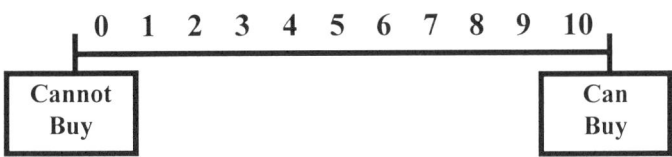

Comments like the following allow salespeople to plainly see that the buyer believes "I can buy it" and B-1 ratings of 10 are appropriate.

- "Yes, I can buy it."
- "It's my decision."
- "Yep, that's my job."

When salespeople hear comments like the following, buyers are stressing that they believe "I can't buy it" and B-1 ratings of 0 are appropriate.

- "It's not my decision."
- "We just don't need this."
- "Sorry, I can't buy it."

Many comments are not clearly "I can buy it" or "I can't buy it." Here are a few examples where ratings other than 10 or 0 are appropriate.

- "I have to get approval, but she goes along with me 9 times out of 10." (This firmly suggests a B-1 rating of 9 on the 10-point scale would be appropriate.)
- "I don't have the money in the budget for this, but I have a 90 percent chance of getting it." (Sounds like a B-1 rating of 9 fits here.)
- "All I do is make the recommendation. They go along with me about half the time." (This 50-50 situation suggests a B-1 rating of 5 appears to be appropriate. However, the person might have a better feel for getting his recommendation accepted on this particular buying decision. One way to find out is get the person to talk by asking a question like, "Do you think they would go along with your recommendation on this?")
- "I have to get approval, but that's seldom a problem." ("Seldom is a problem" shows that the person is "pretty sure" of getting approval and suggests a B-1 rating in the 7 to 9 range. It is appropriate to ask, "Do you think it might be a problem in this case?")
- "I'll just have to present this to my boss. He may want me to handle it. On the other hand, he may decide to make the decision himself. I just don't know." (It sounds like a lot of uncertainty here. The person does not have a clear perspective about who the decision maker is. A B-1 rating in the 4 to 6 range feels right. An exact rating does not matter here. A rating in this range indicates that more information is needed. It would add clarity to ask, "In that case, would you check with him so he can decide how much he wants to be involved on the front end?")

How is B-2 information interpreted? Remember, B-2 is the buyer's belief about performance (buying) leading to outcomes. A rating scale ranging from 0 to 10 can be used again, with a B-2 rating of 10 meaning "I will get the outcome" and a 0 rating meaning "I will not get the outcome." Points in between show varying degrees of this belief. This rating scale is shown as follows.

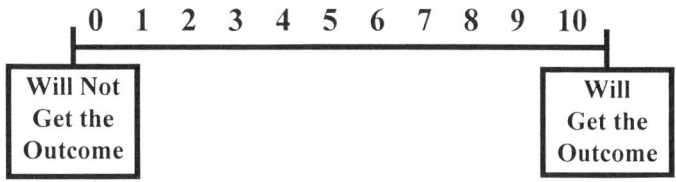

Hearing comments like the following give the salesperson a clear indication of "I will get them," and B-2 ratings of 10 are appropriate.

- "No, I don't have any doubt about things working out like we expect."
- "I'm very confident this will meet all of our objectives."
- "I have every reason to believe we'll get all of these benefits."

Statements like the following sound like the buyer believes "I will not get the outcomes," and B-2 ratings of 0 are a good fit.

- "I just don't believe it will happen."
- "I'm not gullible enough to believe all of that."
- "My analysis totally disagrees with what you are telling me."

Many comments are not clearly "I will get the outcomes" or "I won't." Here are a few responses of this type that fit somewhere between the extremes on the B-2 rating scale.

- "I believe we have an 80 percent chance of everything working out like you project." (This suggests that a B-2 rating of 8 on the rating scale feels right here. This buyer is not certain about getting all of the outcomes. This could be a problem if the buyer has a stronger B-2 for a competing product or service.)
- "Some of these claims are a little hard to believe." (A B-2 rating in the 4 to 6 range looks appropriate, but an exact rating is not necessary. The buyer sounds skeptical enough about the outcomes that a B-2 problem appears certain. The obvious question here is, "Which claims do you find hardest to believe?")
- "Nothing is certain, so I guess having a few reservations isn't anything to worry about." (This suggests a B-2 rating somewhere around the 6 to 8 range. This buyer shows some doubt, certainly enough to explore in greater depth. A question to accomplish this may be as simple as something like, "What are the things you're having reservations about?")

- "I just don't know. I've made a couple of bad decisions lately and I'm skeptical about being promised anything." (Here is a situation that looks and sounds like a B-2 rating in the 4 to 6 range, at best. This represents a B-2 problem that must be resolved for this buyer to feel comfortable making a favorable buying decision. One way to start dealing with this is ask, "What can I do to help you feel comfortable with the information about the services I offer?")

How is B-3 information interpreted? Remember, B-3 is the buyer's belief about how satisfying or dissatisfying the outcomes will be if they are received. A rating scale is used again to get a good feel for information obtained from buyers, but this scale looks different from the B-1 and B-2 rating scales. The B-3 scale ranges from –10 to +10. A rating of +10 clearly is for an outcome that gives maximum satisfaction, with a +1 indicating some, but not much, satisfaction. A rating of –1 shows the outcome would be slightly dissatisfying, while a rating of –10 would indicate maximum dissatisfaction. Points in between represent varying degrees of this belief. This rating scale is an effective way for salespeople to get a good grip on taking what buyers are saying and interpreting it in a way that shows where buyers stand. In other words, it helps salespeople know which outcomes the buyer views as satisfying and, more importantly, which ones are seen as dissatisfying. Let's see how B-3 comments can be interpreted like this using this rating scale.

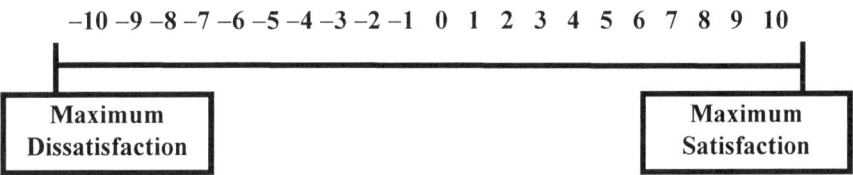

- "The thing I'm looking at more than anything else is whether or not this product will cut our costs." (A B-3 rating of +10 fits here since cost saving is the most important outcome to the buyer.)
- "We've got a smooth running operation here. Upsetting that would be the worst possible thing that could happen." (Since the "disruption" would be the "worst" thing that could happen, a rating of –10 looks appropriate.)
- "I'm more concerned about employees responding positively to the new equipment than I am about price." (A B-3 rating of +10 probably fits for "positive employee response." Just because the buyer says he is more concerned with "a positive employee response" than price doesn't mean price is unimportant. This could be made clear by asking, "How would you rate the importance of employee response compared to price?")

SOLVING B-1, B-2, AND B-3 PROBLEMS

Sales executives have an accurate view that problems are best solved by sounding out causes and choosing solutions that flow from the causes. The causes are the key. Causes lead to hard and firm solutions. The real secret to solving any problem is to identify the causes. Once this is done, it is possible to come up with solutions that will overcome the buyer's lack of motivation to buy.

Using this approach, sales executive are not surprised to hear that three things must be done to solve the B-1, B-2, and B-3 problems which buyers face. The first is to be aware of the most common B-1, B-2, and B-3 causes. The second is to observe which causes are behind the problem. This is easily accomplished simply by asking a few questions and letting buyers talk and tell about how they feel. The third is to choose an appropriate solution in view of the cause(s). Let's take a look at each of these—causes, diagnostic techniques, and solution approaches—for B-1, B-2, and B-3 problems and see how good they sound from the salespersons perspective.

Let's first look at solving B-1 problems. This is a situation where buyers do not believe they can buy (a B-1 problem) because they do not feel they have the need, money, and/or authority or influence to buy the product or service. All of this can be easily diagnosed simply by asking the right questions. Solutions will vary depending on what is causing the buyer to believe "I can't buy." The causes, diagnostic questions, and solutions regarding B-1 problems are summarized as follows.

SOLVING B-1 PROBLEMS

B-1 Causes	B-1 Diagnosis	B-1 Solutions
1. No need	Ask "Do you have a need for this?"	None
2. No money	Ask "Do you have the money to buy?"	Offer credit. Suggest getting a loan.
3. No authority or influence to buy	Ask "Can you make, or get, a decision on this?"	Get to the decision maker.
4. Perception of no need	Ask "Are you sure there is no need?"	Show how a need really does exist.

Solving B-1 Problems
(Continued)

5. Perception of no money	Ask "Is there any way to get the money?"	Show how money may be obtained, when possible.
6. Perception of no authority	Ask "Are you sure you do not have the authority?"	Show how the authority might be obtained, when possible.
7. Perception of no influence	Ask "Will you have any problem convincing the decision maker?"	Show how to persuade the decision maker.

Next, solving B-2 problems. Sales executives often see the situation where buyers do not believe they will get certain things if they buy the product or service (a B-2 problem). This "not believing" can have at least two possible causes. First, the outcome in question does not, in fact, accompany the purchase of the product or service. The salesperson knows it and so does the buyer. Second, the outcome does accompany the purchase, but for a variety of reasons the buyer does not believe it. Both the diagnosis and solution approach depend on what is causing the problem, as shown in the following summary.

Solving B-2 Problems

B-2 Causes	B-2 Diagnosis	B-2 Solutions
1. Outcomes do not accompany purchase of the product/service.	Evaluate the outcomes of buying the product or service.	Add appropriate outcomes when possible.
2. Buyer is not aware of key product/service information.	Ask "What all do you think you will get from this?"	Provide information.
3. Buyer does not understand some product/service information.	Ask "What is your understanding about . . . ?"	Provide clarification.

SOLVING B-2 PROBLEMS
(CONTINUED)

4. Buyer does not believe some of the product/service information.	Ask "Are you skeptical about any of the things I've said?"	Provide explanation.
5. Buyer has had a bad experience with other salespeople.	Ask "Are experiences with other salespeople affecting our situation?"	Gain credibility.
6. The salesperson, the company, or the product/service have a bad reputation.	Ask "Do you have any concerns about the product (or service)? Our company? My ability to deliver?"	Overcome bad reputation.
7. The buyer has had a bad experience with the salesperson, the company, or the product/service.	Ask "How do you feel about what happened before?"	Overcome bad experience.

Finally, solving B-3 problems, where buyers do not believe the outcomes from buying will be satisfying (a B-3 problem). The two main causes, getting unwanted outcomes and not getting desired outcomes, often can be solved by removing undesired outcomes and adding those that are wanted. A third cause comes into play occasionally, namely, when buyers see an outcome as undesirable when it really isn't or desirable when it really isn't. The solution here is to provide clarifying information. All of this is presented in the following summary.

SOLVING B-3 PROBLEMS

B-3 Causes	B-3 Diagnosis	B-3 Solutions
1. Getting unwanted outcomes.	Ask "Are their some things you don't want, but expect to get?"	Remove undesired Outcomes when possible.

SOLVING B-3 PROBLEMS
(CONTINUED)

2.	Not getting desired outcomes.	Ask "What do you want, but don't expect to get?"	Add desired outcomes when possible.
3.	Misperceptions about expected outcomes.	Diagnosis comes from the questions above.	Provide clarification.

Sales executives clearly see that the motivation to buy is based on beliefs that buyers grasp and firmly hold regarding a variety of factors surrounding the buying process. And sales executives are fully aware that when the sales force listens to buyers, particularly about their beliefs, they hear things that allow them to get a firm grasp on the situation and smoothly focus on increasing the motivation to buy. Asking and listening form the basis for diagnosing B-1, B-2, and B-3 problems and causes, and this establishes a solid foundation for solving those problems and strengthening the motivation to buy.

Sales executives can imagine what they will hear salespersons say, and the good feelings they will get, when the sales force is better equipped to motivate people to buy. The sales organization will become more effective when salespeople simply overlay principles of motivation onto the sales approach they already are using. Doing so enables salespeople to hear, see, and understand the beliefs of the buyer. Addressing these beliefs increases the motivation to buy and this leads to closing more sales. Getting better results is the reason sales executives will want to teach Belief System Selling™ to the sales force.

NOTES

1. Thad B. Green, *Performance and Motivation Strategies for Today's Workforce: A Guide to Expectancy Theory Applications* (Westport, Connecticut: Quorum Books, 1992).

2. Thad Green, *A Person's Motivation to Buy Will Be Strengthened If the Person Answers These Ten Questions* (Atlanta, Georgia: The Belief System Institute, 1995).

CHAPTER 3

Selling to Style Is Motivating

One of the constant battles sales executives face is moving salespeople away from the comfortable notion of selling every prospect the same way. The best salespeople view buyers as individuals, hear what they really are saying, get a good feel about where they are coming from, and then vary their sales approach accordingly. The majority of salespeople in most sales organizations, however, are still hanging on to the one-size-fits-all approach. They may claim that they get in tune with their buyers and go about selling to them differently, but going on a few sales calls with salespeople tells another story. While most salespeople do modify their approach to some extent, they don't adjust nearly enough and often not in the right way. This inability to sell in a way that fits the buyer explains why many salespeople and entire sales organizations don't meet quota. Strengthening the ability of the sales force to sell to the individuality of each buyer literally can turn a sales organization around.

Sales executives are aware that every buyer is different. Research on buying behavior confirms this.[1] Buyers have their own unique behavioral tendencies that influence the way they buy and the way they prefer to be sold. Each buyer sees, hears, and feels different things. Some buyers are the no-nonsense type that focus primarily on bottom-line results when they are buying. Others are friendly, fun-loving people who enjoy talking to and interacting with the salesperson during the buying process. Still other prospects are looking for a warm, long-term relationship of commitment and trust when deciding to buy. And some are logical, rational, systematic decision makers who want to touch and feel all of the available information before making a buying decision.

Each buyer has a behavior style and having a good perspective on each individual buyer's style enables salespeople to sell more effectively. When salespeople know the behavior style of the buyer, they can communicate better, gain their acceptance, be more persuasive, and close more sales. All sales executives have to do is go ahead and decide to do something now, if you will, and watch things change, because teaching salespeople to sell to the buyer's behavior style pays off.

Sales executives should be aware that salespeople also have their own behavior style and herein lies a problem. Behavior style influences the way they sell. This is only natural. A salesperson who tends to skip the small talk and get to the bottom-line will tend to sell that way. The salesperson who approaches situations in a detailed, methodical way likewise will tend to sell this way. Sometimes salespeople are successful when they sell to their own behavior style. This happens mainly when the salesperson's behavior style is compatible with the buyer's behavior style. However, when the behavior styles of buyer and seller are incompatible, salespeople are less likely to strengthen the motivation to buy. Needless to say, it isn't reasonable to expect buyers to adjust their behavior style to fit the salesperson. Instead, salespeople must focus on selling to the style of each buyer rather than selling to their own style.

The big question is this: What can sales executives do to move an entire sales organization more in the direction of *selling to style*, of selling to the individuality of each buyer? The answer is simple. Sales executives must give the sales force the skills necessary to handle the task of selling to the behavior style of buyers. And sales executives must be outspoken and motivate salespeople to use those skills. This chapter deals with the skills issue. Chapter 9 addresses the motivation challenge.

BEHAVIOR STYLE

Sales executives who are considering to use Belief System Selling™ will feel gcod to know that the best known and most widely accepted approach to understanding behavior, and the one that yields the greatest results for salespersons, is based on the work of Dr. William Moulton Marsten who classified behavioral responses into four styles, dominance, inducement, submission, and compliance.[2] The names of the four styles have evolved over the years to be called dominant, influencing, steady, and conforming. To simplify discussion of these styles, a buyer whose primary style is dominant will be called a high D. Likewise, high I, high S, and high C will be used throughout the book to refer to buyers whose primary style is influencing, steady, and conforming, respectively

As sales executives begin to get a deep and clear perspective on the concept of behavior style, they will want to keep three things in mind. First, all that body of knowledge presented here is the result of over fifty years of research and testing by many practitioners as well as researchers who have advanced Marsten's original work. Second, the behaviors attributed to each behavior style should be viewed as strong behavioral *tendencies* of the person rather than as behaviors they are certain to show. Finally, each behavior style is comprehensively described. Most of the behaviors in each style are strengths, though some are not. Drawing attention to the shortcomings is not intended to imply a negative view of buyers. Instead, they are mentioned because successful selling requires that salespersons use a sales approach that is a good fit for the strengths and weaknesses of the buyer.

Sales executives will want to learn the fundamentals of behavior style before deciding if Belief System Selling™ makes sense for their own sales organization. One way to get a good feel for behavior style is to read about the high D style and at the same time identify and think about a buyer, from the present or the past, who tends to show the behaviors attributed to the high D style. Do the same while reading about the high I, high S, and high C styles. This provides a frame of reference and allows for quickly grasping the concept of behavior style so you can share it with your sales organization, should you decide to do so.[3] And sales executives may want to, by now, take another step and call on available resources to gain a better understanding of behavior style and see that it can be used to sell more effectively.

The Dominant Buyer

How do high D buyers behave? The following picture provides a glimpse of their behavioral tendencies and gives a sense of what to expect when calling on high D buyers. They normally are time conscious and expect sales calls to finish on time. They tend to speak loudly, ask direct questions, and are short and to the point. They find it hard to concentrate and may look at their watch, their mail, and even talk on the phone during the sales call. Impulsiveness and impatience drive their desire to get to the bottom line. The high D will often look stern or solemn, rarely smiling. It is results, not reasons, that count.

The Influencing Buyer

How do the high I buyers behave? They often will be late for a sales call or have to reschedule because of their lack of time consciousness. They are people oriented and will focus on the people they are with at the expense of people who are waiting to see them. They would rather talk than listen and will talk at length about themselves and their company while often dominating the conversation. They will be upbeat and optimistic, smiling and laughing a lot, and making others feel good. Social relations and having fun are key to the high I.

The Steady Buyer

How do high S buyers behave? They are easygoing and unhurried. They desire a relationship and will not buy on the first visit. They will listen closely and ask questions as to how things will work. Their motivation is to resist change. They are concerned with security and status quo. They seek the salesperson's involvement and support during the sales process. They have a pleasant, comfortable appearance and will try hard to put people at ease.

The Conforming Buyer

How do high C buyers behave? They will be on time for appointments and expect salespeople to do the same. They want to get down to business fairly quickly. They expect salespeople to be fully prepared. They will ask many detailed and fact-based questions. The questions will be indirect to see if things conform to their high standards. Credentials, referrals, and support facts are important to the high C. They do not like to rush, are not quick decision makers, and will not be closed on the first contact. They demand much. The high C shows little expression, preferring to appear indifferent until a basis for business is established.

COMPARING BEHAVIOR STYLES

Many behavioral tendencies of buyers are of special interest from the selling point of view. Several of the more important are highlighted here by comparing the four styles. The necessity for selling to the buyer's behavior style comes through loud and clear.

Decision Making—How Do Buyers Decide?

- High D—Tends to decide quickly without consulting others
- High I—Often talks about it with others before deciding
- High S—Finds out how others feel about it before deciding
- High C—Carefully looks at all alternatives before deciding

Listening—What Do Buyers Do When the Salesperson Is Talking?

- High D—Seems distracted, impatient for others to finish
- High I—Looks for an opportunity to talk, jumps in
- High S—Listens attentively to everything
- High C—Evaluates everything that is said

Change—How Do Buyers React When Buying Would Change Things?

- High D—Likes change, especially if it gives better results
- High I—Wants few details, looks for overall feel of things
- High S—Resists change, needs reassurances
- High C—Wants to look at all the facts

Details—How Much Attention Do Buyers Give to Details?

- High D—Wants to know the bottom line, not the details
- High I—Needs few details, focuses on the way things feel
- High S—Will consider whatever information given
- High C—Wants all the details

Persuasion—How Are Buyers Persuaded?

- High D—With facts and figures about results
- High I—With stories about others, appearance, and enthusiasm
- High S—With evidence of benefits and support from others
- High C—With information about pros and cons, quality and standards

DETERMINING BEHAVIOR STYLE

There is good news for sales executives when it comes to preparing the sales force to determine the behavior style of buyers. The most practical way to determine behavior style is to *listen* and *observe*. What prospects say and do always provide the clues needed to make an accurate assessment of behavior style. In other words, it is not difficult for salespeople to learn how to do this. It simply means taking everything salespeople normally see and hear and interpreting it in the context of behavior style.

Consider this fairly typical scene when making a sales call. The buyer greets the salesperson with a frown, looks like the hard and cold type, and obviously is in a rush. As she looks through some files on her desk she says, "I don't have much time. Can we do this in fifteen minutes?" The salesperson is thinking, "This doesn't feel good" as he says, "Well, ah . . ." but she abruptly interrupts while continuing to shuffle through her paperwork and says, "Just skip the details and give me the bottom line. Why should I buy this product and how much will it cost?" When all that is seen and heard here is interpreted in the context of behavior style, it becomes obvious that the buyer has a dominant (high D) behavior style. Salespeople who accommodate this style have an excellent chance of making the sale. Those who try to sell in there *own* way will be ushered out promptly, and not always in a kind, gentle way, and the opportunity to make a sale is gone.

Sales executives will be excited to know that there are two easy, straight forward ways to show salespeople how to determine a buyer's behavior style. One is by following these four simple guidelines.

- See what you see.
- Hear what you hear.
- Feel what you feel.
- Interpret everything in the context of behavior style.

To help salespeople see and hear with the eyes and ears of a behavior style expert, comprehensive lists of the behavioral tendencies of each of the four behavior styles are presented.[4] All of these tendencies can be seen and heard when salespeople are trained to tune in to what prospects say and do, and interpret everything in the context of behavior style. Salespeople tend to learn this quickly, when trained properly. Sales executives may want to consider this and just jump in and do it. Do it with the entire sales organization, or start with a few sales teams, but do something. Take advantage of an opportunity that is readily available, because you can, if you will, since it is just another decision you have to make.

BEHAVIORAL TENDENCIES OF THE HIGH D BUYER

- Aggressive
- Bottom-line oriented
- Challenges status quo
- Dislikes details
- Likes change
- Decisive
- Needs little information
- Not open to suggestions
- Makes things happen
- All business
- Direct
- Intent is to overcome
- Likes to conquer
- Enjoys a challenge
- Straightforward
- Positive
- Optimistic
- Strong ego
- Impatient
- Values time
- Innovative
- Problem solver
- Risk taker
- Results oriented
- Self-starter
- Likes to be in charge
- Not a good listener
- Always right
- Doesn't smile much
- Frowns
- Cold
- Hard
- Intimidating
- Enjoys conflict
- Confident
- Arrogant
- Dislikes routine work
- Gets bored easily
- Takes on too much
- Oversteps authority
- Argumentative
- Results more important than people
- Defiant
- Dislikes wasting time

BEHAVIORAL TENDENCIES OF THE HIGH I BUYER

- Talkative
- Optimistic
- Enthusiastic
- Emotional
- Impulsive
- Popular

BEHAVIORAL TENDENCIES OF THE HIGH I BUYER (CONTINUED)

- Trusting
- Persuasive
- Creative
- Laughs a lot
- Motivates
- Sense of humor
- Negotiates conflicts
- Articulate
- Smiles
- Enjoys people
- Likes having fun
- Convincing
- Poised
- Meets strangers easily
- Outgoing
- Hates rejection
- Accepting
- Misjudges others
- Warm
- Charming
- Charismatic
- Makes a good impression
- Many acquaintances
- Few close friends
- Not a detail person
- Situational listener
- People more important than results

BEHAVIORAL TENDENCIES OF THE HIGH S BUYER

- Steady
- Predictable
- Possessive of things
- Possessive of people
- Understanding
- Friendly
- Sincere
- Team player
- Good listener
- Dependable
- Patient
- Empathetic
- Dislikes conflict
- Supportive
- Maintains the status quo
- Dislikes change
- Takes time to adjust to change
- Difficulty setting priorities
- Takes criticism of work as personal
- Amiable

BEHAVIORAL TENDENCIES OF THE HIGH S BUYER (CONTINUED)

- Easygoing
- Relaxed
- Low key
- Undemonstrative
- Self-controlled
- Conceals true feelings
- May hold a grudge
- Dislikes pressure of deadlines
- Even tempered
- Approaches things systematically
- Can't say no
- Family oriented
- Emotionally mature
- Relationships are important
- Complacent
- Lenient
- Doesn't like the new and different
- Has a calming effect on others
- Calm
- Wants to know what's expected
- Dislikes urgency
- Procrastinates

BEHAVIORAL TENDENCIES OF THE HIGH C BUYER

- Analytical
- Fact finder
- Accurate
- Detailed
- Conscientious
- Precise
- Systematic
- Sensitive
- Objective
- Clarifies
- Defines
- Gets information
- Criticizes
- Tests
- Maintains standards
- Quality oriented
- Prefers precedents
- Bound by methods and procedures
- Gets bogged down in details
- Yields to avoid controversy
- Does not like to verbalize feelings
- Avoids trouble

BEHAVIORAL TENDENCIES OF THE HIGH C BUYER (CONTINUED)

- Does necessary homework
- Makes few mistakes
- Avoids risk
- Proceeds in orderly way
- Nonargumentative
- Likes established procedures
- Prefers the proven
- Conservative
- Disciplined
- More strict than tough
- Unmovable when mind is made up
- Prefers switching to fighting
- Adapts to avoid confrontation
- Strong need for self-preservation
- Documents everything
- Goes by the book
- Tries to please
- Slow to criticize
- Slow to take independent action
- Once sure, very determined
- Diplomatic
- Complies with authority
- Needs reassurance
- Dislikes challenge
- Prefers personal to public recognition
- Cautious
- Tentative
- Hesitant
- Doesn't like to be rushed
- Organized
- Neat
- Prepares in advance
- Strictly business
- Methodical
- Perfectionist

The second way sales executives can teach salespeople to determine the behavior style of buyers is with the *quick read* method. Simply observe what the buyer says and does for a short period of time, then ask the following questions. This approach generally leads to an accurate determination of the buyer's behavior style.

- When observing the buyer, is she

    active (direct and outgoing) or

    inactive (reserved and quiet)?

- If the buyer is active, is he

    aggressive and competitive? This suggests the *dominant* style.

    enthusiastic and talkative? This suggests the *influencing* style.

- If the buyer is inactive, is she

    attentive and doing? This suggests the *steady* style.

    cautious and observing? This suggests the *conforming* style.

SELLING TO BEHAVIOR STYLE

Sales executives are aware that all buyers are different. Yet, many of their salespeople continue to treat each buyer the same. It is easy to hear the sameness in the canned presentation, the favorite close, and rituals such as "always take them for drinks." It doesn't work, as shown by the consistently low-close ratios in most sales organizations.

Different buyers need to be sold in different ways, as sales executives know from listening to buyers over the years. Selling to the individual calls for a sales approach that is tailored to the uniqueness of the buyer. The best way to do this is for sales executives to go ahead and give the sales force the skills needed to sell to the behavior style of buyers. In other words, sales organizations will be more successful when the sales force sells in a way that fits the behavior style of each buyer. Sales executives may want to get a feel for how to do this.[5]

Selling to the High D

There are several important steps salespeople can take when selling buyers with the high D behavior style, including the following.

- Indicate how much time is needed, agree on the amount of time, remind buyers when the time is almost up, and finish on time unless they choose to continue.
- Say or do something early that gives credibility—to self, company, and product or service.
- Be prepared for their short, direct, pointed questions, and respond with complete—but short—direct answers.
- Emphasize results, deemphasizing details unless they are requested.
- Hit the high points. Get to the bottom line.
- Indicate how they will benefit if they buy, especially by showing how buying meets their need for power, authority, prestige, results, challenge, newness, and variety.

Selling to the High I

High I buyers often provide a challenge as salespeople try to sell to this dynamic and changeable behavior style in the following ways.

- Be warm and friendly, and show acceptance of them.
- They like to socialize and talk about nonbusiness things (small talk, personal conversation, and so on), so plan some time to do this over lunch, dinner, a cup of coffee, or at least by relaxing in their office.
- Spare the details. They don't want to hear a lot of them. Just hit the high points. Put important details in writing.
- Focus on their eagerness to learn about and possess the newest, latest, best product or service, especially if someone they know and respect has bought it. They'll sell themselves under the right circumstances.
- Be prepared for them to make decisions quickly and easily, but sew up the sale tightly because they may change their mind when the next salesperson comes in.

Selling to the High S

Selling high S buyers requires pacing and steadiness, which can be demonstrated as follows.

- Salespeople must sell themselves first, earn trust, establish a relationship, become a friend, then move slowly toward making the sale. Avoid getting friendly too fast and moving too quickly toward the sale.
- Don't rush. Take it slow and easy. Expect to make repeat visits to close the sale.
- They like proven things rather than something totally new or different, so emphasize products and services that have passed the test of time in terms of being simple, workable, and durable.
- Show them how the product or service will meet their need for traditional practices and procedures, security, reliability, predictability, the status quo, being appreciated, identification with a group, and having a happy family life.
- Give plenty of proof, statistics, and evidence that their buying decision will carry minimum risk and maximum benefits.

Selling to the High C

Salespersons will increase their ability to sell high C buyers by carefully following these suggestions.

Selling to Style Is Motivating 37

- Be on time for the appointment. Establish credibility, then get down to business fairly quickly. Don't waste time with friendly small talk, but don't rush once you get down to business.
- They are highly suspicious of anything new and unproven, so emphasize standard products and services that have a solid track record with plenty of evidence and hard data to back up the success of the product/service.
- They will demand a lot, often to the point of frustration, so be patient and meet their requests. Most meetings with high C prospects end with a request for a proposal. This can pay off since they tend to be loyal once they decide to buy.
- Give them plenty of time to make the final buying decision, including time to verify the information presented and carefully analyze the options offered.

THE SALES MODEL AND BEHAVIOR STYLE

Sales executives can plainly see the connection between the sales model (Chapters 1 and 2) and behavior style. It is important to grasp this relationship. Combining the two concepts puts the salesperson in harmony with the buyer. Salespeople end up with a powerful sales approach designed for selling to the individuality of each buyer. Take a look at how this works.

B-1 and Behavior Style

The belief about effort leading to performance (buying) varies with behavior style. This belief varies with whether or not buyers have the need, the money, and authority or influence to buy, as previously discussed.

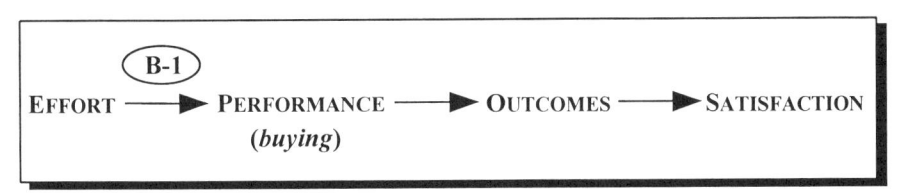

$$\text{Effort} \longrightarrow \underset{(buying)}{\text{Performance}} \longrightarrow \text{Outcomes} \longrightarrow \text{Satisfaction}$$

(B-1)

When they have the authority and money to buy, (1) high D buyers tend to have a high B-1, believing without a doubt that "I can buy"; (2) high I buyers also tend to have a high B-1, being certain in their belief that "I can buy"; (3) high S buyers tend to have a moderately high B-1, believing "I can buy, if I can get the time to do it;" and (4) high C buyers tend to have a moderately high B-1, believing "I can buy, if I can get all of the information I need."

When they do not have the authority and/or the money to buy, (1) high D buyers tend to have a high B-1, believing "I can buy—I'll just use my clout to get what I want;" (2) high I buyers also tend to have a high B-1, believing "I can buy—I'll just turn on my charm until I get what I want;" (3) high S buyers tend to have a low B-1, facing reality and simply believing "I can't buy;" and (4) high C buyers tend to have a low B-1, believing "I can't buy because I'm not the decision maker (no authority)"or "I can't buy because I don't have the money."

People can be either *decision makers* (D), *users* (U), or *influencers* (I). The DUI concept is applicable to the question of whether or not a person can make buying decisions. Experience shows that many of the decision makers have high D and/or high I behavior styles, while persons with high S and high C styles tend to be either influencers or users. Many salespeople also tend to have high D and/or high I styles. This style compatibility between buyer and seller offers a greater likelihood of sales success. Salespeople with high S and high C styles tend to be more service oriented and sell best in long-term relationship selling.

B-2 and Behavior Style

The belief about performance (buying) leading to outcomes (B-2) also varies with behavior style. Two other variables have an effect on B-2 as well: whether the salesperson objectively describes the outcomes that are associated with the product or service, or whether outcomes are overpromised. A close look at how these two variables interact with behavior style gives insight into buying behavior, into the way buyers decide, and presents an advantage, an edge, always an edge, when as sales executives you want your salespeople to use behavior style.

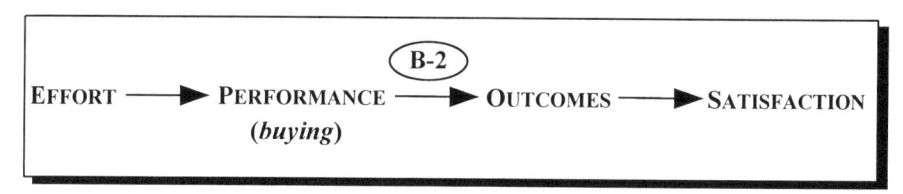

```
                              (B-2)
EFFORT ——▶ PERFORMANCE ——▶ OUTCOMES ——▶ SATISFACTION
              (buying)
```

When the outcomes are objectively presented, (1) high D buyers tend to have a high B-2 if they can relate outcomes to bottom line results; (2) high I buyers tend to have a high B-2 because they are trusting and optimistic; (3) high S buyers tend to have a moderate B-2 because they are realistic; and (4) high C buyers tend to have a low B-2 because they are cautious and pessimistic.

When outcomes are overpromised—and the buyer knows they are overpromised, yet really wants the product/service—(1) high D buyers have a moderate B-2 because they think they can work it out anyway; (2) high I buyers tend to have a relatively high B-2 because of their trusting nature; (3) high S buyers tend to have a relatively low B-2 because they are realistic; and (4) high C buyers tend to have a very low B-2 because of their cautiousness and pessimism.

B-3 and Behavior Style

The belief about outcomes leading to satisfaction (B-3) varies with behavior style, too. Each behavior style feels varying levels of satisfaction or dissatisfaction from the wide range of possible outcomes. However, for each behavior style there is one outcome that tends to be more satisfying than any other. The primary satisfiers are: (1) results for high D buyers, (2) social acceptance for high I buyers, (3) stability for high S buyers, and (4) perfection for high C buyers. Sales executives can plainly see that these outcomes send a message to salespeople that is loud and clear. When it comes to B-3, the motivation to buy is closely tied to offering the primary satisfiers to buyers. So when the most prized outcomes are available, salespeople should scream out and let buyers see—they can have what they want if only they will buy.

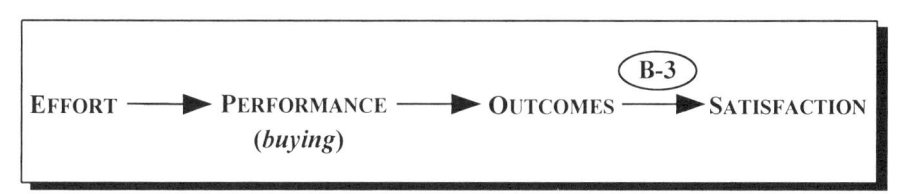

EFFORT ⟶ PERFORMANCE ⟶ OUTCOMES ⟶(B-3)⟶ SATISFACTION
             (*buying*)

Sales executives can have a significant impact on the sales organization by preparing and calling on the entire sales force to show flexibility and fit sales approaches to the individuality of the buyer. This is accomplished best when salespeople integrate behavior style into the sales model. Getting in tune with the individuality of the buyer increases the motivation to buy. Sales executives may want to imagine the value to their sales organization if they would teach the sales force to use Belief System Selling™ and then just go ahead and decide to take action, make things happen, teach some new skills, and get the value that is there waiting for the taking.

NOTES

1. David W. Merrill and Roger H. Reid, *Personal Styles and Effective Performance* (Radnor, Pennsylvania: Chilton Book Company, 1981); Paul Mok, *Communicating Styles Technology* (Dallas, Texas: Training Associates Press, 1982); Larry Wilson, *Social Styles Sales Strategies* (Eden Prairie, Minnesota: Wilson Learning Corporation, 1987); and Anthony Alessandra, Phil Wexler, and Rick Barrera, *Non-Manipulative Selling* (Englewood Cliffs, New Jersey: Prentice-Hall, 1987).

2. William Moulton Marsten, *Emotions of Normal People* (Minneapolis, Minnesota: Persona Press, Inc., 1979).

3. Kurt H. Sutton, *The Only Thing You Can Do!* (Buford, Georgia: Heinz Hertlein Company, 1991).

4. Thomas C. Ritt, Jr., *Understanding Yourself and Then Others* (Tequesta, Florida: People Concepts, 1980).

5. Bill J. Bonnstetter, *Buyer Profile Blending Factors* (Cedar Falls, Iowa: Freiberg-Frederick & Associates, 1982).

CHAPTER 4

Prospecting That Motivates

Prospecting is one of the most troubling problems staring sales executives full in the face. There appears to be little disagreement about what prospecting means. It is the process of finding people who have the need, the money, and the authority or influence to buy. People who have all three—need, money, and authority or influence—are called prospects. Those who do not are not prospects. They will not buy because they cannot buy. On one hand sales executives clearly see the importance of prospecting, yet on the other they feel the painful ordeal of getting it done. Sales executives are aware that reluctance to prospect has a firm grip on the majority of the sales force. And it isn't easy to get the motor running to overcome this kind of pervasive and rather compelling reluctance. While sales executives plainly see the reluctance, the reasons behind it are hazy and there hasn't been a flash of brilliance spelling out a way to overcome it. When the haze is lifted, solutions may well be forthcoming. Viewing reluctance to prospect as a motivation problem offers the potential for understanding and getting a handle on it.

Sales executives also need to come to grips with a second problem with prospecting. This one isn't viewed as troubling because sales executives are less aware of it. It is a problem very much intertwined with the reluctance to prospect, yet sales executives tend to have a dim view of it at best. One of the principal reasons salespeople are reluctant to prospect is because they don't know how. That's right, they don't know how to prospect. Salespeople who are open, honest, and outspoken are quick to say, "I can't make it work. I'm not good at it. I don't know what to say when somebody answers the phone." This feeling of "I can't do it" is a major cause of the reluctance to prospect.

Sales executives, when they think about it, will observe that inadequate prospecting skills cuts two ways, one of which is plain to see and the other disguised and deceptively damaging with harsh consequences. When salespeople do not have adequate prospecting skills, it obviously limits the number of new prospects that are turned up. The companion problem, however, is quiet and often goes unnoticed. The problem is this: Salespeople often appear as though they don't see, don't feel that prospecting is the starting point for motivating people to buy. Yes, prospecting is important because it uncovers new buyers, but it is significant for a second reason as well. Sales executives are aware that first impressions are critical, doubly so in sales, and prospecting represents the first contact with prospects. Inadequate prospecting skills leaves salespeople at a decided disadvantage when coming out of the shoot and needing a solid first impression to start the process of motivating people to buy. This is a second and very compelling reason why sales executives want to focus on strengthening the prospecting skills of the sales force. Let's take a look at all these problems with prospecting, but first some brief talk about the necessity of prospecting.

Sales executives have a sense of agreement about the necessity for prospecting and that it stems from the need to have enough people to sell to. Many things continually happen to customers that put pressure on sales organizations and make prospecting an on-going necessity. For example, customers will:

- move away, retire, or die;
- switch to competitors;
- no longer need the product or service;
- go out of business;
- have a down turn in business;
- no longer have the money to buy; or
- no longer be profitable to sell to.

All customers are vulnerable to the harshness of these changes, and this creates a forceful need to prospect and find potential customers to replace those who are being lost. This replacement can only be successful with a steady stream of prospects. The need for prospecting is even more pressing when new salespeople are brought on board but are not given an existing customer base.

RELUCTANCE TO PROSPECT

Sales executives are aware that in spite of the necessity to continually find new prospects, most salespeople have prospecting reluctance. There is an endless flow of reasons. Here are some of the more common ones salespeople speak out about:

- "I'm just not good at prospecting."
- "It's hard and boring work."
- "It's no fun."
- "It's lonely and lots of people are rude."
- "I get criticized a lot."
- "I get rejected all the time."
- "Few of my prospects end up buying."
- "It's one failure after another."
- "I don't know what I'm doing wrong."
- "I waste so much time."

It takes only one reason to dull the inspiration to prospect. If more than one of the reasons fits and comes into play with a salesperson, there can be considerable reluctance to prospect. And sales executives come face to face with a reluctance factor that can be very difficult to overcome.

Overcoming Reluctance to Prospect

The best way for sales executives to get a handle on prospecting reluctance is to view it in the context of motivation. When doing so, it is easy to see that the reasons most often given for reluctance fall into one of three categories.

The first category of reasons for prospecting reluctance that salespeople are loud and clear about involves the belief about effort leading to performance (B-1), where performance is defined as identifying new prospects. Given this definition of performance, salespeople often conclude, "I can't do it." This is a B-1 problem. The "I can't do it" belief strips the salesperson of the motivation to prospect. It leaves salespeople unmotivated and unwilling to put out the effort needed to perform well (identify prospects). It stands to reason that when salespeople believe "I can't do it," they will not try very hard, and maybe not at all. This is summarized as follows.

B-1 Rating Is Low
"I can't do it."

EFFORT ⟶ PERFORMANCE ⟶ OUTCOMES ⟶ SATISFACTION
(B-1) (identifying prospects)

B-1 Problem

- "It's one failure after another."
- "I'm just not good at prospecting."
- "I don't know what I'm doing wrong."

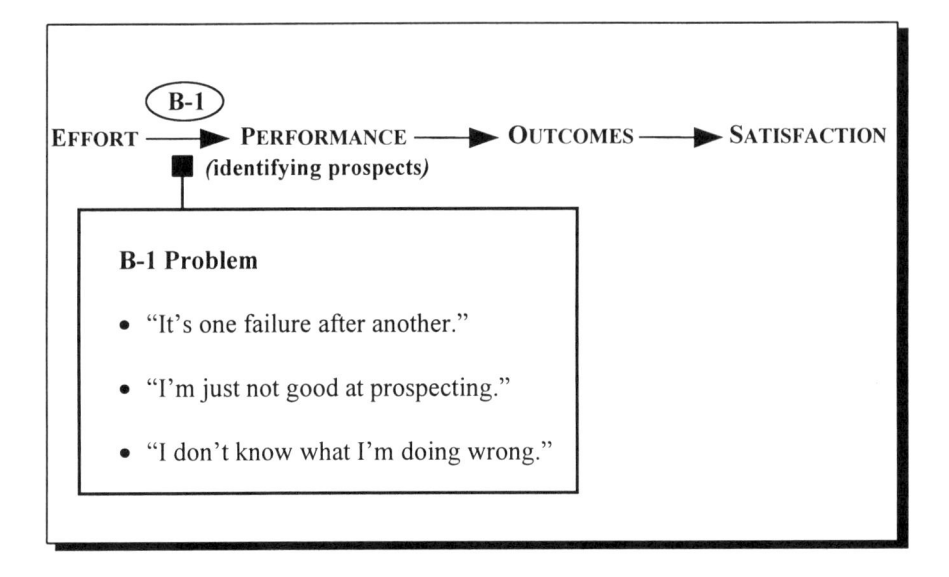

The second category of reasons for prospecting reluctance that salespeople discuss involves the belief about performance leading to outcomes (B-2). Salespeople often conclude, "Sales don't increase much (outcome) when I identify new prospects (performance)." This happens especially when the so-called prospects turn out not to be prospects at all, or when they are hard to sell. This "even when I perform, nothing much happens" belief (B-2) holds salespeople back and leaves them reluctant to prospect. This is summarized on the following page.

The third category of reasons sales executives might hear for prospecting reluctance involves the belief about outcomes leading to satisfaction (B-3). It all boils down to believing that the set of outcomes to be received will be dissatisfying. While some of the outcomes may be satisfying, others will not be and the weight of the dissatisfying outcomes will be greater. Overall, the set of outcomes will be dissatisfying. This is summarized on the next page.

B-2 Rating Is Low

"I will not get the outcomes."

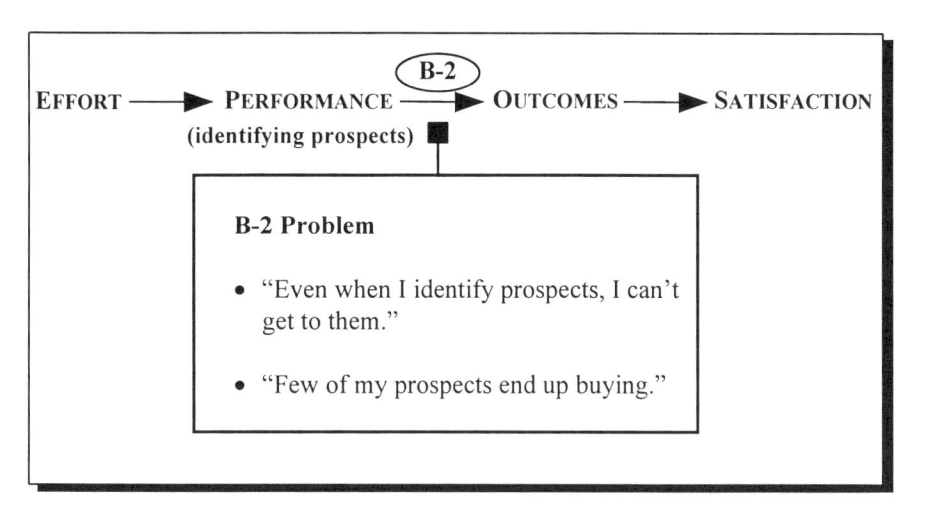

EFFORT ⟶ PERFORMANCE ⟶(B-2)⟶ OUTCOMES ⟶ SATISFACTION
(identifying prospects)

B-2 Problem

- "Even when I identify prospects, I can't get to them."
- "Few of my prospects end up buying."

B-3 Rating Is Low

"The outcomes will not be satisfying."

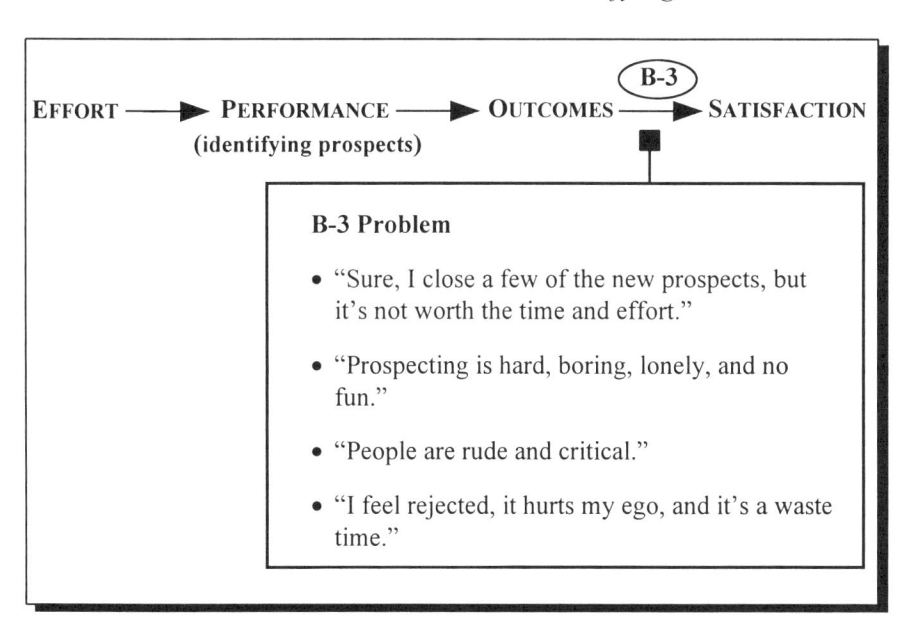

EFFORT ⟶ PERFORMANCE ⟶ OUTCOMES ⟶(B-3)⟶ SATISFACTION
(identifying prospects)

B-3 Problem

- "Sure, I close a few of the new prospects, but it's not worth the time and effort."
- "Prospecting is hard, boring, lonely, and no fun."
- "People are rude and critical."
- "I feel rejected, it hurts my ego, and it's a waste time."

Sales executives are wondering what they can do to overcome the reluctance to prospect that has such a strong hold on salespeople. Viewing reluctance in the context of motivation and defining the problems as B-1, B-2, and B-3 problems has provided a new depth of understanding and now opens the door for solutions that will work. Sales executives should review the solutions from the three lists which follow and pick out the ones that fit, the ones that look, sound, and feel right. Then do something with them. Do something. A handful of options may be enough to turn the corner and overcome much of the prospecting reluctance that has been holding salespeople back. Do something. Give it a try. And sit back and wait for a pleasant surprise.

B-1 SOLUTIONS

1. Make salespeople aware of exactly what has to be done—outline the steps required to successfully identify prospects, steps salespeople believe will work for them.

2. Develop the prospecting skills that salespeople need—provide training.

3. Make available all of the tools salespeople need for prospecting—such as business directories, maps, telephone scripts, appointment book, tickler file, and so on.

4. Have sales managers work with salespeople to agree on realistic prospecting goals—ones they can accomplish on a monthly, weekly, and especially on a daily basis.

5. Have sales managers work with salespeople to develop and implement plans to reach their goals—including a schedule of the times each day to devote to prospecting.

6. Create opportunities for small successes. Have sales managers work with each salesperson to assist and to provide coaching and feedback to ensure prospecting success and allow salespeople to see that they "can do it."

7. Provide words of support and encouragement that will build self-confidence in the salesperson's ability to prospect effectively, even in the face of rejection.

B-2 Solutions

1. Get salespeople to apply logic and realize they are more likely to sell more if they have a steady stream of new people who are genuine prospects, that is, people with the need, money, and authority or influence to buy.

2. Encourage salespeople to talk to a couple of top producing salespersons and find out how much prospecting contributes to their success.

3. Get salespeople to analyze their own experience. How much prospecting have they really done? How many new prospects have they identified? How many of the new and genuine prospects have they actually closed?

4. Gather data on prospecting successes throughout the sales organization and share the results with the entire sales force.

5. Establish incentive programs that offer compelling rewards for salespeople who have success with prospecting. Consider having prospecting quotas with the same outcomes (rewards and otherwise) as for sales quotas.

6. Shift the prospecting burden from the sales force to a temporary or permanent staff responsible for prospecting. Good hiring decisions and sound incentive programs are a must.

B-3 Solutions

1. Get salespeople to recognize the often overlooked outcomes of prospecting that have considerable value:

   a. greater familiarity with the marketplace;
   b. identification of new market segments;
   c. new ways customers can use the product or service to solve existing problems or satisfy new needs and demands;
   d. industry knowledge that will help sell more effectively; and
   e. information about competitors that can give a selling edge.

B-3 SOLUTIONS
(CONTINUED)

---

2. Try to get salespeople to view prospecting as a challenge rather than something that is simply to be dreaded.

3. Encourage salespeople to choose the methods of prospecting that are the most effective and rewarding to them. For example, one salesperson might focus more on getting referrals from current customers while another might stress using the phone for cold calling.

4. Get salespeople to review and consider how they would use the time and money saved by eliminating sales calls to people who are not real prospects.

5. Get salespeople to think about how much easier their job would be if most of their sales calls were with genuine prospects.

6. Get salespeople to calculate what their sales would be if the majority of their sales calls were with people who had the need, money, and authority to buy.

Sales executives may be curious, and may be talking to themselves, and if they are they may began to realize just how easy it is to overcome prospecting reluctance and how beneficial the results can be. And they may able to picture those results and see what they look like, hear what others will say, and feel what they feel with this new success. And they might just like the way it looks, sounds, and feels. They just might. And then perhaps the time is right for sales executives to do something, to make something happen, to take some steps to get prospecting back on track with their salespeople and their sales organization.

THE BIG PICTURE

Sales executives who want to strengthen the performance of the sales force sense by now that preparation and motivation always form the underpinnings of progress. Where to begin? Sales executives should start by helping salespeople see how prospecting fits into the big picture. This can be done by letting them hear and grasp a few things about: (1) prospecting and the sales process, (2) the sales model (Chapters 1 and 2) and the sales process, and (3) behavior style (Chapter 3) and the sales process.

Prospecting and the Sales Process

Sales executives will want to talk about and make salespeople aware that prospecting is the initial step in a sales process that includes four other steps, namely (1) preparation (Chapter 5), (2) the sales interview (Chapter 6), (3) closing the sale (Chapter 7), and (4) follow-up (Chapter 8). The first four steps are essential to making a sale, while Step 5 is necessary for resale. The steps are to be carried out in sequence as shown since the steps are a logical progression that salespeople can easily see.

STEPS IN THE SALES PROCESS

1.	Prospecting	Finding people who have the need, money, and authority or influence to buy
2.	Preparation	Getting ready to motivate prospects to buy
3.	Sales Interview	Identifying the specific objectives and needs of the prospect and jointly determining how the product or service can satisfy those needs
4.	Closing	Getting the prospect's commitment to buy
5.	Follow-Up	Taking steps after the sale to insure customer satisfaction and resale

Sales executives should come across loud and clear with salespeople about the great temptation and danger of not doing justice to each of the steps in the selling process. One of the biggest temptations, and most biting errors, is making appointments with people hoping they are prospects, but not knowing. The goal often is to grab an appointment with someone, anyone, as soon as possible. Yet, getting there doesn't feel right, or end right, if the prospect isn't qualified. Closing rates plummet, precious time flies away, and this flows into the inevitable conclusion that prospecting doesn't pay off. Salespeople must be persuaded and truly feel that in selling there are no shortcuts to success, that every step in the sales process is essential, and that sooner or later prospecting will make or break every salesperson.

The Sales Process and the Sales Model

Sales executives by now are aware that the sales model (Chapters 1 and 2) stresses that people are motivated to buy only when they (1) believe they can buy, that is, believe they have the need, money, and authority or influence to buy—B-1; (2) believe they will get the outcomes promised if they buy—B-2; and (3) believe the outcomes will be satisfying—B-3. This model is summarized, again, as follows.

The Sales Model

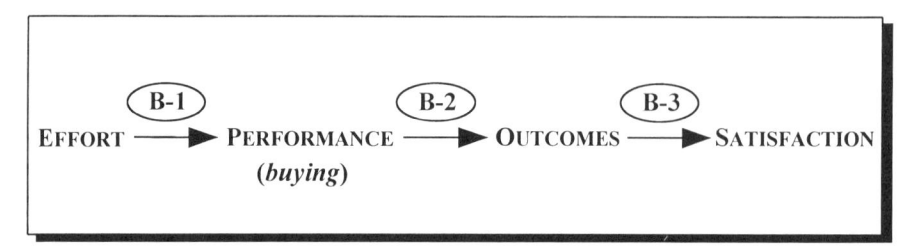

```
                 B-1              B-2            B-3
   EFFORT ──────▶ PERFORMANCE ──────▶ OUTCOMES ──────▶ SATISFACTION
                  (buying)
```

Sales executives will want to help salespeople grasp the notion that the sales model and the sales process go hand in hand. Here is a brief discussion that gives a clear picture of how each step in the sales process closely matches the three elements of the sales model (B-1, B-2, and B-3).

1. *Prospecting and B-1.* Prospecting is getting a feel for whether or not potential buyers believe they have the need, money, and authority or influence to buy (B-1). Salespeople must be reminded that it is the belief that counts because people are motivated to buy, or not to buy, depending on whether they believe they can buy. Determining this belief is essential to good prospecting.

2. *Preparation and B-2, B-3.* Preparation calls on salespeople to do their homework and *get ready* to convince prospects to believe that they will get (B-2) what they want (B-3) and avoid (B-2) what they don't want (B-3), if they buy the product or service.

3. *Sales Interview and B-1, B-2, B-3.* The focus of the sales interview is on *confirming* that prospects have the need, money, and authority or influence to buy (B-1) and *persuading* them to believe they will get (B-2) what they want (B-3) and avoid (B-2) what they don't want (B-3), if they buy the product or service.

4. *Closing and B-2, B-3.* Closing the sale means getting a hard decision, a firm handshake, or a signature on the dotted line. It is reaching an agreement whereby prospects agree to buy the product or service and salespeople agree to give (B-2) prospects what they want (B-3) and not give (B-2) what they don't want (B-3).

5. *Follow-Up and B-2, B-3.* Follow-up is being sure the pictures imagined before the sale are the same ones customers are receiving after the sale, that customers are getting (B-2) what they wanted (B-3) and not getting (B-2) what they didn't want (B-3), as promised during the sales process.

The Sales Process and Behavior Style

Sales executives will find it worthwhile to help salespeople see the value and hold on to the importance of considering the behavior style of prospects, as discussed in Chapter 3, in every step of the sales process. The prospect's behavior style (high D, high I, high S, or high C) determines the best way to: (1) handle people when prospecting, (2) prepare to meet with prospects, (3) conduct sells interviews, (4) close the sale, and (5) follow-up after the sale. In this and all of the remaining chapters, it will become evident how awareness of behavior style provides an easy and invaluable way to get in tune with prospects and strengthen their motivation to buy. Yes, strengthen their motivation to buy. That is the name of the game. Sales executives would do themselves an enormous favor if they would make the decision to equip the sales force to use behavior style. It leaves one wondering how long it will take to do yourself a favor now.

PROSPECTING WITH STRUCTURE

Sales executives who want to teach salespeople how to prospect effectively will give them a structure, a structure they can get a firm grip on. Some sales executives have a natural touch for creating structure (establishing model ways of doing things, designing methodology that spells out what and how), some don't. That doesn't matter. Some sales executives have an appreciation for structure, some don't. That does matter. Structure is the way people learn, the way they see what to do, the way they get a feel for how to do it. Effective prospecting has a structure. It spells out what has to be done to find people who have the need, money, and authority or influence to buy, and it provides guidelines for how to do it. This is what sales executives want to give their salespeople. Think about it. And just go ahead and do it. Give some structure. Or maybe not. Don't give structure. That way things can stay the way they are now. Avoid all the problems that come when everybody learns how to uncover big bunches of new prospects. Everybody sells more. Everybody gets paid more. Everybody likes their job more. Sales executives wouldn't want to deal with all that.

A structure like the one discussed here that has proven to work can cause a scene in any sales organization. Someone needs to teach salespeople to do four things that will give them a fresh perspective on prospecting: (1) set prospecting goals; (2) use prospect qualifications; (3) identify suspects (i.e., people who salespeople suspect *may* have the need, money, and authority or influence to buy); and (4) qualify suspects to find out which ones are prospects (i.e., people who *do* have the need, money, and authority or influence to buy). Let's take a close look at each step.

Step 1—Set Prospecting Goals

Sales executives have a good sense for how much difference goals make and that difference holds true with prospecting. High-performing salespeople have them. Everyone needs them. Sales executives will want to guide each salesperson to have at least one prospecting goal and others can be articulated as well:

1. number of prospects to identify per time period;
2. percentage of suspects who turn out to be prospects;
3. number of attempted contacts per time period;
4. percentage of appointments relative to contacts; and
5. percentage of closes relative to appointments.

Setting a firm goal for the first area is particularly important because it is quite clear that finding a certain number of prospects is the ultimate goal of prospecting. (Remember, a prospect is a person who is qualified to buy, i.e., a person who has the need, the money, and the authority or influence to buy.) An example of such a goal would be, "One qualified prospect per week, four per month." Other goals can make sense, too. For example, since some people who look and sound like prospects at first turn out not to be prospects at all, a second goal could be set to stress the importance of accurate judgments on the front end. An example of this kind of goal would be, "Seventy–five percent of all prospects called on each month will turn out to be legitimate prospects."

Step 2—Use Prospect Qualifications

Sales executives need to tell their salespeople how to know if a suspect is qualified to buy. These guidelines should come from the top of the sales organization and every salesperson should use them. Sales executives should provide firm leadership in establishing a list of qualifications. The conditions that must be met for the person or organization to be considered a prospect should be clearly spelled out to the sales force. There are several necessary qualifications.

1. *There must be a minimum need for the product or service (in units or dollars).* Example: "If they don't need at least five units per month, they are not a prospect."
2. *A minimum amount of money or credit must be available for the purchase of the product or service.* Example: "They must have at least $500 in cash or credit for the initial purchase."
3. *The person must have the authority or influence to buy.*
4. *The time frame for purchase must be acceptable.* Example: "We must be able to finalize the sale within three months."

Other qualifications may be established related to profitability, sales potential, location of the buyer, type of the buyer, and so on. The point is this. Sales executives are responsible for being sure prospect qualifications are established and communicated to the sales force so everyone knows what a prospect looks like when they see one.

Okay, let's say the sales executive has clearly defined the minimum prospect qualifications. Since prospects can be qualified in varying degrees, salespeople need a way to prioritize them. The most common way and one that is easy to grasp is the A-B-C rating system where prospects are rated as first, second, and third priority, respectively. The A-B-C rating system will be discussed by using it for each of the qualifications which follow to paint a picture of how the system can be applied. The ratings used here are subject to amendment, and that's fine. The system and ratings can be tailored to any organization and product or service being sold.

QUALIFICATION REGARDING NEED TO BUY

Quantity Needed				
Rating	A	B	C	Not a Prospect
1. The quantity of the product or service needed is below the minimum amount. (no rating, not a prospect)				X

QUALIFICATION REGARDING NEED TO BUY
(CONTINUED)

2.	The quantity needed is below the minimum now, but there is potentially a high need in the future. ("C" rating)			X	
3.	The quantity needed is just over the minimum requirement. ("B" rating)		X		
4.	The quantity needed is substantially over the minimum. ("A" rating)	X			
Time Frame of Need					
1.	The purchase can be made within the required time frame. ("A" rating)	X			
2.	It is likely, but not certain, the purchase can be made within the required time frame. ("B" rating)		X		
3.	It is possible, but not likely, the purchase can be made within the required time frame. ("C" rating)			X	
4.	It is impossible for the purchase to be made within the required time frame. (no rating, not a prospect)				X
Evidence of Need					
Rating		A	B	C	Not a Prospect
1.	Similar products or services are routinely purchased from a competitor, but the buyer is dissatisfied and wants to change suppliers. ("A" rating)	X			
2.	The organization is routinely buying and is willing to make a change in suppliers if circumstances are right. ("B" rating)		X		
3.	The buyer is reluctant to change suppliers. ("C" rating)			X	

QUALIFICATION REGARDING NEED TO BUY (CONTINUED)

					Not a Prospect
4.	The need for products and services has recently been created because of decisions, problems, or changes in the organization and one supplier has a strong inside track. ("C" rating)			X	
5.	There is a newly created demand and everyone has a fair shot at making the sale. ("A" rating)	X			
6.	The organization has a need for the product or service, but the organization does not realize it yet. ("B" rating)		X		
7.	The organization does not need the product or service. (no rating, not a prospect)				X

QUALIFICATION REGARDING MONEY TO BUY

Rating		A	B	C	Not a Prospect
1.	Money is budgeted for the products or services needed. ("A" rating)	X			
2.	Money is not budgeted, but it is believed to be available upon request. ("B" rating)		X		
3.	Money is not available, but it is believed the organization is willing and able to obtain a loan. ("B" rating)		X		
4.	Money is not available, but it is believed the organization is willing and able to obtain credit. ("B" rating)		X		
5.	Money is not available, and it is possible, though not likely, that the organization can secure either a loan or credit. ("C" rating)			X	
6.	The organization does not have and cannot obtain the money to buy. (no rating, not a prospect)				X

QUALIFICATION REGARDING AUTHORITY AND INFLUENCE TO BUY

Rating	A	B	C	Not a Prospect
1. The person unquestionably has the authority to buy. ("A" rating)	X			
2. The person has authority to buy, subject to approval. ("B" rating)		X		
3. The person does not have the authority to buy but has considerable influence over the decision maker. ("B" rating)		X		
4. The person's recommendations are routinely approved by the decision maker. ("A" rating)	X			
5. The person does not have either the authority or influence to buy. (no rating, not a prospect)				X

How can the individual ratings on each qualification be combined? If all individual qualifications have the same rating (say, an "A" rating), then the overall rating would be the same. If the individual ratings differ, as typically they do, the overall rating probably should be the same as the lowest rating.

Step 3—Identify Suspects

Sales executives know it all boils down to names. Salespeople need a hard list of names, names of individuals suspected of having the need, money, and authority or influence to buy. It is from this pool of names that salespeople will find the individuals who are legitimate prospects that have the potential to eventually buy. Getting the names of suspects, and a steady flow of them, is the only way salespeople can succeed. Names and more names. That's the name of the selling game.

Is there a clear-cut way that sales executives can lead and direct the sales force to find people suspected of being potential buyers? The best way is to make salespeople aware, to remind them, of the many proven approaches available to them. They can all work, but salespeople have to find the ones that feel right and will work best for them. Sales executives should encourage salespersons to consider the options that appear here and think about which ones best fit them, given their behavior style, the product or service they sell, and the market they're in. They also should be called on to reevaluate the way they have been identifying suspects, decide how they can improve, and move ahead to generate that constant stream of suspects so vital to their success. Let's review the options.

Publications

Sales executives should talk up the use of publications that show the names of organizations and individuals who are potential buyers. Industry directories allow salespeople to see a synopsis of companies in the industry, including names of key individuals, addresses, products manufactured and/or sold, sales figures, and so on. This information alone may be sufficient to determine if the organization should be called, or called on, and qualified. Sales executives should make appropriate directories available to their salespeople. Directories can be found in local libraries, by calling companies in the area and asking about directories for their industry, or contacting associations that represent the various industry groups. Industry directories are indispensable to prospecting. Other published sources that can be helpful are the yellow pages, newspaper articles, want ads, and Chamber of Commerce publications. Sales executives should make it easy for salespeople to prospect, and making key listings available to them is a great start.

Cold Calls

Sales executives will want to be very outspoken about the importance of cold calls as one of the most effective, though most hated, methods of prospecting. This is the method of calling unknown persons to find out if they are qualified to buy. The publications mentioned earlier are good sources of names for cold calling. Reluctance to make cold calls is perhaps the single greatest cause of failure among promising salespersons. Salespeople can be as sharp as a tack, but when they have call reluctance, the result is not enough suspects, not enough prospects, and not enough sales.

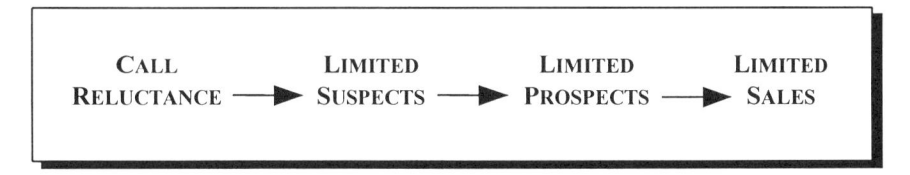

CALL RELUCTANCE ⟶ LIMITED SUSPECTS ⟶ LIMITED PROSPECTS ⟶ LIMITED SALES

Sales executives are well aware that most salespeople are reluctant to make cold calls. This is easy to understand. Reluctance stems from the distracting noise ricocheting around in their heads, like "I hate doing it" (a B-3 problem), "It's too painful" (a B-3 problem), "It's like hunting a needle in a haystack" (a B-1 problem), "Prospecting is filled with rudeness and rejection" (a B-3 problem), "It will not lead to anything anyway" (a B-2 problem), or "I can't do it" (a B-1 problem).

Sales executives can help salespeople get a handle on call reluctance, so just go ahead and help them. Just do it. Give encouragement, be supportive, and offer guidelines like the following. Then follow up and be sure that sales managers, as well as the salespeople, are doing their part in converting these guidelines into action that will pay off and help the sales force take a step forward in overcoming reluctance to make cold calls.

1. Set specific goals related to cold calls, such as number of attempts or percentage of appointments to contacts.
2. Block time for prospecting. Then do it. One hour, two hours, then take a break. Count successes and start again.
3. Use positive self-talk to get ready. Remember that people may need the product or service, that it can help them.
4. Use self-rewarding for small successes.
5. Remember, it is a numbers game. More calls lead to more suspects.

Drop-bys

The drop-by is a form of cold call. Some salespeople feel comfortable and find it effective to "drop by" a place of business, without an appointment, in an attempt to find someone with the need, money, and authority or influence to buy.

Centers of Influence

Persons who have a lot of contacts can identify suspects, if salespeople can get them to talk and help. People active in the business community are the best bets. It may not be easy to win them over, but they can be a gold mine.

Networking

Developing a network of people who are suspects themselves, or who know suspects, can be very beneficial. This means spending a considerable amount of time mingling with people at meetings, restaurants, clubs, parties, and so on.

Referrals

Sales executives know that referral prospecting screams out as the easiest and most overlooked opportunity in prospecting that salespeople will ever see or hear about. It also is one of the most effective and is nothing more than focusing on current customers and asking them for names of people they suspect to be potential buyers. Salespeople have a good sense for when they have strong relationships with customers, and referrals from these customers can result in an endless source and flow of prospects. Most satisfied customers are willing to give referrals. Sales executives who have an image of a brighter future for their organizations should not rest until they take steps to educate every salesperson on the merits of getting referrals from current customers and motivate them to do so. This clearly is a method for sales executives to make a scene about.

Nesting

Sales executives will want to push and be outspoken about nesting, the concept of identifying suspects by developing a particular industry or geographical area. This restricts the world in which the salesperson sells and makes it easier to identify possible buyers. Being nested in a particular industry or in a specific geographic area, makes it relatively easy to identify all of the suspects there. For some products and services, this can be an effective way of identifying the limited number of suspects in a defined market.

Lead Swapping

Swapping leads with other salespeople can be a good way to identify suspects. Not only are good leads possible this way, useful information about the company and the person to call on often is forthcoming. Salespeople can see that lead swapping can be a valuable approach for identifying suspects.

Company-generated Leads

Sales executives need to make good decisions about the use of advertising, direct mail, trade shows, and so on to generate leads. Some sales organizations find this to be a very effective way to identify suspects.

Step 4—Qualify Suspects

Sales executives will want to speak out and focus on giving structure to their salespeople because when the background work is over and suspects have been identified, it's time for salespeople to start talking to them to find out which ones are qualified to buy. Here is some structure that will help salespeople relax and feel comfortable using: (1) guidelines to follow when qualifying suspects; (2) asking qualifying questions; and (3) confirming qualifying conclusions. Providing structure like this is very important when salespeople have a history of not performing as well as they would like. The structure clearly maps out what to do in a step-by-step fashion and this elevates self-confidence, an essential ingredient when motivating salespeople to overcome their own inertia.

Qualifying Guidelines

There are several basic points that sales executives will want to stress to guide salespeople when qualifying suspects. Here are some of the important guidelines.

1. Keep in mind that there are two ultimate goals to hang on to: (1) finding out if the suspects are qualified to buy and (2) getting an appointment with them if they are. Everything should be done with this in mind.

2. Do the qualifying over the phone, whenever possible, because qualifying is talk, it's asking and listening. Then requalify in person.

3. Do the qualifying with decision makers. This should be the focus. Others are not in a position to answer all of the key questions about the need, money, and authority or influence to buy. They may say "not interested" when the decision maker would say "let's talk." *Remember, don't take a "no" from a person who can't say "yes."*

4. Use each person to get closer to the decision maker. It is not uncommon to talk with several people in a company before finding the right one, namely the one who has the need, money, and authority or influence to buy.

5. Save the selling for the sales call. It flows better that way. Mixing selling with qualifying can be tempting, but resisting makes sense. Take care of first things first. Find out if the person is a prospect. Selling over the phone rarely works and ending up with little more than a lost opportunity is discouraging.

6. Press hard for information because that's the only way to decide if the person is qualified to buy. The temptation can be overwhelming to give up when the person is playing hard to get. It is equally tempting

to give in to an appointment with people who are not qualified to buy if they show an interest.

7. Set appointments only with persons who are qualified to buy. Remember that the goal is not to get appointments, but to get appointments with qualified buyers. To do otherwise is a costly waste of time.

Asking Qualifying Questions

Sales executives are aware of how important it is to constantly remind salespeople that to be qualified to buy, a person must: (1) need the product or service, (2) have the money to buy it, and (3) have the authority to make the buying decision or the influence to get it made. Two other qualifiers should be discussed with salespeople and clearly understood by them. One is the time frame in which the buying would take place. There was mention of this earlier in the chapter. The other is the "no sale" condition. Let's look at the latter briefly.

Sometimes salespeople will see uncontrollable circumstances under which a sales transaction cannot take place even though the prospect is qualified in terms of need, money, and authority or influence to buy. This is called a no sale condition. For example, a company may be squarely in the middle of a buyout or merger and certain purchasing decisions have been placed temporarily on hold. Or the death of a business partner may result in pressure for the delay of major expenditures. Sales executives may need to remind salespeople that when a no sale condition is present, it sometimes is best to walk away until the issue is resolved and concentrate on prospects who can buy *now*.

Sales executives definitely should make a loud cry for salespeople to get a good grasp of, and then use, a wide range of questions available to obtain the information needed to determine if a person is qualified to buy. Here are some examples. Sales executives should urge salespeople to pick and choose a few from each category and try them out until they have a handful that work for them.

QUALIFYING QUESTIONS REGARDING NEED TO BUY

- "Are you using a product or service like this now?"
- "Are you considering a change in suppliers?"
- "Are you willing to review your current situation?"
- "What are your objectives and needs regarding . . . ?"

Qualifying Questions Regarding Need to Buy (Continued)

- "Have you ever considered using . . . ?"
- "Are you thinking of purchasing . . . ?"
- "Do you need a product (service) like this?"

Qualifying Questions Regarding Money to Buy

- "Do you have the money to buy this?"
- "Is money budgeted for this kind of thing?"
- "Is enough money available to buy this?"
- "How much money do you have allocated for this?"
- "Can you come up with the money you'd need?"
- "Can you meet our credit terms and requirements?"

Qualifying Questions Regarding Authority to Buy

- "Who would make the decision on this?"
- "Are you the decision maker?"
- "Who is the decision maker?"
- "How will the decision get made on this?"
- "Do you have to get approval on this?"
- "Where is the decision made for this kind of thing?"
- "Is there anyone else who would need to be in this meeting to make a decision?"

QUALIFYING QUESTIONS REGARDING INFLUENCE TO BUY

- "What is your relationship with the decision maker?"
- "Can you influence the decision maker?"
- "Can you push this decision through?"
- "Can you get approval on this?"
- "Does she normally go along with your recommendations?"

QUALIFYING QUESTIONS REGARDING TIME FRAME TO BUY

- "What is your time frame for making this decision?"
- "When would you want delivery on this?"
- "How pressing is your need for this?"
- "How soon would you want to get started?"
- "What kind of priority does this have?"

QUALIFYING QUESTIONS REGARDING NO SALE CONDITIONS

- "Can you think of anything that could keep us from getting together on this?"
- "Are there any unusual circumstances that could delay doing what you want to do?"
- "Is there anything else I need to know?"

Confirming Qualifying Conclusions

Salespeople may need to be reminded and hear that sometimes a person clearly is a prospect and sometimes it's more than a little hazy. There may not be any doubt about the person's qualifications to buy—at least everything sounds good. At other times there can be some uncertainty floating around and it just isn't clear. In either case, it is always best to reach out and get confirmation. Doing so can prevent costly mistakes. It's simple, easy, and fast. Just summarize what the person has said and state the conclusion that logically flows from it. Here are two examples sales executives can offer salespeople who are being prepared for prospecting.

- "So you definitely need this product, you have $1,200 budgeted for it, and you're the decision maker and don't have to get approval from anyone. Is that correct?
- "You have an ongoing need for this, it's in your budget each year, getting approval to buy is a formality, you're locked into a contract with your current supplier for five more months, but you are willing to consider changing suppliers at that time. So, you're not ready to talk now, but you will be in about three months. Did I get that right?"

Sales executives need to stress that when people hear their own words repeated back to them, and hear the conclusion the salesperson has reached, a valuable thing happens. They will confirm whether they are a prospect or not. Either way, the salesperson comes out ahead. If the person acknowledges being a prospect, it is only a formality to get an appointment. If the person is not a prospect, this is a clear signal to saddle up and ride off to the next order of business. Getting confirmation pays off.

PROSPECTING AND THE SALES MODEL

Sales executives see the relationship between prospecting and the sales model. The focus in prospecting is on finding out who the suspects are and then qualifying them. Prospecting calls for the salesperson to gather information to determine this. In doing so, the salesperson is asking, "Do you have the need, money, and authority or influence to buy?" The answers obviously are based on the suspect's *perception* of the situation, which in essence means the salesperson is asking, "Do you *believe* you have the need, money, and authority or influence to buy?" This is exactly the meaning of B-1—"Can I buy?"—in the sales model.

PROSPECTING AND BEHAVIOR STYLE

Sales executives may or may not see the relationship between prospecting and behavior style, but they certainly will feel curious about how this affects the way prospects should be qualified. This is information sales executives will want to pass along to their salespeople. Let's take a look at the impact that each of the four behavior styles has on prospecting.

Prospecting (B-1) and the High D

Persons with the high D behavior style are willing to stretch the bounds of their authority and sometimes see themselves as having the authority to buy, even when they don't. They tend to feel they can accomplish anything, so they have a tendency to believe they can get the money to buy, even when they can't, and the tendency to believe they can convince the real decision maker to buy, even when they can't.

The bottom line is that high Ds tend to have high B-1s and hold on to them in an unshakable way. In fact, their B-1s sometimes are unrealistically high; that is, they believe they can make the buying decision, even when they can't. This problem is further magnified because high Ds tend to have a strong ego which sometimes leads them to overstate things. When high Ds say, "I can make this buying decision," it may be an overstatement that is misleading because it gives the mistaken appearance that the high D is a prospect.

When working with high Ds, there are at least three things sales executives should advise salespeople to focus on doing. First, when high Ds say they can buy, their tendency to overstate things should be recognized and confirmation should be obtained to see if they really *can* buy before getting too far into the sales process. Second, it should be recognized that once they say "I can buy," they will do everything possible to prove they are right. This can work in the salesperson's favor by subtly encouraging them to back up their claims. Third, when high Ds don't have the money, authority, or influence to buy, remember that they have a dogged determination to get what they want. They can be challenged to get whatever it takes to make the purchase. They might just do it. They also can be challenged to convince the real decision maker to do the buying. They may be successful here, too.

Prospecting (B-1) and the High I

The most commonly heard strength of people with the high I behavior style is their ability to influence others. This means that when persons with the high I style don't have the money to buy something they want, they tend to firmly believe they can get it. When they have neither the authority nor the money, they often believe they can influence the right person to buy it for them. Not only do they believe they can get what they want, they generally are not hesitant about using their influence to get it. In other words, persons with the high I style tend to have high B-1s. That is, they believe they can buy, even when the odds appear to be against them.

In fact, they often have feelings that are overly optimistic when it comes to believing they can buy. Not only do they convince themselves, they sometimes convince salespeople they can buy, even when they can't. This problem is worsened to some extent because they wish to be seen in a positive light and this leads them to often overstate what they can do. This can mean that salespeople might aggressively pursue the sale only to find out in the end that the high I was not a prospect at all. In view of this, what advice can sales executives give salespeople about working with prospects who have the high I behavior style? There are several suggestions. First, recognize that because high Is tend to have unrealistically high B-1s and often overstate things, there is a need to focus on closely qualifying them to be sure they are legitimate prospects. Second, even when they don't have the authority or money, consider them a prospect if they have a strong motivation to buy and the willingness to use their influence to get it.

Prospecting (B-1) and the High S

When persons with the high S style don't see themselves as having the money and/or authority or influence to buy, they are not likely to take steps to get it. Doing so is not their style. But being open, direct, and up front about it is not their style either. This can be very misleading and give a false sense about being a prospect. At least two other high S tendencies make it hard to know if they are prospects. One is the difficulty they have in saying "no." They simply find it rough to say, "No, I can't buy." The other is their need for relationships. This can be incorrectly perceived as an interest in buying when it really is an interest in the salesperson as a person. When high Ss don't believe they can buy, they definitely are not prospects. Again, it's time to saddle up and move on.

Even when high Ss have the money and authority or influence to buy (high B-1), it may be hard to get a handle on it. Here's why. First, it is not their style to provide an open flow of information, instead preferring to be indirect in their communication. The salesperson might ask, "Do you have the need, money, and authority or influence to buy?" The response typically is a soft-spoken, ambiguous, indirect answer rather than a simple "yes" or "no." Second, they often are hesitant and uncertain. They feel the need to ask for the opinion of others, and having no strong sense of urgency and preferring a more paced approach, they tend to procrastinate. This results in constant delays, like taking forever to talk to others who are using the product or service, or repeatedly postponing the review of product information. This eventually may leave the salesperson wondering if the high S really has the need, money, and authority or influence to buy.

How can sales executives get salespeople to stand up and take notice of these problems and deal with high Ss more effectively? Two things: (1) Remind them not to jump to conclusions too quickly. Recognize that people with the high S behavior style can give a false appearance, either that they can or can't buy. (2) Be friendly and develop a *relationship* before going for direct answers with them. When using questions like "Do you have the budget to buy?" be prepared to follow up with, "Does that mean 'yes' "? Continue clarifying their ambiguity until things are clear, but do it carefully and without pressure.

Prospecting (B-1) and the High C

High Cs are interesting because they almost always feel pressure around the question "Can I really do this?" Consequently, salespeople often find themselves seeing B-1 problems, regardless of the circumstances. People with the high C style tend to: (1) be very, very cautious, seek to avoid risk, and are reluctant to do anything that has the appearance of stepping beyond their bounds; (2) believe in following the rules on everything, including rules about who has authority to make buying decisions; and (3) believe "If I don't have it (money or authority), I can't get it." When it sounds like they don't have the money or authority to buy something they want, they are not likely to try to get it. When they do try, it may be a halfhearted effort that falls short and leaves them empty-handed.

Okay, then, what does it mean when high Cs talk and say, "I really want this product (or service), but I'm not the decision maker." High Cs usually speak in a firm way, so it probably means just that, and it's not likely to change. Unlike high Ds and high Is who often are willing and able to get the authority and money needed to buy, or get someone else to buy it for them, high Cs aren't. As a rule, it is best to quickly move on to the person who does have the money and authority to buy. However, it is important to remember that high Cs often are gatekeepers, so they can be invaluable in helping identify the decision maker, providing information about that person, and maybe even clearing a smooth path in getting there.

On the other hand, when high Cs have the money and authority or influence to buy, salespeople still may be faced with a B-1 problem of sorts. High Cs tend to be skeptical and feel a strong need for all the facts and details, preferably in writing, before making a buying decision. Because of their money and authority or influence, they may conclude, "I can buy," but they also are firmly saying, "I can't buy unless I follow all of the rules for buying that I've set up for myself." One of the main rules is "I can't buy unless I have all the information." When they talk about wanting all the information, they literally mean "all" and they prefer getting it on paper. This need for completeness and perfection usually results in a request for a written proposal and often causes them to take forever to make buying decisions. They tend to procrastinate and stall until they have every possible assurance that they are making the perfect buying decision.

Salespeople clearly see that high Cs are hard to sell, so they feel a need for good advice from sales executives on dealing with them. Salespeople must first decide whether to stick it out with the high C or not. There are cases when it is best to forget them and move on. Sometimes the value of a sale is less than the time, cost, and frustration of making it.

If high C prospects are worth holding on to, then what must salespeople do? First, come to grips with the fact that the selling process will be lengthy, very lengthy. Second, expect to jump through all the hoops, which invariably include constant demands for information and frequent requests to put it in writing. Third, prepare mentally for the frustrations that are certain to be experienced throughout the selling process. Fourth, dig deep down for the kind of patience that is certain to be needed.

Selling to high Cs is like having a long, hard road to travel, and it is easy to turn back and not get to the destination unless the journey begins with full knowledge of the road that lies ahead and a willingness to put in the time, yield to the demands, and be patient in spite of trying times. All of this goes with the territory when selling to high Cs. Salespeople who are persistent enough to complete the journey are in for a special reward because high Cs are loyal. Once they make a decision, they tend to stick with it for a long, long time. That's the way it should be. Getting in tune with the high C's behavior style earns the right to have a loyal customer.

SUMMARY

- It is easy to see that reluctance to prospect is a common cause of failure in sales, but it can be overcome when sales executives go ahead and do something about it and apply basic principles of motivation to identify and eliminate the causes of the reluctance.

- There is a pressing need for sales executives to step up to the challenge and equip the sales force and give people the skills they need for effective prospecting.

- Sales executives can help convert prospects into customers if they will decide to show salespeople that prospecting is the starting point for motivating people to buy.

CHAPTER 5

Preparing to Motivate

Sales executives see it all the time. They hear about it from the sales force. They feel the impact of it. The amount of time salespeople spend with prospects is brief. Too brief. And sales executives feel the sting from it. Time runs out before the prospect's needs are fully understood, before everything is explained, before critical questions are asked and answered, before misunderstandings are clarified, and before objections are overcome. It happens often. Too often. Sales executives know that prevention is the best way to deal with it, and that means *preparation*. Sales executives must stand up and take notice. They must listen to those who stress the importance of getting the sales force prepared for battle. They must get a firm grip on readying their salespeople to be prepared to motivate people to buy.

In light of the complexity of selling, it isn't possible for salespeople to be prepared for everything, no matter what sales executives do, but insisting on a little more preparation gives a loud and clear signal that getting a better handle on the situation in advance can go a long way toward meeting sales quotas. Sales executives can be outspoken on the need for more preparation and can nudge the organization forward by equipping the sales force to prepare for sales calls by: (1) anticipating questions prospects might ask and preparing, in advance, to answer them; (2) anticipating objections and preparing to deal with them; (3) anticipating stalls and preparing to respond to them; (4) anticipating "no" and preparing to handle it; (5) anticipating the need to ask and preparing questions in advance; and (6) anticipating the need to listen and preparing psychologically and skill-wise to do so.

Sales executives get the picture. They've seen it, heard it, and felt it. They've learned it the hard way. They know from their own experience that people aren't motivated to buy from salespeople who aren't prepared to make the sale. Sales executives know that salespeople close more deals when they are prepared. And every sales executive should focus on equipping and motivating the sales force to be prepared to make the sale.

ANTICIPATING QUESTIONS

Prospects always have questions and they expect answers. Getting caught off guard makes salespeople look bad. It may do more. It may cause the sale to slip right out of their hands. Salespeople can handle most questions that flow their way by anticipating and preparing for them. Sales executives must take the necessary steps to equip the sales force to anticipate the questions and train them to have a firm grasp on the answers. This is especially important when new products are introduced and new salespeople come on board. Sales executives can imagine how smooth it goes when they have prepared the sales force to articulate the information prospects need and request.

No matter how well salespeople are prepared, they'll get stuck from time to time with questions they can't answer. When this happens, salespeople should be taught to plainly see it is best to respond in a straightforward and clear way by saying something like, "That's a good question. I don't know the answer, but I can talk to my sales manager (or a service technician, engineer, specialist, etc.) and get back to you right away." Prospects generally feel better with an honest "I don't know" than with a slick answer that has a hint of being wrong or a clumsy or smooth response that dodges the question. Sales executives need to stress that salespeople don't have to always be perfect with customers, and the right kind of preparation will get them close enough to perfect.

The best way for salespeople to prepare for the questions they will hear is to anticipate the questions in advance. Sales executives will find it interesting to learn that behavior style is perhaps the best way to get a glimpse into the future and anticipate the questions prospects will ask. This means that teaching salespeople how to clearly identify the prospect's behavior style also teaches them to anticipate the questions they are most likely to face. Let's take a look at the kind of questions frequently asked by each of the four behavior styles.

Typical High D Questions

High D prospects tend to ask short, pointed questions. They ask straight forward questions to get a feel for the salesperson's competence. Their questions focus on the bottom line, not the details. They ask questions to get a handle on whether the product or service will yield results, improve performance, and strengthen their position of dominance. Their questions reflect a preference for the sales call to be short and to the point, yielding the necessary information for a quick buying decision. Here are some typical high D questions.

- "What have you got for me?"
- "Are you sure you know what you're talking about?"
- "Can I change it?"
- "Is it the biggest and best you have?"
- "How much does it cost?"
- "Can I get it immediately?"
- "What's the bottom line?"

Typical High I Questions

Prospects with a high I behavior style tend to ask questions that focus on people rather than the product. They ask questions to see how others will be affected. They especially want to know how others will view *them* if they buy. Their questions will show how much they want the product or service to please others, to make people feel good, and lead to the acceptance and approval of others. Their questions will probe to see if buying will extend their scope of influence. They ask questions that reflect their desire for the sales call to be a warm, pleasant experience. A list of typical high I questions follows.

- "Will our employees like it?"
- "Will it make me look good?"
- "Do you mind if I tell my friends about it?"
- "How can I get some publicity out of it?"

- "Will it help me win the contest?"
- "Is this the best price you have?"
- "This has been a real pleasure. When can we get back together?"

Typical High S Questions

High S prospects tend to ask questions that focus on their concern for stability and predictability. They will ask questions to be sure the purchase will avoid, or at least minimize, change. Their preference is to keep things as they are, so their questions will be to justify continuing with the same products, same brands, and same suppliers. They will ask questions to be sure that new products and services are proven, predictable, risk-free, and maintain the status quo. In addition, they ask questions that reflect the importance they place on trust in any relationship. A list of typical questions that salespeople can expect from high S buyers follows.

- "I've been using the same supplier for years. Why should I change?"
- "I've been buying the original brand for years. Why change now?"
- "Is the original model still available if I want it?"
- "Why did you have to change it just when I'm getting used to it?"
- "Is this a proven product?"
- "Can you call me back in a week?"
- "What is everybody else buying?"

Typical High C Questions

High C prospects tend to ask a million very probing, detailed questions. They will ask questions that help them feel like they are making the perfect buying decision. Their questions will stress the importance of products and services meeting both the technical requirements of the organization and their own personal standards with respect to what they are buying, how they buy it, and from whom they are buying it. They ask questions that reflect their need to have a firm grasp of all of the available information before making a buying decision. They also ask questions that show their preference for sales calls to be detailed, thorough, information oriented, and all business. Here are some typical questions high C buyers ask and salespeople will want to be prepared in advance to answer them because this is what the high C expects.

Preparing to Motivate 75

- "Who are you?"
- "What is your background?"
- "Do I know anyone who knows you?"
- "How long have you been selling this product (or service)?"
- "Is this a high-quality unit?"
- "What facts do you have to back up that statement?"
- "What kind of warranty does it have?"
- "I don't have to make a decision on this now, do I?"
- "Can you get me a proposal on that?"

One of the important ways sales executives can prepare salespeople to anticipate questions is by training them to look for and get a handle on the behavior style of their prospects. But this only the first step. Salespeople also have to be prepared to answer the questions. Although this is easy for some questions, it is not for others. However, this kind of preparation flows immediately into better sales results. It keeps salespeople from stumbling over questions, it makes the sells process smoother, it reduces the number of sales calls that have to be made, and it increases sales. Sales executives who equip their sales force with the ability to anticipate questions and be prepared to answer them view doing so as a wise investment that pays big dividends. It is clear that people are more motivated to buy from salespeople whose preparation shows a firm grasp of the situations that arise with each prospective buyer.

ANTICIPATING OBJECTIONS

Sales executives plainly see that the best way for salespeople to deal with objections is to prepare for them ahead of time. This means that salespeople have to have a sense for what the objections will be. In other words, the objections first must be anticipated, then preparation to prevent or overcome them can begin. Sales executives will be pleased to hear that anticipating objections is not hard to do.

There are many techniques for handling objections[1] and sales executives are well aware of most of them. As a result, sales executives may be wondering if they will like the approach presented here. Is a comprehensive approach important? Is simplicity an advantage? Is ease of application a benefit? Well, if the answer is yes, this approach is well worth considering. When all is said and done, it gives results. So, here is the approach recommended for anticipating objections.

When a prospect has a need for the product or service, there are three, and only three, objections to buying. Salespeople can get a good grip on understanding and anticipating objections when they are viewed in the context of the sales model. Translated into the language of the sales model, here is the best way to classify and picture objections.

Objections to Buying

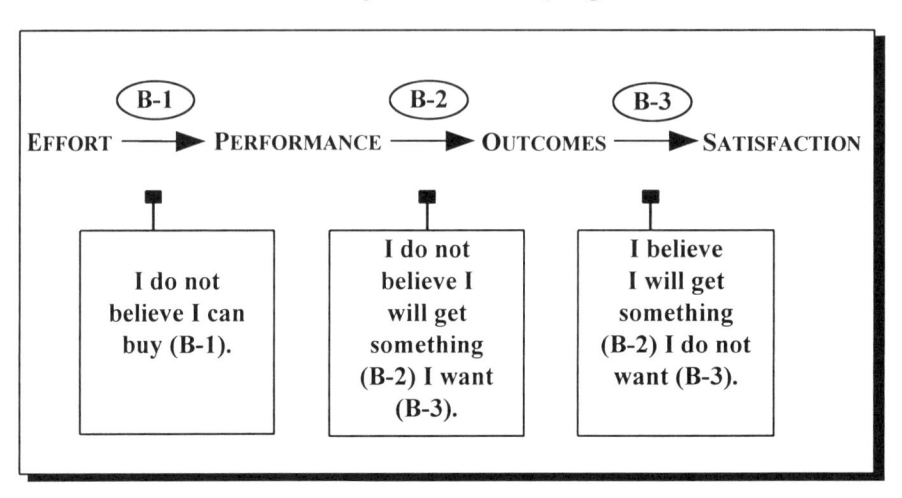

EFFORT —(B-1)→ PERFORMANCE —(B-2)→ OUTCOMES —(B-3)→ SATISFACTION

| I do not believe I can buy (B-1). | I do not believe I will get something (B-2) I want (B-3). | I believe I will get something (B-2) I do not want (B-3). |

These objections are derived from the six possibilities illustrated in the sales model. Three of the possibilities are objections, motivating prospects away from buying. Three are favorable, motivating prospects in the direction of buying. Sales executives, take special notice here. This is one of the most important sets of information salespeople can learn. It is simple. It is easy to learn. It is easy to use. And it gives results, but only if you, as the decision-making sales executive, give this information to the sales force.

1. *Effort is expected to lead to buying (B-1).* No objection to this.
2. *Effort is not expected to lead to buying (B-1).* Objection 1:

    "I can't "buy."
3. *Outcome is wanted (B-3) and expected (B-2).* No objection to this.
4. *Outcome is wanted (B-3) but not expected (B-2).* Objection 2:

    "I will not get something I want."
5. *Outcome is not wanted (B-3) but expected (B-2).* Objection 3:

    "I will get something I don't want."

6. *Outcome is not wanted (B-3) and not expected (B-2).* No objection to this.

Objection 1—"I Can't Buy"

Prospects naturally object to buying when they don't believe they can buy (B-1). This is a common objection among those who were not properly qualified as prospects. When people feel like they aren't in a position to buy, they don't buy.

Statements

When salespeople are trained to listen, they will hear people voice the "I can't buy" objection in a variety of ways, including those shown below.

Regarding Money

- "It cost too much."
- "Your price is too high."
- "I can't afford it."

Regarding Authority and Influence

- "I'll have to talk to my boss."
- "I can't push this through."
- "I'm not the decision maker."
- "I don't have enough influence."

Regarding Circumstances

- "The timing isn't right."
- "This isn't a good time."
- "Maybe later."

Causes

There are three possible *causes* of the "I can't buy" objection, namely, people believe they do not have: (1) the money to buy; (2) the authority or influence to buy; or (3) control over other circumstances.

Regarding the latter, people may feel it is impossible to buy, at least at the present time, because of a pending merger or acquisition, recent death of a partner, or the person is too swamped to consider buying now, to name a few.

How to Handle "I Can't Buy"

Sales executives should sound off about how to handle the "I can't buy" objection. Different approaches are required. It all boils down to and depends on the underlying causes. In light of this, here are some suggestions that will work. But they work only when sales executives pass them along to the sales force. These suggestions probably are nothing new to salespeople, except sometimes, and maybe often for some salespeople, they have knowledge that they fail to use. Sales executives may need to do nothing more than give salespeople a reminder. This is not a situation that requires training, and one that can have considerable payoff.

HOW TO HANDLE "I CAN'T BUY"

B-1 Objection/Causes	How to Handle the Objection
"I can't buy *because* I don't have the money."	Find a way to free up some money from the budget.
	Discover a way to get someone to make the money available.
	Show how the money can be borrowed.
	Extend credit, delay billing, or arrange monthly payments.
"I can't buy *because* I don't have the authority or influence."	Show the prospect how to persuade the decision maker.
	Go with the prospect and sell the decision maker.
"I can't buy *because* of the circumstances."	Get a time frame and come back when circumstances have changed.

Objection 2—"I Will Not Get Something I Want"

Prospects naturally speak out against buying when they want something (B-3) they don't believe they will get (B-2). That is, when prospects believe that buying will not lead to certain outcomes (B-2) that would be satisfying (B-3), they sense a strong opposition to buying. In other words, it has a negative impact on their motivation to buy.

Examples

Many outcomes may be "wanted but not expected" by prospects. Some that can easily be imagined are:

- timely delivery;
- shipments without problems (no breakage, no shortages, and so on);
- quality;
- responsiveness to problems;
- good, timely service;
- no surprises; and
- an honest salesperson.

Statements

Prospects mention the "I will not get something I want" objection in a variety of ways, including those shown below.

- "So you're telling me I will not get it."
- "Do I have all the information?"
- "I'm confused about what to expect."
- "I'm not sure I believe you."
- "I've had a bad experience with other salespeople."
- "It's hard to overcome that kind of reputation."
- "I can't forget what happened last time."

How to Handle "I Will Not Get Something I Want"

How should sales executives stress handling the "I will not get something I want" objection? The focus should be on B-2, namely, changing the belief from "I will not get it" to "I will get it." The best way to do this depends on the underlying cause of the B-2 objection. Here are some appropriate ways to handle each cause. Notice that the first solution includes substitution. Sales executives know that substitution is a bright, clever, creative, and powerful way to overcome the "I will not get what I want" objection. The idea of substitution is for the salesperson to replace the thing that can't be given to the prospect with one or more other outcomes the prospect may find equally desirable. Sales executives may want to make a point to convince the sales force how valuable substitution can be.

HOW TO HANDLE
"I WILL NOT GET SOMETHING I WANT"

B-2 Objection/Causes	How to Handle the Objection
The prospect correctly believes "I will not get what I want" (*because* it is not available).	Find a way to give what is desired, or a satisfactory substitute, when possible.
The prospect incorrectly believes "I will not get what I want" (*because* she does not know it is available).	Provide information.
The prospect incorrectly believes "I will not get what I want" (*because* he does not understand generally what he will get).	Provide clarification, and more information.
The prospect incorrectly believes "I will not get what I want" (*because* she doesn't believe what has been promised).	Provide evidence of outcomes.
The prospect incorrectly believes "I will not get what I want" (*because* he has had bad experiences with salespeople).	Gain credibility.
The prospect incorrectly believes "I will not get what I want" (*because* the salesperson, the product or service, or the company has a bad reputation).	Overcome bad reputation.
The prospect incorrectly believes "I will not get what I want" (*because* she had a bad experience with the salesperson, the product or service, or the company).	Overcome bad experience.

Some of the ways to provide evidence of outcomes, gain credibility, overcome a bad reputation, and overcome a bad experience are: (1) documented results; (2) product demonstrations; (3) observation of the product or service in action; (4) testimonials; (5) persuasive arguments; and (6) free samples or a free trial.

Objection 3—"I Will Get Something I Don't Want"

Prospects naturally object to buying when they believe they will get (B-2) something they don't want (B-3). That is, when prospects believe that *buying* will lead to certain *outcomes* (B-2) that would be dissatisfying (B-3), they are opposed to buying. Getting something that is not wanted doesn't feel good and this strips away their motivation to buy.

Examples

Prospects, for example, might believe that buying will lead to (B-2) the following unwanted outcomes (B-3):

- regret for paying a price that is too high;
- regret for not spending the money on something else;
- problems with the product or service purchased;
- no improvement in productivity;
- increased operating cost;
- feelings of uncertainty or loss of control;
- employee complaints;
- rejection from others;
- negative attitudes;
- resistance to change;
- greater stress;
- interpersonal conflicts; and
- dissatisfaction with the product or service.

Statements

The "I will get something I don't want" objection gets mentioned in a variety of ways. Here are some of them.

- "That would be a problem."

- "Your price is too high."
- "I'm concerned about how people would react."
- "I'm afraid changing suppliers will disrupt things."
- "You don't understand my business (product, people, circumstance)."
- "I don't see how your product (service) meets my needs."

How to Handle "I Will Get Something I Don't Want"

Sales executives want to call on salespeople to handle the "I will get something I don't want" objection effectively and strengthen the prospect's motivation to buy. There are four ways and they all feel right because they work. The first focuses on B-2, namely changing the belief from "I will get it" to "I will not get it." The other three look to B-3. One of the three simply is to get a hold on a unique way to remove the unwanted outcome, when possible. Another is to offer one or more desirable outcomes that will offset the unwanted outcome. The last is to change the belief from "I don't want it" to "I do want it." Let's take a closer look at each of these four ways, recognizing that the most appropriate one to handle the situation depends on the underlying cause of the "I will get something I don't want" objection.

The first way is to take a B-2 focus. This is appropriate when buying doesn't feel right because the prospect has a misperception such as, for example, when the prospect mistakenly believes "I will get the unwanted outcome" when in fact the unwanted outcome will not be received. There are numerous ways to correct such misperceptions, including:

1. providing information;
2. providing clarification;
3. providing evidence of outcomes;
4. providing documentation of results;
5. giving product demonstrations;
6. planning opportunities for prospects to observe the product or service in action;
7. arranging for prospects to get first hand testimonials from users;
8. offering persuasive arguments that are well thought out; and
9. offering samples, free trials, or test cases to be paid for only if the product is satisfied.

Preparing to Motivate

What about handling the "I will get something I don't want" objection with a B-3 focus? Sometimes unwanted outcomes can be removed. This can be done, for example, by looking to a model of the product that doesn't have the unwanted feature, modifying the product or service to eliminate unwanted functions, or coming up with a design tailored to the customer's specifications. Removing unwanted outcomes isn't always possible, but being open minded and flexible to use this approach whenever feasible sometimes can be the simplest and easiest way to handle the "I will get something I don't want" objection.

When unwanted outcomes cannot be removed, often it is possible to offer additional outcomes that will *offset* the unwanted outcomes. One way to do this is to give something that customers normally pay for. Free products, free services, or free training often offset unwanted outcomes, for example. Salespeople do this all the time. Yes, it often is possible to offset unwanted outcomes that cannot be removed by offering additional outcomes that prospects would want. Sales executives may want to encourage salespeople to use this approach and define any guidelines and limits appropriate for them to keep in mind.

What about getting prospects to change their mind and picture something as desirable when they currently don't want it? While this often is not plausible, sometimes it is. For example, prospects sometimes don't buy because one of the unwanted outcomes is having to learn to do something a different way. However, if it is brought to their attention that learning a new way would give them additional skills that would increase their chances for a badly wanted raise or promotion, or give them better opportunities in the job market, the unwanted outcome of "learning something new" may become desirable.

Sales executives know how difficult it is to make the sale when prospects believe they will get something they don't want. Sales executives also know that this is one of the most formidable obstacles salespeople face. But there are some solution approaches that have proven to work. And here they are. Four ways to handle the "I will get something I don't want" objection and rebuild the motivation to buy. They are summarized as follows.

HOW TO HANDLE
"I WILL GET SOMETHING I DON'T WANT"

B-3 Objection/Causes	How to Handle the Objection
The prospect incorrectly believes "I will get something I don't want" (*because* of a misperception).	Correct the prospect's misperception.

HOW TO HANDLE
"I WILL GET SOMETHING I DON'T WANT"
(CONTINUED)

The prospect correctly believes "I will get something I don't want" (*because* it comes with the product or service).	Identify a unique way to remove the unwanted outcomes. Offer additional outcomes to offset the unwanted outcomes. Show how an unwanted outcome really is desirable.

ANTICIPATING STALLS

It isn't a pretty scene when prospects stall and delay progress toward closing the sale. Sales executives have noticed that salespeople are more effective when they are able to quickly and clearly recognize when prospects are stalling and move hard and fast to get a firm grip on counter measures that will nullify, or at least minimize, the impact on the prospect's motivation to buy. Let's get a feel for recognizing stalls, understanding their causes, and deciding how to handle them.

Recognizing Stalls

There are several things sales executives can train salespeople to listen for prospects say, and watch for them to do, that will give a sense that prospects are stalling in their motivation to buy. Here are some typical stall statements and stall actions.

Stall Statements

- "I'll think it over."
- "Come back in thirty days."
- "I'll wait until business is better."
- "Leave your catalog."
- "Call me next week."
- "Send me some literature and I'll review it later."

Stall Actions

- Not returning calls
- Canceling appointments
- Unwilling to set appointments
- Not reviewing materials
- Not following up on references provided

All of these signal *potential stalls*. Recognizing these signals is not that difficult for most salespeople. The trick is for sales executives to train them to be perceptive enough to have a good sense for distinguishing a real stall from a legitimate delay. Let's see how to do this.

Interpreting Stalls

How can salespeople get a feel for accurately interpreting stall signals? Two things. First, they must have a clear insight into the possible causes of stalls. There are many reasons buyers stall. Salespeople who are aware of the wide range of causes will be better equipped to understand and accurately interpret them. Here are some of the main ones.

The prospect isn't interested and is stalling because she:

- has trouble saying "no" to everything (high S);
- doesn't want to hurt your feelings (high I, high S); and/or
- wants to see what others think (high I, high S, and high C).

The prospect is interested but is stalling because he:

- doesn't have time to decide now (any of the four styles);
- doesn't have the money now (any of the four styles);
- doesn't have the need now (any of the four styles); and/or
- doesn't have the support of others yet (high I).

The prospect has not decided yet but is stalling because she:

- is a procrastinator (high S);

- is indecisive (high S and high C);
- wants to wait and see what others think (high I, high C);
- wants to evaluate everything carefully (high C);
- can't make the decision (high I);
- has a hidden objection (high S);
- needs time to think (high S, high C); and/or
- wants to test the salesperson (high D, high C).

Second, salespeople must accurately perceive what stalls do and do not mean. This will keep them from hearing a stall and then getting unnecessarily discouraged. And it will help them get a quick and firm hold on some positive steps that will convert the stall into a sale.

What Stalls Do and Do Not Mean

Stalls Do Not Mean
• The sale is lost.
Stalls Mean
• The prospect hasn't said "no."
• There still is a chance to make the sale.
• The salesperson must do something.

How to Handle Stalls

Okay, so how do sales executives coach salespeople to handle stalls? It's simple. Salespeople have to be trained to look behind the stall, see what is causing it, then handle it accordingly. This means not blindly accepting what the prospect says or does. Instead, salespeople have to get a sense for what is going on. The best way is to ask. Sales executives easily can imagine how meaningful it is when they convince the sales force to embrace and apply the principle, "If you want to know, ask!" Asking provides information, and information is essential for salespeople to effectively handle stalls.

- "What do you expect to happen between now and the next time we get together?"
- "What specifically do you need to think about?"
- "What will you be looking for in this product?"
- "What can I do in the meantime to help you reach a decision?"
- "What has to happen next for us to get together again on this?"

The purpose of asking is to find out what the real issue is. Salespeople simply cannot get a firm grip on handling stalls unless they have been able to identify the real issue behind the stall. Once salespeople know this, deciding what to do generally is pretty obvious. Information is the key and most buyers willingly give it when salespeople skillfully ask for it.

THE REAL STALL ISSUE

Issue	Action to Take
Prospect does not intend to buy.	Move on and sell someone else.
Prospect really does need more time.	Agree on next steps, including when to meet again.
Prospect is reluctant to buy.	Reevaluate diagnosis of: (1) B-1, B-2, and B-3; and (2) behavior style. Then decide what to do.

Stalls and Behavior Style

High D Prospects

Since high Ds tend to rush into decisions based on limited information, they seldom stall unless they really need the extra time. They tend to stall when the picture frame of things fills up or when they feel the decision can be made better later. What can the salesperson do? It's simple. Use the principle "If you want to know why they are stalling, ask!" They normally will give a direct answer, one that will help salespeople decide what steps to take next. High Ds tend to have no secrets and usually are willing to tell all when they are asked. The hurdle to be overcome with high Ds is not to become intimidated and unwilling to ask.

High I Prospects

Salespeople can expect to see two kinds of stalls from high I prospects. One, the high I is busy interacting with everybody and simply finds it hard to get around to making a decision. It is best to nail down a specific action to be taken by high I prospects; then, they are more likely to be willing to take phone calls or set appointments, and they will not mind being pushed a little to close the sale. Another common stall from high I prospects centers on their concern about the way others see them. This often causes them to take a "wait and see" position before making buying decisions. The best way to strengthen their motivation to buy and speed up the buying process is to help them clearly see and get a feel for the favorable responses of the people who influence them.

High S Prospects

Several things about high S prospects show up as factors that contribute to their stalling. First, they tend to take on more than they can do, so they get around to making a buying decision when they can. Second, they don't feel comfortable buying unless they have developed a trusting relationship with the salesperson. This takes time. Third, they sometimes have difficulty saying no and tend to put off doing so. Since high S prospects are the stable people who steadily plug away at things, they don't mind when salespeople do the same with them. Pushing hard and using pressure likely will backfire, but gently and steadily directing and strengthening their motivation to buy will be received well.

High C Prospects

High C prospects can be seen stalling more than anyone. Their tendency is not to make decisions until they have thoroughly evaluated all of the information available. This takes time. The decision process can be hastened to some extent by getting information to them quickly and in a form easy to evaluate. That's about the only way salespeople can push high C prospects away from stalling and toward making a decision. The word of the day when selling high C prospects is to "hang in there." Salespeople have to keep giving them the information they want and remember that they don't like to be pushed. Patience is not only a virtue, but a necessity when selling to high C prospects. Otherwise they will never be motivated to buy.

ANTICIPATING "NO"

"We've decided not to buy" is the response every salesperson can visualize as if it were in glaring bright lights. Sales executives know how discouraging this can feel. To hear "no," even the thought of it, is so distasteful that most salespeople go to enormous lengths to avoid it. Sales executives have found that the best way to get a grip on this problem is to teach salespeople to anticipate "no" and to prepare them in advance to deal with it. How can this be done do? There are several ways.

The Meaning of "No"

One way is to help salespersons see that "no" can have many different meanings. Prospects may say "no" because they:

- don't have the money or authority to buy, and aren't willing to admit it;
- are too busy to deal with the buying decision now;
- are facing business or personal problems (power struggles, conflict with the boss, problems at home) that overshadow their need for the product or service;
- can't figure out how to justify buying even though they want to;
- want to challenge the salesperson to overcome a final objection that is standing in their way of buying;
- believe saying "no" prematurely is easier than doing so later after they know the salesperson well; and
- do not want or need the product or service.

Handling "No"

Sales executives must be sure the sales force has a sense for the many ways to handle "no." Some are effective. Some are not. Watch any group of salespeople and it is easy to see them using all of the following ways.

- Give up. Leave. Don't go back.
- Beg. Plead. Promise anything.
- Fight back. Blame. Antagonize.

- Keep trying. Probe. Overcome.
- Accept "no." Keep the door open.

Greatest success comes when salespeople use the latter two while applying their own personal touch. Not giving up and keeping the door open pays big dividends. Specifically, here is what every sales executive wants their salespeople to do.

1. *Find out the reason for "no."* This is accomplished best by asking questions, listening carefully, and looking for B-1, B-2, and B-3 problems that continue to dull the prospect's motivation to buy.

2. *Try to close the sale.* This works by revisiting all that has been learned about the prospect's B-1, B-2, and B-3 and pulling the handle on another attempt to close the sale.

3. *If no sale, keep the door open.* The picture here is to accept "no" with an eye on the future. Set the stage to come back again. Remember, no is not forever!

4. *Ask for leads.* Why not? When salespeople have shown their hand and played their cards well, asking for leads gives prospects a way to shed a little guilt and pain for saying "no" and feel better about themselves and the salesperson. This can help keep the door open and allow the salesperson to easily slip back in again. Getting a couple of leads also is a form of therapy for the salesperson as it eases the sting and burn of the "no" and makes the effort somehow seem a little more worthwhile.

"No" and Behavior Style

It is possible to get a feel for and, therefore, anticipate the way prospects will say "no" when their behavior style is known. Here is a glimpse of what can be expected from each behavior style. Sales executives find this interesting.

High D Prospects

The tendency is for high D prospects to make it short and sweet when saying they aren't buying. A straightforward "no" can be expected, and perhaps the bottom-line reason for not buying. Brevity and honesty are their guidelines for giving the bad news. While it may be hard to take the directness of their "no," the salesperson typically can plainly see why the deal fell through. If the salesperson needs to know more about the reasoning that led to "no," high D prospects will tolerate a few short, direct questions.

High I Prospects

Prospects with the high I behavior style wouldn't hear of saying "no" in a direct, abrasive way because they want the salesperson to like them. The way they say "no" typically is characterized by a lengthy sugar-coated explanation, considerable indirectness, an apology for not buying, and assurance that it isn't the salesperson's fault. Salespeople can have a hard time with this because: (1) it leaves the salesperson not knowing why they didn't buy, and (2) it may even give false hope of selling them later. Salespeople have to work to get high I prospects to indicate why they are not buying, but they will explain if given enough time to do so.

High S Prospects

Prospects with the high S style tend to work hard at saying "no" in a way that preserves the relationship that has been developed with the salesperson. They tend to soften the blow and try to make the salesperson feel good and somewhat relieved that although the sale was lost, the relationship was maintained. However, the salesperson will not have a clear picture of why the sale didn't close or what to do to close it the next time. Considerable probing is required to get more information, but high S prospects will be patient if the salesperson wants to pursue it.

High C Prospects

Prospects with the high C style tend to be willing to give a complete, detailed perspective of why they decided not to buy. They may even discuss the pros and cons of the product or service and where it did not measure up. If the salesperson wants to know more than is volunteered, more is there for the asking. There is no reason to rush away from a high C prospect not knowing why the sale was lost.

ANTICIPATING THE NEED TO ASK

The days are gone when the salesperson does all the talking. The best ones never did. Salespeople can't sell if they don't know what prospects want and need, think and feel, like and dislike. Sales executives are very much in touch with this. It is essential to get prospects to open up and provide a flow of information salespeople need to make the sale. It is impossible to motivate buyers to buy unless salespeople have the right information. This includes information such as behavior style and readiness to buy (B-1, B-2, and B-3), both of which are crucial to making the sale.

Here is the point. It all boils down to getting information. If salespeople can't get information from prospects, they can't sell. Sales executives know this. They can flash back to the days when they were on the street making sales calls every day. Yet, they may be surprised at how fast and easy it is for salespeople to get the information needed, especially when they are trained to go about it the right way.

What is the right way? What guidelines can be used? What are the steps to follow? It's all based on the simple concept, "If you want to know, ask." Research clearly shows that asking is fundamental to effective selling. If sales executives want to get better sales results, they should grab hold of the research findings and spread the news to the sales force. The research findings are simple and clear—*ask more, sell more*.[2]

It should be stressed that asking alone is not sufficient. There's more to it than that. The salesperson must ask, then get in tune with the prospect. The real secret is to ask, then "shut up," and listen. This requires two important skills—how to ask and how to listen. If salespeople have these skills, they will get the information they need and they will ring up the sales. Let's take a look at how to ask, then how to listen.

Sales executives should prepare the sales force to use three kinds of questions that are especially helpful in getting information from prospects. Each question has a unique purpose and is intended to be used at the right time and place. Let's take a look at and get a feel for each of them: *open questions, direct questions,* and *clarifying questions.*

Asking Open Questions

Open questions are designed to open the door for prospects to say whatever is on their minds. They are more likely to give the information the salesperson wants and needs if the questions asked don't influence what they say. Open questions are noninfluencing; they do not confine, limit, direct, or focus what prospects say.

Suppose the salesperson is trying to sell a high S prospect who has that kind and gentle, soft-spoken nature and is hearing this nagging thought running around in her head: "If this product will do everything it is supposed to do, it will be exactly what we need. But it's so new I'm afraid to take a chance on it." The prospect is experiencing a B-2 problem. In other words, she feels uncertain about getting all that has been promised. But the salesperson doesn't know this. A good question would be to inquire, "Would you like to have all of the benefits I've described?" What will the prospect say? Most likely she will speak out loud and clear with something like, "Sure." With this response, does the salesperson get the information requested? Yes. Is this information needed? Yes, it reveals the prospect's B-3, that is, her belief about how satisfying the outcomes (benefits) will be, if she gets them. But does the salesperson get all of the information that is needed about what the prospect is thinking? Definitely not. Why? Because the wrong question was asked, one that limited the prospect to the issue of "liking or not liking the benefits."

An open question such as "What do you think?" gives the prospect a better opportunity to voice what is on her mind. With this kind of question, the salesperson likely will hear the prospect say something like, "If this product will do everything you claim, it's exactly what we need. How long did you say it has been on the market?" Pay dirt. The sweet smell of success. The prospect is letting her skepticism show. And the salesperson gets the scene in vivid color. The issue swirling around in the prospect's mind is a B-2 problem. Now the salesperson knows. Now, and only now, can something be done about this previously unvoiced objection.

Here are some examples of open questions that invite prospects to mention what they're thinking rather than limiting how they respond.

- "What has to happen for you to buy this?" rather than "Does this exceed your budget?" (The first question allows the possible diagnosis of B-1, B-2, and B-3; the latter question limits the diagnosis to only one part of B-1.)

- "What could keep us from getting together on this?" rather than "Are you worried about getting approval to buy this?" (The latter question confines the diagnosis to only one aspect of B-1; the former allows the possible diagnosis of B-1, B-2, and B-3.)

- "What are your concerns?" rather than "Are you concerned about getting reliable service?" (The first question again allows for the possible diagnosis of B-1, B-2, and B-3, while the second question is confined to the diagnosis of B-2 for one outcome.)

- "What do you like most (least) about this product?" rather the "Do you like the labor savings this offers?" (The second question confines the diagnosis to the prospect's B-3 for one outcome, whereas the first question allows for the possible diagnosis of the prospect's overall B-3.)

- "How do you go about making a decision like this?" instead of "Do you want me to give you the details or just bottom line?" (The first question allows for any response regardless of the prospects behavior style; the second question addresses only the high C and high D styles.)

- "What can I do to help you make this decision?" rather than "Do you want me to give you all of the information on this so you can make an informed decision?" (The latter question is confined to only one aspect of behavior style, while the first question allows for many aspects to be revealed.)

Open questions like these "open the door" for prospects to be complete and clear about what they're thinking. This means they are most likely to talk about what the salesperson needs to know. When salespeople don't want to confine and limit what prospects say, open questions are the word of the day.

Asking Direct Questions

There is a time and place to ask direct questions, too. These are questions designed to get prospects to focus and talk directly to a certain point. This helps the salesperson get specific information about a specific issue. Direct questions are especially helpful with prospects who tend to ramble and get off track, or when time is of the essence and there is a need to quickly zero in on the main issues. Salespeople who use direct questions effectively can obtain a wealth of information that will help them make the sale. Here are some examples of direct questions.

- "Do you have at least $15,000 budgeted for this?" (This diagnoses one aspect of B-1.)
- "Does anyone have to approve your decision on this?" (This diagnoses one aspect of B-1.)
- "Do you believe you'll get the results others have been getting with this product?" (This diagnoses B-2.)
- "Are you concerned about us meeting the delivery date?" (This diagnoses B-2 for one outcome.)
- "All things considered, do you believe this is the best product for your needs?" (This diagnoses B-3.)
- "Do you like the added capability this optional feature offers?" (This diagnoses B-3 for one outcome.)
- "Are you concerned about the reaction others will have if you buy this?" (This diagnoses one aspect of B-3 that is tied to behavior style.)
- "Is getting results your main concern?" (This diagnoses one part of B-3 that is related to behavior style.)

When the aim is to get prospects to give specific information on specific issues, direct questions are a smooth way to do this. This confines and limits the prospect's responses to the specific issues of interest to the salesperson. If that's what's needed, direct questions will do the job.

Asking Clarifying Questions

The third kind of question is the clarifying question. Its purpose is to get prospects to clarify something they have said or implied. Prospects often say things that are ambiguous, confusing, incomplete, even contradictory. When this happens, it is important for the salesperson to sniff out information that is more reliable and move ahead and motivate the prospect to buy.

Consider the situation where the salesperson listens to a prospect say with a whimper, "I just don't know if I can win the battle of the bureaucracy on a purchase like this." This suggests a B-1 problem. The prospect seems to be saying, "I'm not sure I can buy." The salesperson could respond in several ways here including a sympathetic "I know it's not easy" or an encouraging "You can do it" or a helpful "Maybe I can do something." But it's hard to know what to say without having more information.

The right clarifying questions will stimulate the flow of information needed. Salespeople simply have to get a sense for this. The idea is to focus on the ambiguous parts of the prospect's statement by asking questions like "What do you mean *on a purchase like this*?" or "What kind of *bureaucracy* are you dealing with?" or "What do you mean by *don't know if I can win*?"

Another approach is to get a clear perspective of what has happened in the past in a similar situation. This can be done by asking questions like "Thinking back to the last time this happened, what were the circumstances?" or "How did you try to handle it that time?" or "What were the results?" or "Based on that, do you think you could be successful this time?"

The salesperson also can get a good feel for what is happening by giving the prospect a chance to tell the full story. This can be done by asking one or more standard clarifying questions, then following up with questions that zero in on specific points that may need to be clarified. Here are some standard clarifying questions that allow salespeople to get a firm grip on most any situation.

- "Can you tell me more?"
- "Can you tell me exactly what happened?"
- "Can you be more specific?"
- "Can you give me an example of what you mean?"
- "I don't understand." (This has the same effect as a question.)

Here are some examples of how the standard clarifying questions can touch on specific situations.

- "Could you tell me more about why you are reluctant to push for the approval to buy this?" (This diagnoses B-1.)
- "What exactly is behind your uncertainty about having enough money to buy this?" (This diagnoses B-1.)
- "Can you be more specific about not trusting salespeople?" (This diagnoses B-2.)
- "Can you tell me more about what's behind your concern that this product will not live up to expectations?" (This diagnoses B-2.)
- "Can you give me a couple of examples of the things you're dissatisfied about with the product you're using now?" (This diagnoses B-3.)
- "I can see you are unhappy with your current supplier. Can you tell me exactly what's happening?" (This diagnoses B-2 and/or B-3.)
- "You've mentioned that purchasing is not what you're cut out to do. I'm not sure I understand what you mean." (This diagnoses B-3 and behavior style.)

Here's the point. Salespeople can't afford to get burned by not knowing what prospects mean. When clarification is needed, salespeople have to be trained to ask for it. Sales executives know that salespeople do not ask enough questions. This can result in moments of panic because prospects often aren't articulate and don't communicate clearly and completely. And salespeople find it hard to stay calm and not get frustrated. But blaming and complaining doesn't make it better. One of the jobs of salespeople is to get clarification. And they can. Easily. But they have to be trained. They have to be alert to the need to clarify and they must be prepared to ask clarifying questions to get the clarity and completeness they want and need. Asking questions is a skill. It can be developed, but it takes time. It requires coaching and practice.

Okay, how can sales executives make some loud noise about this and help the sales force get the feel for asking questions? It means one thing. Provide training. There is no shortcut. Provide training. Not classroom lectures, but training where salespeople have to practice the skill of asking questions and then get feedback and coaching to improve their skills. If sales executives want the sales force to ask more and sell more, there is only one thing to do. Provide training.

Remember, the secret to getting information from prospects is to ask, then "shut up," and listen. As sales executives can readily imagine, there is more to asking than appears on the surface. It includes asking the right question at the right time and in the right way. This means looking at the situation, choosing the right kind of question to ask (open, direct, or clarifying), and asking it in a suitable way. It's easy to do. The battle is half won just realizing the need to do it. The rest of the battle is won when salespeople develop the skills they need. Sales executives love the way it feels to win battles, so they may want to consider, when all is said and done, to step up and move forward and just go ahead and do it. Provide training.

ANTICIPATING THE NEED TO LISTEN

Asking questions is not enough. Salespeople have to listen. Sales executives intuitively know this. And their intuition is backed up by research. Studies on the subject shine a bright spotlight on the importance of listening when selling. The findings are crystal clear. *Listen more, sell more.*[3]

Sales executives have a good sense that listening is more than keeping ones ears open. A lot more. Good listeners aren't passive. There is more to listening than maintaining good eye contact, paying attention, and concentrating on what prospects are saying. Good listeners are active. They do things. Five things, actually. Active listeners have a good perspective of, and a strong handle on, paraphrasing, restating, summarizing, responding to nonverbal messages, and responding to feelings. These active listening techniques enable salespeople to hold three important things in their grasp. One, listening results in a better understanding of what prospects are saying. Two, listening causes a greater flow of information from prospects. Three, listening is the basis for tailoring a sales approach that matches the prospect. All of this can be accomplished when salespeople use the following five active listening techniques.

Paraphrasing

Paraphrasing is repeating in one's own words what another person has said. Let's see how it works.

Prospect:	"I just don't know if I can buy this." (This suggests a possible B-1 problem.)
Salesperson:	"Sounds like your hands are tied." (This is a try for more information for a B-1 diagnosis.)
Prospect:	"Things are tight now. I can't get approval to buy anything that's not in my budget, and this isn't in it." (This confirms that you paraphrased correctly.)

What does paraphrasing in this example accomplish? First, it lets the prospect know the salesperson was listening. Second, it shows the prospect that the salesperson had a clear understanding of what was said. Third, it lets the salesperson know he got the drift.

There are other reasons to paraphrase. Suppose the salesperson in the same example paraphrased differently.

Prospect: "I just don't know if I can buy this."

Salesperson: "Sounds like we're never going to get together on this."

Prospect: "All I'm saying is I can't buy this quarter." (This is a correction of the paraphrase.)

This actually is a bad paraphrase, and that makes it good. Here's why. Look at what happens. Two things are accomplished. First, it allows the prospect to offer a correction. He basically says, "Not true. While it would be tough to buy from you now, it will not be later." Second, the paraphrase encourages the prospect to give more information, in this case, "I can buy next quarter." That is, if he waits until next quarter, the B-1 problem will be solved.

To summarize, then, five different things can be accomplished by using the active listening technique of paraphrasing. Two of them involve salespeople giving information, namely letting prospects know they are (1) listening and (2) understanding. Three involve the salesperson getting information, namely (3) getting confirmation that the prospect's message was received correctly, (4) getting corrected if not, and (5) getting additional information. All of these can cause the sales force to charge sales executives with having a flash of brilliance for providing the listening skills they need. Now the sales force realizes what the sales executive already knew. Listen more, sell more.

Summarizing

The second active listening technique salespeople need to get their arms around is summarizing. This is the technique of repeating, in one's own words, one or more main points another person has said. An example of summarizing is illustrated in the previous paragraph. Another example would be to say, "Some standard ways to summarize are: (1) 'I'm hearing you say three main things . . .' (2) 'Okay, you're making four major points . . .' and (3) 'In summary, then, you're saying . . .'"

Summarizing accomplishes the same five benefits derived from paraphrasing, plus one more. When the summary takes place at the end of the sales interview, or at the end of any segment of a discussion, it pulls the essence of the discussion together, lets the prospect hear it, and gives a feeling of closure. This makes the prospect feel the time spent has been worthwhile and that any next steps agreed upon will be completed. This is a good way to conclude any discussion.

Restating

The third active listening technique salespeople find helpful is restating. This is repeating verbatim all or part of what someone, like a prospect, has said, but placing emphasis on one part of it. For example, a prospect may say, "Everyone says it's impossible to get your unit installed in time to do us any good." Several restatements can be made here. One would be to restate by saying, "Everybody says it's *impossible. . .*" (emphasis on impossible). The prospect's natural tendency will be to explain why it seems impossible. The prospect responds with, "Everybody knows delivery normally takes two weeks, and we don't have that much time." This is a B-2 problem, one that can be easily solved—if delivery can be faster than usual.

Another way to restate would be to say, "*Everybody* says it's impossible . . ." (emphasis on everybody). The prospect is encouraged to talk more and indicate who believes it can't be done. She may say, "A couple of people in maintenance said you cost us a lot of money with a late delivery on some special order equipment several years ago." Okay, so everybody is two people and they are comparing apples with oranges, namely a piece of made-to-order equipment several years ago versus standard units carried in inventory daily.

The point is clear. The main purpose of restating is to get prospects to give more information. This helps salespeople get to the root of the problem and lets them know how to deal with it. Additional information can be the difference in making the sale or not.

Responding to Nonverbal Messages

The fourth active listening technique is responding to nonverbal messages. This technique calls for the salesperson to get a feel for picking up nonverbal messages and then being willing and able to respond to them. Rather than wondering what the message means, or wrongly assuming what it means or doesn't mean, the idea is for the salesperson to respond in a way that yields more information from the prospect.

Sales executives may want to stress the following three-step process when training the sales force to respond to nonverbal messages.

1. Name the nonverbal signal.

- "I can't help but notice that *worried look* on your face."
- "I see that you are *frowning*."
- "That looks like a *blank stare* I see."
- "I notice you are *nodding*."

2. State what the message seems to mean.
   - "You look like you are skeptical about the results."
   - "It sounds like you really want to buy this."
   - "I feel like you may be anxious about an expenditure this size."
   - "You look like you are disappointed that it doesn't have all the options you wanted."

3. Respond in a way that encourages the prospect to talk more.
   - This can be done with a question like, "Is something bothering you?"
   - Or simply make a statement like, "Maybe there are some issues we need to discuss further" and wait for the prospect to comment.

Regardless of how the salesperson responds, it is important to be brief, then clearly put the ball in the prospect's court and listen. The purpose of responding to nonverbal messages is to encourage the prospect to talk. Here are some examples of responding to nonverbal messages.

- "You have a worried look on your face, like you're not sure you can get approval to buy this." (This diagnoses B-1.)
- "You're frowning like you're skeptical about getting all of the results." (This diagnoses B-2.)
- "You've got that blank stare on your face again." (This diagnoses B-1, B-2, and/or B-3.)
- "You look anxious about this size expenditure." (This diagnoses B-1.)
- "You look disappointed that the lower priced model doesn't have all the options you want." (This diagnoses B-3.)
- "You look like you enjoy working with people more than numbers." (This diagnoses behavior style, probably high I.)
- "You get excited when you talk about how this will increase productivity." (This diagnoses B-3 and behavior style, probably high D.)
- "You don't seem to relax until all of the details are worked out." (This diagnoses behavior style, probably high C.)

Responding to nonverbal messages does several things. It lets the prospect know the salesperson is sensitive to everything the prospect is projecting. It gives the prospect a chance to: (1) confirm the message the salesperson is picking up; (2) offer clarification; or (3) correct the salesperson's perception. Overall, responding to nonverbal messages facilitates more and better communication. And this gives the salesperson a better handle for motivating prospects to buy.

Responding to Feelings

These same things are accomplished with the fifth active listening technique, responding to feelings. When responding, sales executives want their salespeople to say something to acknowledge the prospect's feelings. There is no need to say a lot—certainly no need to be negative. Instead, follow this four step process: (1) name the feeling, (2) name the thing that seems to be causing it, (3) respond in a way that encourages the prospect to talk, and (4) "shut up" and listen. Here are some examples.

- "You look *frustrated* (Step 1) that you can't decide this on your own (Step 2)." Then wait for a response (Step 3) and listen (Step 4). (This diagnoses B-1.)
- "You sound *angry* (Step 1). Do you think I deliberately misled you about the results (Steps 2 and 3)?" Then listen (Step 4). (This diagnoses B-2.)
- "You seem to feel *pleased* (Step 1) with all the benefits this offers (Step 2)." Wait for a response (Step 3) and listen (Step 4). (This diagnoses B-3.)
- "You looked *upset* (Step 1) after talking with your boss about this (Step 2). What happened (Step 3)?" Then listen (Step 4). (This diagnoses B-1, B-2, and/or B-3.)
- "I sense that going over the details (Steps 2 and 3) *frustrates* you (Step 1)?" Stop and listen (Step 4). (This diagnoses behavior style.)

Sales executives get the picture. One of the secrets of motivating prospects to buy is to ask questions *and* listen. Asking and not listening is a clumsy way to approach prospects. Listening is the key. Actually, active listening is the key. By using the five active listening techniques—paraphrasing, summarizing, restating, responding to nonverbal messages, and responding to feelings—salespeople will see a big difference in their sales performance. Also, they will be pleasantly surprised with the positive way prospects react to this. Prospects communicate more. They feel better about the salesperson. And salespeople will sell more.

So, how do sales executives prepare the sales force to listen? Active listening is a skill. This means it is necessary to provide training. The only way is to provide training. And when sales executives provide training, it is essential to provide training that includes an opportunity for three things: *practice, practice, practice.* And feedback and coaching. When salespeople feel comfortable using the five techniques, they will use them and they will sell more. Listen more, sell more. Listen, just go ahead and provide listening training.

SUMMARY

- Salespeople can anticipate questions prospects will ask and prepare ahead of time to answer them.

- Objections can be anticipated and prepared for in advance to put the salesperson in an excellent position to prevent or overcome the objections and make the sale.

- There are only three objections (reasons to oppose buying) to anticipate and prepare for: (1) "I can't buy," (2) "I will not get something I want," and (3) "I will get something I don't want."

- It also is possible to anticipate and prepare for stalls and "no." This enables the salesperson to prevent—or minimize—delays and possibly turn around decisions not to buy.

- Knowing the behavior style of prospects can make a significant difference in the salesperson's ability to accurately anticipate and adequately prepare for prospects to ask questions, voice objections, stall, and say "no."

- Salespeople sometimes talk too much and listen too little. This makes it difficult to motivate prospects to buy.

- Successful salespeople focus on getting information from their prospects. They use a simple two-step process—ask and listen.

- Three kinds of questions aid the asking—open, direct, and clarifying questions.

- Five techniques aid the listening—paraphrasing, summarizing, restating, responding to nonverbal messages, and responding to feelings.

- Getting a good balance between talking, and asking and listening, can have a dramatic impact on sales.

NOTES

1. Alan J. Dubinsky, "A Factor Analytic Study of the Personal Selling Process," *Journal of Personal Selling and Sales Management* (Fall–Winter 1980–1981), p. 30.

2. Camille P. Schuster and Jeffrey E. Davis, "Asking Questions: Some Characteristics of Successful Sales Encounters," *Journal of Personal Selling and Sales Management* (May 1986), p. 17.

3. Monci Jo Williams, "America's Best Salesmen," *Fortune* (October 26, 1987), pp. 122–134.

CHAPTER 6

Selling That Motivates

The sales presentation doesn't cut it anymore, and most sales executives see this. It is not an effective way to motivate people to buy. Never has been, never will be. The very nature of the sales presentation precludes its success. It doesn't feel right to buyer or seller. Sales presentations deprive salespeople of the opportunity to truly tailor the sales approach and to focus on what is important to the prospect—the prospect's objectives, what is wanted, the way the buying decision is made, the preferred way of being sold. Without this information, selling is a roll of the dice, a shot in the dark. And the odds are hard to overcome. Sales executives see greater success when they persuade their sales force to move away from the one-wayness of sales presentations and focus more on a kind of interaction that allows salespeople to adapt their behavior to match the prospect.[1]

THE SALES INTERVIEW PROCESS

The sales interview process gives salespeople the maximum opportunity to motivate prospects to buy. The process centers on three things: (1) getting a clear picture of the prospect's objectives and showing how the product or service will meet those objectives; (2) getting a feel for the prospect's motivation to buy by incorporating the sales model (Chapters 1 and 2) to be sure prospects believe they can buy (B-1), believe that buying will lead to promised outcomes (B-2), and believe that the outcomes will be satisfying (B-3); and (3) getting a sense for the prospect's behavior style (Chapter 3) and selecting a sales approach that matches the way prospects like to be sold.

Several steps constitute the sales interview process. All of them are essential.

1. Getting the prospect's attention
2. Confirming the B-1 diagnosis
3. Determining behavior style
4. Identifying the prospect's objectives (B-3 diagnosis)
5. Translating objectives into needs
6. Stating benefits in terms of objectives
7. Showing how features provide the benefits
8. Handling questions and objections
9. Diagnosing the motivation to buy
10. Strengthening the motivation to buy
11. Closing the sale
12. Summarizing follow-up actions

Step 1—Getting the Prospect's Attention

Sales executives need to teach their salespeople how to grab the attention of every prospect.[2] And how to do it quickly and maintain a firm hold on it. One of the most effective ways to do this is for the salesperson to focus on the prospect's B-2 and B-3. Regarding B-2, it is essential for prospects to conclude right away, "I can believe what this salesperson tells me." If the salesperson isn't believable, the prospect will conclude, "I don't believe I will get the outcomes being promised (a B-2 problem)." It's simple. When prospects don't believe the salesperson, they don't buy. With respect to B-3, it is necessary for prospects to conclude right away, "This is a product (service) that I just might want." When prospects are saying to themselves, "I don't need that product (a B-3 problem)," they aren't motivated to listen, certainly not motivated to buy.

Becoming Believable (B-2)

There are many ways to become believable. One that is effective is an introductory statement with a focus on believability. This can be done by preparing salespeople to tell the prospect: (1) why they are there, (2) the sales approach they plan use, and (3) their sales philosophy. Prospects like to hear this. It can be brief, yet have the desired impact. Here is an example.

- "Let me tell you *why I'm here*. I want to see if my product (or service) will help you make more money (or increase your sales, productivity, quality, service, profit, or whatever)."
- "The *approach* I'd like to use is for us to spend a few minutes jointly determining if my product (or service) will do this."
- "If it doesn't, I'll leave and not bother you again. That's my *philosophy*. I don't want to sell you something you don't need."

There are other things that also can be mentioned to gain and reinforce believability. Here are some examples.

- "Some people say being honest hurts me. It probably does, but I sleep better that way."
- "I lost a sale recently because I leveled with a plant manager. The problem wasn't his equipment. It was his operators."
- "I see my job as being open and honest so you'll have the information you need to make the decision that is right for you."

Sales executives can well imagine the number of buyers who have negative and stressful experiences with salespeople everyday. Warm feelings of trust often are overshadowed by a cold sense of doubt, skepticism, and mistrust for salespeople in general. To overcome these feelings, salespeople have to make a special effort to gain the trust and confidence of their prospects.

Something to Offer (B-3)

The two best ways for salespeople to show they have something to offer is to emphasize the longevity and credibility of their company and product or service. Regarding longevity, it is helpful for salespeople to mention how long their company has been in business and how long it has been selling the product or service being presented to the prospect. With respect to credibility, salespeople can indicate who some of their major clients are and how long have they been buying. Salespeople should not underestimate the importance of their company's history and client base. A track record is very strong evidence of having something worthwhile to offer. This is important to prospects! Salespeople should stress it.

Step 2—Confirming the B-1 Diagnosis

Sales executives are all to familiar with the problem of salespeople trying to sell people who are not prospects at all. They see it all the time. It is necessary for sales executives to constantly hammer away on this issue. *People don't buy when they don't have the need, money, and authority or influence to buy.* This is B-1. People have to believe they can buy; otherwise they will not be motivated to buy. Salespeople should determine this when making a sales appointment. And they should confirm it early during the sales call. Doing so can save a lot of time and disappointment. Salespeople can meet some interesting people, have an enjoyable visit, and foster the illusion that something will happen, but it is a bitter pill to swallow when a lot of time is invested only to discover late in the process that the person doesn't have the need, money, or authority or influence to buy.

So, how can salespeople get a handle on a prospect's B-1? It's simple. Just apply the principle, "If you want to know, ask." Getting attention (Step 1 above) sets up the opportunity to confirm whether or not the prospect has the need, money, and authority or influence to buy (B-1). Answers are needed to just three questions.

- "Are you the decision maker on this?"
- "Do you have a need for this product (service)?"
- "Do you have the budget for it?"

If the salesperson hears a "yes" answer to all three questions, it obviously makes sense to move ahead toward making the sale. If *all three* answers are *not* "yes," a different strategy altogether must be used. Salespeople must make their own assessment of the need to buy and not depend entirely on what prospects say, for often there can be an unrecognized need. Regarding money and authority or influence to buy, salespeople must (1) figure out who the decision maker is and how to get a face-to-face sitting and (2) get a feel for whether money is really a problem and, if so, dig up ways to deal with it, like extending credit or whatever.

Sales executives observe that the sales force spends countless hours trying to sell people who don't have the money or authority to buy. On the one hand, salespeople know this, yet on the other they continue to feel the sting of this transgression. Sales executives would do well to stress two points over and over with the sales force: (1) sell to people who have the need, money, and authority or influence to buy and (2) leave the rest to the competition.

Step 3—Determining Behavior Style

Like several of the steps in the sales interview process, this one does not necessarily fall in the sequence as shown. Diagnosing behavior style begins when the appointment is made and continues when the salesperson arrives for the appointment. First, the secretary or other employees can provide a valuable glimpse into the prospect's behavior style, especially when asked. A simple question may be all that's needed, like "What is she like?" or "Any suggestions about what I should do with him?" Second, everything visible in the prospect's office can be at least a rough gauge as to behavior style. Finally, from the minute the talk begins, everything said can and should be used to diagnose the prospect's behavior style. A review of Chapter 3 will provide guidelines regarding what to look for, what to ask, and how to interpret everything seen and heard.

Sales executives may want to speak out and implement a special initiative to prepare the sales force to determine the behavior style of their prospects. This is a very teachable skill. And important. Behavior style provides the basis for deciding how to sell prospects the way they want to be sold.[3] So, sales executives, consider the possibility and maybe just *take a bold step*. Provide the leadership and prepare the sales force. Provide training. Sales executives know it. Learn more, sell more.

Step 4—Identifying the Prospect's Objectives

Many things are crystal clear to sales executives. One of them is that prospects will not buy unless they believe they will get what they want and avoid what they don't want. This means salespeople can't motivate people to buy unless they know what those "things" are. And they have to know them up front, before getting too far into the sales process. A "perfect pitch" misses the mark unless it matches what the prospect wants and wants to avoid. The sales approach must be tailored to, and focused on, those things. The odds of a hit-or-miss approach working are slim. Why take the chance? Especially when it's easy to find out what prospects want and don't want. All salespeople have to do is use the principle, "If you want to know, ask." When asking, though, remember to keep three things in mind.

First, salespeople must have a clear picture of both the organizational objectives and personal objectives of the prospect. The former includes objectives like increasing performance, reducing cost, improving quality, increasing sales, reducing turnover, modernizing the office, and so on. Personal objectives can be related to a wide variety of things such as promotions, raises, respect, looking good, job security, power, influence, acceptance, stability, and so on. The chances of making the sale are limited unless salespeople can help prospects achieve both personal and organizational objectives.

Second, salespeople can get a good sense of these objectives by asking questions and listening. It starts by simply having one or two standard questions that the salesperson feels comfortable using. Some that other salespeople use with good results include the list that follows. All of them will work. Salespeople can pick out a couple and try them.

- "Can you give me a feel for your objectives?"
- "What do you want to see done?"
- "What do you want to happen?"
- "Why did you decide see me?"
- "What are you looking for?"
- "Can you give me a sense for what you are trying to accomplish?"

Putting the initial question in context makes it work better. It can seem a little awkward, not quite so smooth, and may inhibit some prospects if the salesperson plunges directly into the sales interview by asking, "What are your objectives?" This approach can be softened by putting the question in context, as shown in the following examples.

- "When we talked briefly by phone to set this meeting, you said my call was timely in view of something new you're trying to accomplish. Could you tell me more about it?"
- "To get started, could you tell me what prompted you to meet with me?"
- "As we discussed earlier, I'm here to talk with you about . . . What are your objectives regarding this?"
- "You mentioned a couple of problems you wanted to talk about. Could you tell me about them?"

Salespeople want to be bright and encourage prospects to relax and talk and be willing to disclose whatever they will. Salespeople need to remember that information is the secret to selling and that additional questions usually result in a rush of information. Here are some follow-up questions that will accomplish this.

- "Anything else?"
- "Anything you haven't told me?"
- "Anything you are reluctant to share?"
- "Anything else I need to know?"

As prospects hear a question and start to talk, salespeople cannot forget to listen. This means using the helpful techniques of paraphrasing, restating, summarizing, responding to nonverbal messages, and responding to feelings, as discussed in Chapter 5.

Third, sometimes it is necessary for salespeople to listen between the lines to identify a prospect's objectives. Some prospects, even when pressed, will not talk in terms of objectives. Instead, they talk about problems and concerns. Salespeople can deal with this simply by converting what prospects say into objectives.

IDENTIFY PROSPECT OBJECTIVES

Prospect Response	Converted to an Objective
"My problem is . . ."	"So, your objective is to solve the problem of . . ."
"I'm concerned about . . ."	"So, your objective is to eliminate the concern for . . ."
"I'm not getting . . . and I want it."	"So, your objective is to get . . ."

A specific example of this appeared in a sales call to a telephone company. Notice how the salesperson grasps the situation and restates the manager's response in the form of an objective. Converting what prospects say into well-stated objectives can quickly get the sales interview on the right track and allow salespeople to formulate and use a sales approach that matches the needs that must be satisfied to reach the prospect's objectives.

Prospect: "Our biggest problem is dealing with customers whose phone service is terminated because of billing errors we make."

Salesperson: "So, your objective is to reduce the number of customers whose service is mistakenly terminated because of billing errors."

The process of identifying objectives may be nothing more than asking one question and getting a short answer, or it can flow into a rather extended exchange of questions, response, and a variety of active listening techniques. Once the salesperson has a fix on the prospect's objectives, the salesperson probably will monopolize the conversation, but only for one or two critical minutes as Steps 5, 6, and 7 are covered.

Step 5—Translating Objectives into Needs

Now comes the challenging part. The salesperson has a good grasp of the prospect's objectives. The big challenge is for the salesperson to show how the product or service is *needed* to meet the prospect's objectives. When this can't be done, it is difficult to motivate prospects to buy.

What, then, must sales executives teach the sales force about translating objectives into needs? Four things. First, it is essential for salespeople to know and understand the prospect's objectives. Second, extensive product knowledge also is essential. Third, salespeople must quickly see how the product or service can meet the prospect's objectives. Here are some examples of objectives and the needs they create.

TRANSLATING OBJECTIVES INTO NEEDS

Objective	Products/Services Needed
Energy savings	Insulated windows, energy-saving equipment, insulation.
Increased sales	Advertising, sales incentives, sales training
Fewer defects	Higher quality raw materials, reliable equipment, skill development

Fourth, the salesperson must respond immediately with a statement that translates objectives into needs. Here are some examples. Notice how simple, yet effective, they can be.

Selling That Motivates 113

Salesperson: "If you want to have energy savings (the objective), you certainly are going to *need* to use insulated windows (or energy saving equipment or more insulation)."

Salesperson: "If you want to increase sales (the objective), you definitely *need* to target your advertising more effectively (or offer better sales incentives or do more sales training)."

Salesperson: "To have fewer defects (the objective), you'll *need* to use higher quality raw materials (or get better equipment or do more skill training)."

Step 6—Stating Benefits in Terms of Objectives

In the previous step the salesperson is saying, "If your objective is . . . that means you *need* . . ." Now, the salesperson can say, "The *benefit* of buying this product or service is that it will accomplish your *objective*." This is simple to do. Here are some examples.

Salesperson: "The *benefit* of these insulated windows is a substantial energy saving (the objective)."

Salesperson: "The *benefit* of targeting your advertising more effectively is increased sales (the objective)."

Salesperson: "The *benefit* of higher quality raw materials is fewer defective units (the objective)."

Step 7—Showing How Features Provide Benefits

The next step is for the salesperson to talk about and give the prospect a sense of how the features of the product or service will yield the benefits claimed in the previous step. That is, it would be appropriate to say, "The benefits are made possible because of the following features . . ." This is simple and straightforward, as can be seen in the following examples.

Salesperson: "These windows have two main *features*—the thickness of the double panes and the amount of space between them. This protects you better from the heat and cold and gives you the energy savings you want (the objective)."

Salesperson: "There are two special *features* of our targeted ad program. First, it is directed to people who match the profile of your buyers. Second, the ads are designed specifically to appeal to that group. This generates greater interest in your product and more people will buy it (the objective)."

Salesperson: "The main *feature* of our raw materials is that they are unusually tolerant to stress. They hold up better during production and that's why you end up with fewer defects (the objective)."

Step 8—Handling Questions and Objections

While Steps 5, 6, and 7 have been discussed at length here, notice that the actual amount of time required to complete these steps is very brief, probably no more than two or three minutes. Once this has been done, the salesperson should stop and throw the ball into the prospect's court. That is, give the prospect an opportunity to ask questions and raise objections. Questions and objections allow the salesperson to focus on the issues of interest and concern to the prospect. Salespeople are more effective this way, much more effective than talking about whatever the salesperson thinks is most appropriate. Prospects always convey what it takes to sell them, if they are given a chance talk.

Step 9—Diagnosing the Motivation to Buy

Timing is critical in closing a sale. Trying to close too soon is a problem—so is waiting too long. The best way to deal with the timing issue is to assess the prospect's *motivation to buy*. This makes it possible to know when it's time to close. Remember, it is not time to close until the prospect believes: (1) "I can buy" (B-1), (2) "I will get the outcomes" (B-2), and (3) "The outcomes will be satisfying" (B-3). Diagnosing the prospect's motivation to buy typically begins simultaneously with Step 8 when the prospect is encouraged to ask questions and raise objections.

Diagnosing B-1

The salesperson needs to focus on and reconfirm the prospect's B-1 again at this point. It was first diagnosed when the appointment was set, then again at the beginning of the sales interview. Checking again is critical, especially when there is a need for the product or service. Salespeople waste days, even weeks or months, trying unsuccessfully to make a sale when the person has the need, but not the money and authority or influence to buy. Sometimes the person simply has misled the salesperson up to this point, while in other cases new information results in an "I can't buy" conclusion.

How is the prospect's B-1 confirmed at this point? Simply observe the diagnostic guidelines suggested in Chapter 2. The only difference is that the diagnostic questions need to be modified slightly to put them in the context of the sales interview. Here are some examples of how this can be done.

QUESTIONS TO CONFIRM B-1

Questions Regarding "Money to Buy"

- "Do you have the budget for what we're talking about?"
- "Will this amount of money be a problem?"

Questions Regarding "Authority or Influence"

- "Can you make the decision on this?"
- "Does anyone else have to approve an expenditure this size?"

Questions Regarding No Sale Conditions

- "Is there anything that could keep you from buying now?"

Diagnosing B-3

The initial diagnosis of B-3 flows out of Step 4 (identifying prospect objectives) with additional information derived from Step 8 (handling questions and objections). When the time comes to check the prospect's motivation to buy in terms of B-3, it can be done by: (1) summarizing the outcomes the prospect seems to want and not want, and then (2) asking the prospect for conformation. Here is an example of how this would work.

> *Salesperson*: "The way I see it, based on what you've told me, you are looking for something that will . . . (state the preferred outcomes here) and at the same time you want to avoid . . . (state outcomes the prospect doesn't want). Does that about sum it up?"

Diagnosing B-2

In terms of B-2, prospects are not ready to buy until they see, feel, and believe they will: (1) get what they want and (2) avoid what they don't want. The information prospects give the salesperson in Step 8 (handling questions and objections) generally reveals their B-2. To be sure, simply apply the principle, "If you want to know, ask." Following are some questions that will work.

- "Does this meet your needs?"
- "Will this accomplish all of your objectives?"
- "Do you have any reservations or concerns about this?"
- "Are you comfortable with the results you'll get?"

If the prospect's B-1, B-2, and B-3 all are strong, the prospect is motivated to buy and it is time to move ahead to close the sale. If not, steps must first be taken to strengthen the prospect's motivation to buy before the sale can be closed.

Step 10—Strengthening the Motivation to Buy

How can a prospect's motivation to buy be strengthened? After getting an accurate grasp on the prospect's motivation to buy (Step 9), two other steps must follow: (1) identify what is *causing* the prospect not to be motivated to buy and (2) apply *solutions* that match the causes. See the discussion in Chapter 2 on guidelines for identifying causes and developing matching solutions.

Keep in mind that Steps 8, 9, and 10 are interrelated and often are not applied in sequence. For example, when a prospect is asking questions and raising objections (Step 8), the salesperson simultaneously is using that information to determine the motivation to buy (Step 9); and when the salesperson is handling questions and objections (Step 8), this also is strengthening the motivation to buy (Step 10). This means salespeople should be more concerned about *how* to accomplish each of these steps rather than *when* in the sales interview process they are accomplished.

Step 11—Closing the Sale

When the prospect's motivation to buy is checked out and is strong, it is time to close the sale. This will be discussed in Chapter 7, the entirety of which is devoted to closing the sale and includes discussion on reluctance to close as well as closing techniques that match the behavior style of prospects.

Step 12—Summarizing Follow-up Actions

When a closing agreement is reached with the prospect, several follow-up steps normally must be taken. These will be discussed in Chapter 8 which focuses on and stresses reluctance to follow up, kinds of follow-up, dealing with buyer remorse, and follow-up preferences given the behavior style of the buyer.

THE SALES INTERVIEW AND BEHAVIOR STYLE

The twelve-step process recommended here for guiding salespeople through the sales interview offers a fresh, comprehensive, and very effective way to sell. However, sales executives clearly see that all prospects are not the same and the same approach does not work with all of them. Taking individual differences into account is important and necessary to maximize the motivation to buy. How is this done? The best way is for salespeople to focus on the prospect's behavior style and then modify the sales approach as appropriate in view of this. Okay, so how does the prospect's behavior style tell how the sales interview should be conducted? Let's take a look, step by step, and get a feel for how salespeople can best respond to buyers with each of the four behavior styles. Sales executives will then be in a good position to think about and maybe go ahead and decide to equip the sales force with the knowledge and skills discussed here.

Behavior Style and Step 1 (Getting the Prospect's Attention)

High D Prospects

Sales executives have come in contact with a lot of high D prospects and know how tough they can be. They know that the salesperson should be brief and to the point when getting their attention. They know that being there on the sales call means the salesperson passed the high D's screening test when the appointment was set; otherwise the sales call wouldn't be taking place. The high D is ready to get down to business and often will begin with something like, "Sit down and tell me what you've got." The salesperson should be subtle in doing so, but it is important for the salesperson to take control of the sales interview and not relinquish it to high Ds. In other words, salespeople cannot let high Ds force them to start the sales interview some place other than Step 1 (getting the prospect's attention) as "tell me what you've got" would do. Taking control also is important because high D prospects will boot out salespeople they don't respect.

High I Prospects

Since high I prospects may want to chit-chat first, the salesperson can hold off on Step 1 for a few minutes until prospects are ready to get down to business. It makes sense to get their attention around their interests as well as the credibility the salesperson brings to the table. This is an ego/prestige thing with them. High I prospects will want to know certain things about the salesperson. They are looking for commonality in career, background, jobs, friends, experiences, schools, organizations, social matters, interests, hobbies, and so on. Regarding *credibility*, they especially want to see that the salesperson has done business with the "right" people.

High S Prospects

High S prospects want salespeople to feel at ease and will do things like sit beside them rather than behind their desk. Getting the attention of high S prospects should be designed around their interest in the salesperson, especially in terms of relationships, stability, and security. They will want to know about the salesperson's longevity and clients who are like them. In view of this, it is appropriate to say something like, "I've worked with several companies like yours for a long time and have a good relationship with the people there. Do you know Bill, one of my customers, over at . . . ?"

High C Prospects

Remember that high C prospects want to know and hear about everything and that includes the salesperson. They will allow Step 1 to be completed in its entirety and will be especially interested in the salesperson, the company she represents, and the credibility and longevity the salesperson brings to the table. The guideline with high C prospects is to be brief and to the point, yet give them a lot of specific information.

Behavior Style and Step 2 (Confirming the B-1 Diagnosis)

Sales executives hope that, at the time the appointment was set, the salesperson asked the right questions and concluded that the prospect was the decision maker and had the money to buy—in other words, that the prospect believes "I can make this buying decision." In confirming this, and salespeople do need to confirm it, they will want to keep the following in mind.

High D Prospects

High Ds usually are decision makers. Even when they are not, they may sound, feel, and act like they are. For this reason it is important not to let their over-confidence be misleading when confirming their B-1.

High I Prospects

It is a good guess that high I prospects are either decision makers or influencers. Like high Ds, they tend to believe they can get what they want, even when they can't. They also have a tendency to overstate their authority. Salespeople should keep this in mind when confirming their B-1.

High S Prospects

They tend to be influencers or users rather than decision makers. Salespeople should probe to see: (1) if high Ss really do have decision-making authority, (2) if they have the necessary influence and are willing to use it, or (3) if they are serving a screening function for the real decision maker.

High C Prospects

Like high S prospects, high Cs often are influencers or users, rather than decision makers. The same precautionary, probing approach recommended for high S prospects should be used with high Cs.

Behavior Style and Step 3 (Determining Behavior Style)

Sales executives would do well to be sure the sales force has a thorough understanding of behavior style as presented in Chapter 3. Steps were outlined in that chapter to guide salespeople to quickly and accurately assess and determine the behavior style of their prospects. There is absolutely no reason, with this knowledge available, why salespeople should not be able to know the behavior style of each and every prospect they call on. *Provide training.*

Behavior Style and Step 4 (Identifying the Prospect's Objectives)

Sales executives know that selling can be a clumsy, stressful, unsuccessful experience when salespeople don't have a clear picture of the prospect's objectives. Salespeople simply cannot move too far along in the process without first hearing the complete story of the prospect's objectives.

High D Prospects

Identifying objectives is easy with high D prospects. They usually have clear objectives and will gladly share what they are. Simply use the principle, "If you want to know, ask."

High I Prospects

High I prospects normally can and will state their objectives, but the salesperson will have to read which ones are organizational as opposed to personal. When a high D says, "I want my salespeople to prospect better so they can sell more," he is saying, "I want results." Often when a high I says it, the meaning is, "I personally need for my salespeople to prospect better so they can sell more so I will look good." With high I prospects, the salesperson cannot focus solely on meeting organizational objectives. It is necessary to clearly point out how the product or service can help them reach their personal objectives. This is important to high I prospects and is evidenced by their tendency to state personal objectives more often than organization objectives.

High S Prospects

Of the four behavior styles, high S prospects tend to have the least clarity regarding objectives because they are noncommittal fence sitters. They will talk about objectives tentatively, using words like might, maybe, probably, possible, and so on. They will say things such as "I think we might like to . . ." or "Maybe we'll want to . . ." or "That's probably something we'll consider." They will state objectives with lack of clarity and sometimes with considerable ambiguity. The salesperson must probe and help high S prospects define their objectives, which always deal in some way with maintaining the status quo.

High C Prospects

It is hard to get a good sense of the objectives of high C prospects. They don't like to list their objectives for salespeople. Instead, they are indirect, often stating objectives as questions. For example, they may ask the question, "Can you do such and such?" What they are saying is that the "such and such" is an objective. They don't want to share objectives directly unless they trust the salesperson. This means salespeople have to listen to their questions, convert them into objectives, and restate them. If they ask, "How would you go about so and so?" it is important not to miss the point and simply answer their question. The "so and so" is the objective. This means the salesperson can say something like, "Okay, then, one of the things you want is 'so and so.'"

Behavior Style and Steps 5, 6, and 7

It is very important for prospects to believe, as sales executives know, that buying will lead to (B-2) *personal* as well as organizational outcomes that are satisfying to them (B-3), and not lead to (B-2) outcomes that would be dissatisfying (B-3). One important category of personal outcomes is related to the prospect's behavior style. Focusing on these is recommended for Step 5 (translating objectives into needs), Step 6 (stating benefits in terms of objectives), and Step 7 (showing how features provide benefits). While having this focus on all three steps may seem unnecessarily redundant, it is what prospects want to hear.

High D Prospects

The bottom line is the main interest of high D prospects. They want to see results, and their objectives reflect the results they want to hold in their hands. This means the salesperson should tie the *need* as closely as possible to what high D prospects say their objectives are (Step 5). *Benefits* and *features* also should focus on results (Steps 6 and 7). For example, if "getting the newsletter out on time" is the objective, Steps 5, 6, and 7 might be applied in the following way.

>*Salesperson*: "So you *need* a computer with desktop publishing that will get the newsletter out on time. The *benefit* of our equipment is that it will do just that—it allows you to meet your publishing deadlines. The main *feature* of the system is that it has the speed to knock things out fast."

High I Prospects

Trying new things, being the first to do something, and looking good tend to be important to high I prospects. This should be acknowledged in Steps 5, 6, and 7. It can be done easily by closely tying these outcomes to needs, benefits, and features.

>*Salesperson*: "So you *need* a computer with desktop publishing that will get the newsletter out on time, and at the same time make you look good. The *benefit* of our equipment is that everybody will be impressed that you're the first one to regularly get out a good-looking newsletter on time. This

equipment has the latest *features* in terms of speed and quality."

High S Prospects

Stability, security, and the status quo are important to high S prospects. Each of these should be reflected in Steps 5, 6, and 7. High S prospects must have a strong sense that any product or service will not jeopardize the stability, security, and status quo they desire. For example:

Salesperson: "So you *need* a computer with desktop publishing that will get the newsletter out on time but has a layout similar to the one you are using now. The *benefit* of our equipment is that you'll get the newsletter out on time by continuing to do things pretty much the same way you've been doing them. This equipment has the same old reliable *features* you are accustomed to having."

High C Prospects

Perfection, standards, and quality are especially important to high C prospects. They can really warm up to products and services that meet these three criteria. Steps 5, 6, and 7 should reflect this. For example:

Salesperson: "So you *need* a computer with desktop publishing that not only will get the newsletter out on time, but also will have a high-quality appearance. The *benefit* of our equipment is that you will be able to meet both your publishing deadlines and your production standards. This equipment is designed to operate with the ultimate in precision and perfection (the *features*)."

To summarize, one of the keys to effective selling is the repeated focus on the things of personal importance that make prospects feel good. By knowing the prospect's behavior style, the salesperson will have a clear picture of what is important to the prospect. When the salesperson knows this, it only takes a little practice to state needs, benefits, and features in a way that will convince prospects that they will get (B-2) the personal outcomes they want (B-3) and avoid (B-2) those they don't want (B-3). Salespeople who do this will sell more. Sales executives can see this clearly and may want to determine ways to equip the sales force to get better results. This is yet another nudge toward equipping salespeople to understand the behavior style of their prospects and take advantage of that understanding and use it to sell more effectively. Only sales executives can decide to make it happen.

Behavior Style and Steps 8, 9, and 10

As mentioned earlier, Steps 8, 9, and 10 are interrelated and often are not applied in sequence. At the same time a prospect is asking questions and raising objections (Step 8), the salesperson can use that information immediately to determine the prospect's motivation to buy (Step 9). And handling questions and objections (Step 8) actually is a way of strengthening the motivation to buy (Step 10). With this in mind, let's take a look at the behavior style implications of these three steps.

High D Prospects

Prospects with the high D style do not hesitate to ask questions and voice objections (Step 8). They usually talk in a straightforward way when doing so. For example, they might say, "I've been promised that before and nothing happened (a B-2 problem)." This straightforwardness can be misleading in determining their motivation to buy (Step 9) because it makes their objections sound stronger than they really are.

High D prospects can be misleading in another way. It is their nature not to indicate a high degree of satisfaction (B-3). They tend not to voice or show it even when they feel it. Consequently, this may cause salespeople to see a B-3 problem when there isn't one. If high D's don't voice dissatisfaction, they most likely are satisfied. When handling questions and objections (Step 8) and strengthening the motivation to buy (Step 10), it is best to be open, honest, straightforward, to the point, and brief. This is a strong preferred by prospects with the high D behavior style.

High I Prospects

One of the problems with high I prospects is that they have a tendency not to voice objections directly. For example, "I wonder how people will react to this" may mean "One of my objections is that I'll have some resistance." They often state objections in the form of something they need to do. For example, "I'll have to convince Bill that this is a fair price" may be their way of saying, "Another objection is that your price is too high."

Their tendency toward indirectness can create three problems. One, it makes it hard to identify their objections (Step 8). Two, it makes it tough to accurately determine their motivation to buy (Step 9). Three, it compounds the difficulty of strengthening the prospect's motivation to buy (Step 10). All of this simply means that the salesperson has to be tuned in to what prospects are saying and probe to understand the true meaning of their indirectness.

High S Prospects

Salespeople can expect to hear objections from high S prospects regarding B-1. They tend to be influencers and users rather than decision makers. So, they may object to buying, for example, because they are afraid they can't get approval to buy or because they feel their budget is not quite big enough.

B-2 and B-3 objections of high S prospects can be expected to focus on relationship issues. They want to know if the buyer-seller relationship will be strong and if the salesperson will be around when they need help. For example, they want to know if the salesperson will ensure prompt delivery, service the product, and handle problems related to shipping (shortage, breakage, defective units), invoices, and utilization of the product.

The sales interview with high S prospects can completely break down if the salesperson hasn't developed a good relationship. The basis of such a relationship is trust, and without it high S prospects tend to withhold information that is critical to making the sale. This withholding includes things like not letting the salesperson know if they really have the money and authority to buy (B-1), not stating doubts about getting the outcomes (B-2), not indicating outcome preferences (B-3), and not voicing objections (B-2 and B-3) or withholding them until the last minute.

Withholding this information creates three major problems. First, it is hard to overcome objections when they haven't been voiced (Step 8). Second, it is easy to believe they are motivated to buy (Step 9) when they are not. Third, the lack of information makes it difficult to know how to strengthen their motivation to buy (Step 10). The behavior style of the high S dictates that salespeople develop a good, trusting relationship; otherwise Steps 8, 9, and 10 fall apart, making the sale unlikely.

High C Prospects

Prospects with the high C style want to know everything, so the salesperson can expect a lot of questions from them. They also have, and voice, more objections than prospects with other behavior styles. Salespeople have their hands full handling the questions and objections (Step 8) they voice, particularly if it is necessary to dig up all the facts and details they want.

High C prospects will have B-1 objections similar to high S prospects because they, too, tend to be influencers and users rather than decision makers. Regarding B-2, they will challenge and want proof, proof they can touch and feel, that they will get the promised outcomes.

Determining the motivation to buy (Step 9) comes fairly easily with high C prospects because they make it clear where they stand. The problem comes with strengthening their motivation to buy (Step 10) because doing so requires so much time and energy. The seemingly endless number of questions and objections, and the extensive amount of detailed information required to handle them, can drag the salesperson down, making it easy to become discouraged and tempting to give up. The hardest part is "sticking with it." This, however, is a requirement for motivating high C prospects to buy.

Behavior Style and Steps 11 and 12

The behavior style implications of making closing agreements (Step 11) and summarizing follow-up actions (Step 12) will be discussed after a detailed treatment of these steps is presented in Chapter 7.

Selling to Behavior Style

Sales executives sometimes feel discouraged because they observe that some salespeople use the same sales approach with all of their prospects. The salesperson may fine tune it and get it polished, and this will fit well with a few prospects. The problem, however, is that it misses the mark with the majority. People are different, and the way salespeople deal with each prospect must recognize those individual differences. Using the sales interview process with a focus on behavior style is a way to effectively do this. Every step in the sales interview process can and should match the behavior style of the prospect. Sales executives can imagine the impact on sales results when salespeople sell to the behavior style of prospects. Sell to behavior style, sell more.

THE SALES INTERVIEW AND THE SALES MODEL

The sales model discussed in Chapters 1 and 2 shows how buyers buy. The model is based on the recognition that: (1) prospects put out effort to perform (i.e., to make buying decisions), (2) buying leads to certain outcomes, and (3) the outcomes lead to satisfaction or dissatisfaction.

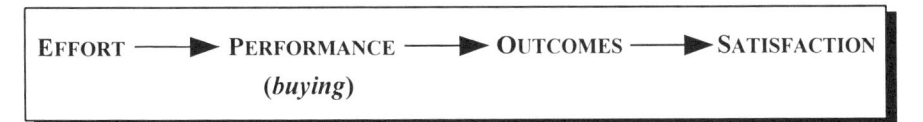

EFFORT ⟶ PERFORMANCE ⟶ OUTCOMES ⟶ SATISFACTION
(*buying*)

The sales model observes that prospects are most likely to buy when they believe three things. First is the belief (B-1) that they can make the buying decision, i.e., that effort will lead to performance (buying). Second is the belief (B-2) that performance (buying) will lead to certain outcomes. Third is the belief (B-3) that the outcomes will be satisfying.

The Sales Model

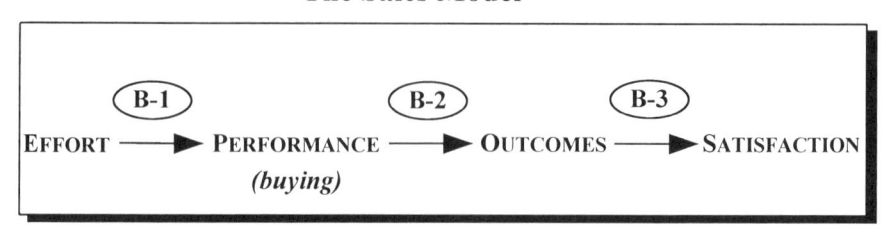

EFFORT $\xrightarrow{\text{B-1}}$ PERFORMANCE *(buying)* $\xrightarrow{\text{B-2}}$ OUTCOMES $\xrightarrow{\text{B-3}}$ SATISFACTION

The sales interview has been formulated with the sales model in mind. Every step is designed to focus specifically on the prospect's B-1, B-2, and/or B-3. Let's quickly review this by looking at each step.

1. Getting the Prospect's Attention—The thrust is on gaining credibility (B-2) and showing that the salesperson has something to offer (B-3).

2. Confirming B-1 Diagnosis—The obvious emphasis is on B-1.

3. Determining Behavior Style—When salespeople know the style of their prospects, they will know: (1) many of the things the prospect likes and dislikes (B-3); (2) their skepticism about promises (B-2) made to them; and (3) the likelihood they can make or influence the buying decision (B-1).

4. Identifying the Prospect's Objectives—The prospect's personal and organizational objectives indicate the things they want and don't want (B-3).

5. Translating Objectives into Needs—The salesperson is telling the prospect that the product or service will give them (B-2) what they want (B-3) and not give (B-2) things they don't want (B-3).

6. Stating Benefits in Terms of Objectives—This is a restatement that they will get (B-2) what they want (B-3) and not get (B-2) what they don't want (B-3) if they buy the product or service.

7. Showing How Features Provide the Benefits—The features indicate *how* the product or service will give them (B-2) what they want (B-3) and not give (B-2) what they don't want (B-3).

8. Handling Questions and Objections—This is where prospects indicate what they are thinking. The focus usually is on B-2 and B-3 issues, and occasionally B-1 issues.

Selling That Motivates 127

9. Diagnosing the Motivation to Buy—The diagnosis addresses B-1, B-2, and B-3.

10. Strengthening the Motivation to Buy—The focus here is on B-1, B-2, and B-3, depending on which beliefs need to be strengthened.

11. Closing the Sale—All aspects of closing the sale must be consistent with the prospect's B-1, B-2, and B-3.

12. Summarizing Follow-up Actions—All follow-up action must fit the B-1, B-2, and B-3 of the prospect.

Sales executives understand why the sales interview looks, sounds, and feels so *powerful*! The sales model describes what motivates people to buy, and every step in the sales interview process is tied directly to the model. Salespeople will become more effective when they use this approach. That's a promise they can bank on.

SUMMARY

- Making sales presentations doesn't cut it anymore. Successful salespeople tailor the sales approach to the individuality of each prospect.

- Salespeople find it easier to sell when they know certain things about their prospects—what their objectives are, what they want, how they buy, and how they like to be sold.

- It's easy for salespeople to get the information they need from prospects. Just follow the principle, "If you want to know, ask." Getting prospects to give the information is better than making assumptions and playing a guessing game.

- Rather than a hit-or-miss sales presentation, a sales interview that is tailored to the prospect is recommended as the format for selling to the individuality of each prospect.

- The sales interview is based on the sales model, which recognizes that prospects have the greatest motivation to buy when they believe they can buy (B-1), believe they will get (B-2) what they want (B-3), and avoid (B-2) what they don't want (B-3).

- Sales executives may want to consider, maybe just make the decision now, to move the sales force in a new direction. Provide training. Prepare and motivate the sales force to use an approach where *selling is motivating* will pay off. Just go ahead and do it.

NOTES

1. Barton Weitz, Harish Sujan, and Mita Sujan, "Knowledge, Motivation, and Adaptive Behavior: A Framework for Improving Selling Effectiveness," *Journal of Marketing* (October 1986), pp. 174–191.

2. Richard Bandler and John LaValle, *Persuasion Engineering* (Capitola, California: Meta Publications, Inc., 1996), p. 4.

3. William Moulton Marsten, *Emotions of Normal People* (Minneapolis, Minnesota: Persona Press, Inc., 1979).

CHAPTER 7

Closings That Motivate

Sales executives get a bird's-eye view of the problem salespeople have in closing the sale. One part of the problem flows out of reluctance to ask for the order; another part is more skills related. This is a serious problem and it holds back the performance of a countless number of both seasoned and new salespeople. Sales executives would do well to step up and zero in on this problem. The impetus to take action begins with the realization that: (1) too many sales are lost, or unnecessarily delayed, because salespeople are not adequately accepting the challenge of closing sales; and (2) fixing the problem across the entire sales force calls for turning up the volume on motivation and education, as will be seen in this chapter. When all is said and done, it is nothing more than a matter of deciding to just go ahead and fix the problem.

This chapter deals first with motivating salespeople to overcome the reluctance to close and then takes an in-depth look at the skill issue by covering the final two steps of the sales interview, namely, how to close the sale (Step 11) and summarize the follow-up actions that must accompany the close (Step 12), as described earlier in Chapter 6. The focus is on Step 11, with special emphasis on when and how to close the sale. A brief discussion of Step 12 then follows.

WHAT DOES "CLOSE" MEAN?

Sales executives know that in the context of sales, the word "close" is used in two different ways. First, it refers to an *end result*, as in the question, "Did you close the sale?" Used in this way, "close" means "Did you get a commitment to buy from the prospect?" In this case, "close" refers to the end result of the salesperson's efforts, namely, a commitment to buy. Second, it is used as a *method*, as in the question, "What kind of close did you use?" In this way, "close" refers to what the salesperson does to get the buying commitment. This chapter will use both of these meanings of the word "close."

What "Close" Means

Way "Close" Is Used	Meaning
As an end result	Commitment to buy
As a method	What the salesperson does to get the commitment to buy

WHAT DOES "CLOSING" MEAN?

Sales executives know that salespeople do not always have a good feel for the basics when it comes to closing a sale, like having a clear picture of exactly what closing the sale means. Many salespeople cannot articulate that closing refers to the three-step process of getting prospects to make a commitment to buy. The steps are: (1) selecting and using one of the many closing methods, or a combination of them, that feel right to the prospect; (2) asking the prospect to buy; and (3) reaching a closing agreement. This process is the core of the chapter and each of the three steps is discussed at length. But first, let's look at a few other related issues.

CLOSING IS MORE THAN A SKILL

Salespeople find it helpful when sales executives cause them to plainly see that skill is only one of the essential ingredients in closing a sale. It goes without saying that every salesperson must have closing skills, like sensing when to close, deciding which closing method to use, and then using it effectively. But closing is more than a skill. Knowledge is a necessity, too. Lots of it. Especially important is knowledge about the prospect's behavior style and motivation to buy, for example. And having the right attitude, namely a *closing attitude*, is important as well. This means salespeople need to have a state of mind about closing that is dominated by a commitment to four things: (1) the goal is to close; (2) always try to close; (3) close for something; and (4) deal with reluctance to close. Let's take a look at each of these.

CLOSING ATTITUDE

Means a Commitment to
1. Focusing on "the goal is to close"
2. Always trying to close
3. Always closing for something
4. Dealing with reluctance to close

The Goal Is to Close

The ultimate goal of any sales effort is to close the sale. As strange as it may seem, many salespeople lose sight of this. Instead, they wander around, going through the motions rather than setting their sights on closing the sale as soon as possible. When the goal isn't to close, it's easy to procrastinate and rationalize, to get off track and stay there. And it shows in sales performance. The goal is to close. High-performing salespeople seldom forget this. They have a kind of tunnel vision when it comes to closing the sale. Sales executives may need to remind the others that the goal is to close.

Always Try to Close

Sales executives can imagine the difference if salespeople were always trying to close.[1] Maybe a gentle reminder or, better yet, a short, tightly designed training program that would nudge the sale force to focus more on closing, closing, closing. Go for it and provide training. Give the sales force a reminder. There is no standard time and place for when to close. While some prospects are a long time in deciding to buy, others decide quickly. Some even decide during the first few minutes of the sales interview. Closing can come anytime, anywhere. The goal is to close, and salespeople should always be trying to close.

Only bad things happen when salespeople don't close the sale when the prospect is ready. Time and money slip away as the selling process drags on, which is poor utilization of limited resources. The likelihood of closing the sale decreases. Anything can happen to change the prospect's mind, like losing confidence in the salesperson, finding a better product or service, getting a lower price somewhere else, or coming under the influence of a more effective salesperson, for example. To avoid these problems, salespeople should always be trying to close.

Close for Something

Sales executives want to stress that when it isn't possible to close the sale, salespeople should close for something, anything, to keep the sales process alive. Closing for something heightens the commitment, brightens the picture, strengthens the motivation to buy. Salespeople can have many intermediate closes, including closing the prospect to: (1) meet again, (2) review product literature, (3) accept a bid or proposal, (4) attend a product demonstration, (5) use the product or service on a trial basis, (6) talk with others who are using the product or service, or (7) arrange a meeting with the decision maker. When the sale can't be closed, the idea is for salespeople to close for something, anything, that will represent progress toward eventually closing the sale. Salespeople need to be trained to do this. Just another reason to provide training, at least to consider to provide training.

Deal with Reluctance to Close

While the ultimate goal is to close, sales executives have observed the closing behavior of salespersons and have a good grasp of why the goal often is not reached. Salespeople obviously close some sales, and try to close others but fail. However, sales executives have observed, and research confirms their observation, that salespeople often do not even make an attempt to close. It is estimated that as much as 60 percent of the time there is no attempt to close the sale! Sales executives may want to sit back and imagine the impact on sales results if all of their salespeople simply *attempted* to close more often. More attempts to close will result in closing more sales. There are several questions sales executives may want to consider. One, how much would sales increase, overall, if every salesperson had more attempts to close? Two, how much would it cost to equip and motivate them to attempt more closes? Three, what can be done to be certain there is a big payoff?

Closings That Motivate

> **Closing Attempts**

40%—salesperson attempts to close

60%—salesperson does not attempt to close

Sales executives, take notice. It is easy to see why there is so much reluctance to close. The picture becomes clear by applying the sales model discussed in Chapters 1 and 2. The model explains the salesperson's motivation, or lack of motivation (reluctance), to close the sale. Specifically, the model can be applied to the salesperson by defining performance as closing the sale (rather than applying the model to the prospect and defining performance as buying). In this context, the model indicates that salespeople put out a certain amount of effort which leads to some level of performance (closing the sale); the performance leads to certain outcomes; and the outcomes lead to some amount of satisfaction or dissatisfaction.

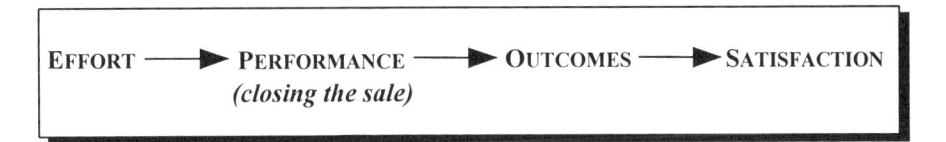

EFFORT ⟶ PERFORMANCE ⟶ OUTCOMES ⟶ SATISFACTION
(closing the sale)

Salespeople are motivated to put out the most effort and perform best when they: (1) believe effort will lead to performance (B-1); (2) believe performance will lead to outcomes (B-2); and (3) believe the outcomes will be satisfying (B-3).

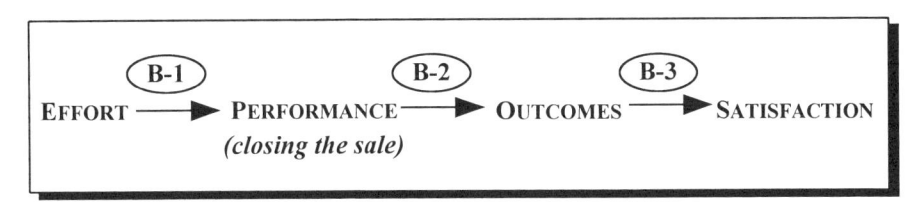

EFFORT —(B-1)→ PERFORMANCE —(B-2)→ OUTCOMES —(B-3)→ SATISFACTION
(closing the sale)

If any of the three beliefs are weak, the salesperson will not be highly motivated. This lack of motivation accounts for the reluctance to close the sale. Let's take a closer look at this.

Reluctance and B-1

There is a B-1 problem when salespeople do not believe effort (attempting to close) will lead to performance (closing the sale). Here is the way salespeople often talk to themselves. Notice how this self-talk naturally leads the salesperson to conclude "I can't close this sale."

Reluctance and B-1

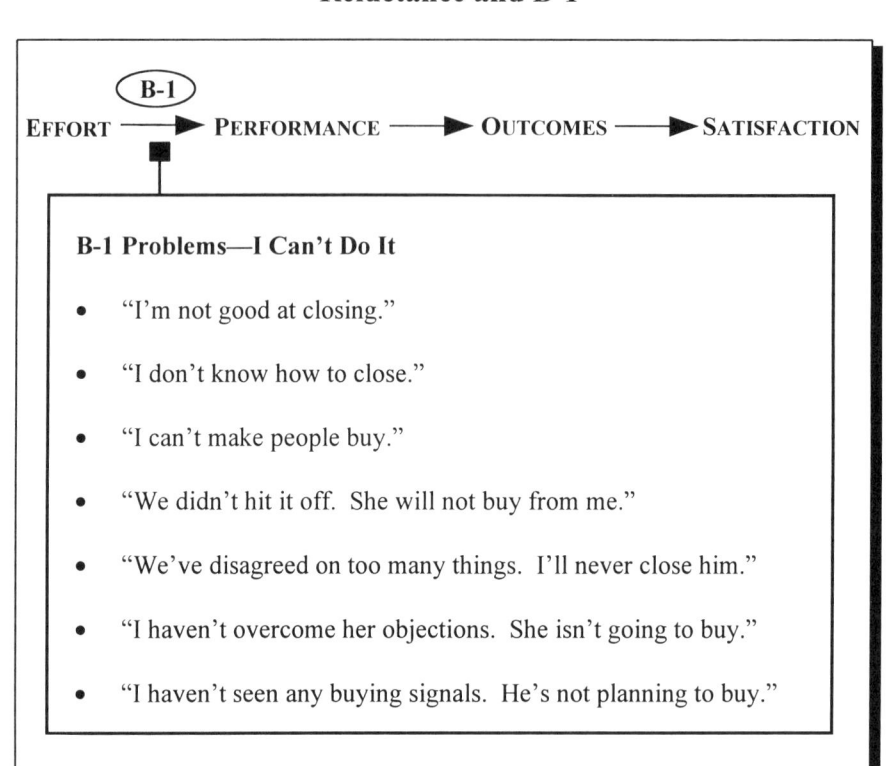

EFFORT ⟶ PERFORMANCE ⟶ OUTCOMES ⟶ SATISFACTION

(B-1 marker on the Effort→Performance link)

B-1 Problems—I Can't Do It

- "I'm not good at closing."
- "I don't know how to close."
- "I can't make people buy."
- "We didn't hit it off. She will not buy from me."
- "We've disagreed on too many things. I'll never close him."
- "I haven't overcome her objections. She isn't going to buy."
- "I haven't seen any buying signals. He's not planning to buy."

What causes B-1 problems and how can sales executives get a handle on them? Sales executives have observed two common causes. One is inadequate closing skills. The other is a history of failure in closing the sale. There are three concrete solutions that sales executives can get a firm grip on. One is to offer skill building through training or coaching. A combination of the two works best. Sales executives may be wondering if they shouldn't come to grips with the need to do more to help the entire sales force and just go ahead and provide training. Another solution is for the sales manager to build the self-confidence of the salesperson by using a structured approach to building self-confidence (see Chapter 9). The third solution is to create opportunities for small successes, like guiding the salesperson through a small sale with a prospect she finds easy to work with and then gradually move her into closing bigger sales with tougher prospects. The point is this. Salespeople who are reluctant to close the sale typically do not overcome the reluctance on their own. They need help. Sales executives can provide the needed support if they will go into the construction business and specialize to build skills and self-confidence in the sales force.

Reluctance and B-3

Sales executives can see and sense B-3 problems when salespeople believe performance (closing the sale) will lead to outcomes (B-2) but believe the outcomes will not be satisfying (B-3). Here are a few of the common things salespersons say.

Reluctance and B-3

EFFORT ⟶ PERFORMANCE ⟶ OUTCOMES ⟶ SATISFACTION (B-3)

B-3 Problems—Don't Want but Expect to Get

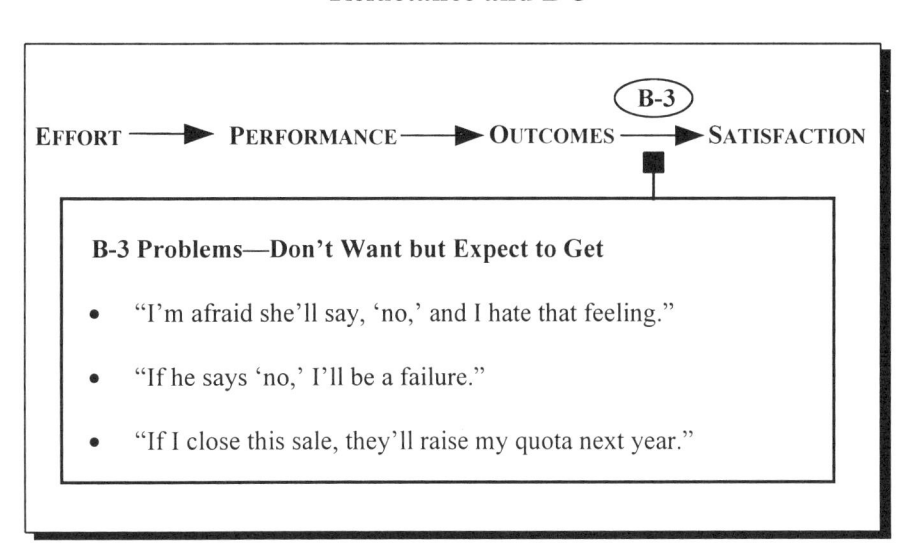

- "I'm afraid she'll say, 'no,' and I hate that feeling."
- "If he says 'no,' I'll be a failure."
- "If I close this sale, they'll raise my quota next year."

B-3 problems like this are simply a case of salespeople getting, or having a fear of getting, outcomes they don't want. Sales executives must do something to keep salespeople from getting what they don't want, or at least do something to minimize the impact. While this solution is simple in concept, it may be tough to implement. Even when the outcomes are in the sales executives hands, as in the case of setting quota, there may be little that can be done because quotas do increase and special favors are not appropriate when it comes to setting quota. However, sales executives would do well to examine the way quotas are determined and be sure salespeople are motivated, rather than demotivated, to sell as much as possible.

Sometimes the unwanted outcomes are not given to the salesperson by someone else, but instead are something salespeople give to themselves. For example, if a salesperson feels rejected when a prospect says "no," the salesperson is choosing to feel that way. The same is true for feelings of failure, inadequacy, frustration, disappointment, and so on. Salespeople can use their imagination and do something about these unwanted outcomes. It may be easier than they think, but sales executives may need to teach them how to do it. The way salespeople interpret an unsuccessful attempt to close a sale depends on their expectation. If they expect to close on the first attempt, they are in for a rough emotional ride. Prospects seldom are closed quickly. It is a process of making numerous attempts to close, hoping each time to be successful, but realizing that the main purpose of most closing attempts is to get more information, to get better in tune with the prospect, to get closer to eventually closing the sale. More about how to do this later in the chapter. A closing attempt is never unsuccessful as long as it results in information that in some way pushes the salesperson a step further along the path toward closing the sale. Sales executives may have to help salespeople grasp what is happening to them and view it in a more positive light.

Reluctance and B-2

Sales executives are familiar with the two kinds of B-2 problems salespeople see. One is when the salesperson wants certain outcomes (B-3) but does not believe performance (closing the sale) will lead to them (B-2). Here are some typical things salespeople might say that indicate this problem.

Reluctance and B-2

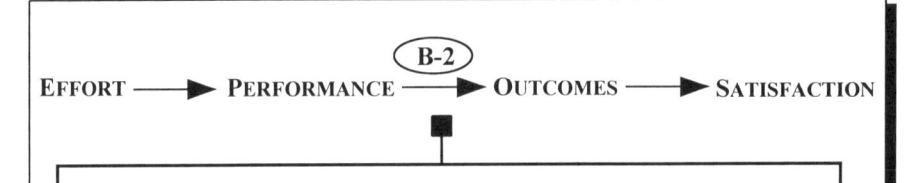

EFFORT ⟶ PERFORMANCE ⟶(B-2)⟶ OUTCOMES ⟶ SATISFACTION

B-2 Problems—Want but Don't Expect to Get

- "I'm not on a sales commission. I don't get anything extra for selling more."

- "Even if I close this sale, I will not get a bonus."

- "When I make a nice sale, what happens? Nothing. Not even a pat on the back."

This problem screams out when outcomes are not tied to performance. The solution is obvious. Tie outcomes to performance. Sales executives have to make this decision. No one else can. Now may be the time for sales executives to play a heavy hand, to exert the authority and influence of their position. Sales executives are paid to make these kinds of far-reaching decisions. The decision to tie outcomes to performance has an impact on every person in the sales organization. When salespeople get what their performance deserves, they are motivated to sell. When they don't, when outcomes are not tied to performance, the motivation of every salesperson is diminished. Tie outcomes to performance, and not just pay. This is one of the most important decisions a sales executive can make. So think about it and just do it.

The other B-2 problem sales executives see is when the salesperson currently is getting (B-2) certain desired outcomes (B-3), and does not believe performing poorly (not closing the sale) will cause the desired outcomes to be taken away. Here are some examples.

Reluctance and B-2

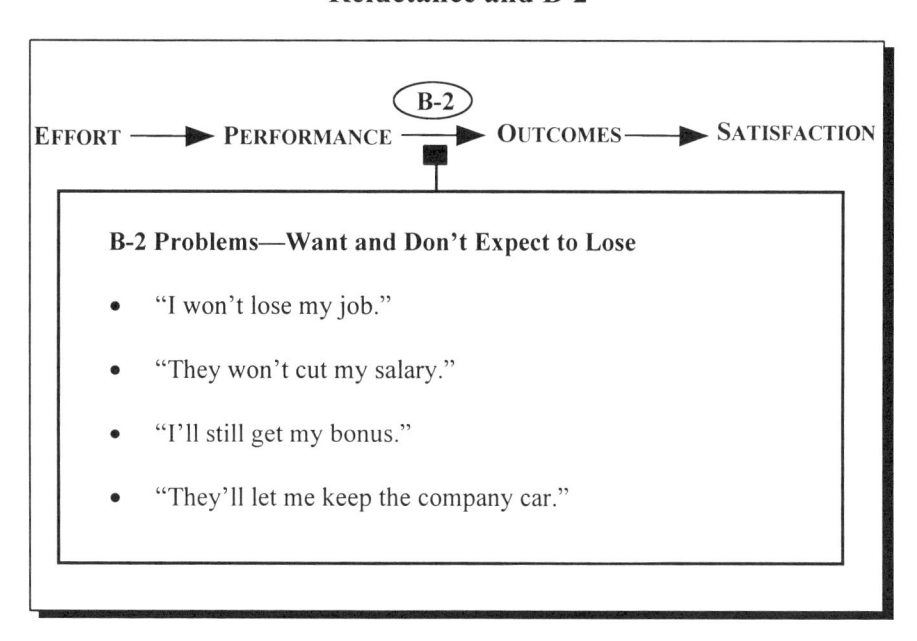

EFFORT → PERFORMANCE —(B-2)→ OUTCOMES → SATISFACTION

B-2 Problems—Want and Don't Expect to Lose

- "I won't lose my job."
- "They won't cut my salary."
- "I'll still get my bonus."
- "They'll let me keep the company car."

Some salespeople can't be expected to do the job if they believe they will continue to get what they want even if they don't perform? The solution is simple. Sales executives can change what salespeople get. Tie outcomes to their performance. The solution to this problem rests squarely on the shoulders of the sales executive. When you think about it, now may just be the time to stand up and scream and shout and *do something about it*. Just go ahead and do it. Tie outcomes to performance. Get the sales force on track. Give them a reason to perform. Give them what their performance deserves, good or bad, whatever it is. Act now. Make a difference. Just do it. Now is the time. Motivate the sales force to sell. Tie it down. Tie outcomes to performance. If doing it feels overwhelming, if taking the right steps isn't clear, get some help. There are plenty of motivation and performance experts out there. Just go ahead and find somebody to help.

WHEN TO CLOSE

Sales executives are aware that *motivation* goes a long way in getting salespeople to close the deals, but motivation is not enough. The problem is that salespeople must have many, many skills and motivation alone will take them only so far. Learn more, sell more. Motivation and *preparation* go hand in hand. One without the other falls short. When it comes to closing the sale, salespeople need to see that knowing when to close is important. Ideally, salespeople should be closing at the first opportunity. There are several reasons. First, it may jeopardize the sale if they don't. This happens because some prospects decide to buy early in the sales interview, and then change their mind as the salesperson talks on. If salespeople miss the first opportunity, it may not come around again. Second, even if they do close the sale later, it is costly. They will: (1) spend more time than necessary, (2) work harder than called for, (3) experience unneeded frustration and stress, (4) increase travel and other expenses, and (5) neglect other prospects they could be selling. Yes, salespeople need to hear and plainly see that knowing when to close is important.

Closing when the Prospect Is Ready

Sales executives want their salespeople to close at the first opportunity. This means they should close when the prospect is motivated to buy. As mentioned many times, prospects are motivated to buy when they believe buying will lead to outcomes (B-2) that they want (B-3) and avoid (B-2) the outcomes they don't want (B-3). Salespeople will know when to close if they are constantly evaluating the B-1, B-2, and B-3 of their prospects.

Most prospects make it pretty clear when they are ready to close. In fact, some prospects even close the sale for the salesperson.[2] Here are some examples.

- "Okay, I'll take it."

- "I'm sold."
- "Sign me up."
- "I've decided to go with you."

Closing Signals

While only a few prospects will speak out and take the initiative to close the sale, they all give closing signals. When salespeople are in tune with their prospects, they will quickly learn to notice these signals. Some prospects are very direct, saying in one way or another, "I am ready to buy." Closing signals that are straightforward and easy to interpret include statements like the following.

- "If I give you a decision now, can you guarantee delivery on Monday?"
- "What has to be done to finalize this?"
- "It all sounds good to me."

Some closing signals are less obvious, but still easy to pick up. Here are some examples that *may* suggest the motivation to buy.

- "What is the price?"
- "What kind of terms do you offer?"
- "What kind of warranty does it have?"
- "When could you make delivery?"
- "What is the smallest order I could give you?"
- "When will you have the new model?"
- "Can I get it in this color (size, style)?"
- "How big does the order have to be to get a good price?"

When a closing signal appears, salespeople should be trained to stop everything and go for the close. It should dawn on them, "Hey, time to close this one. Let's put some money in the bank." This is not a time to wait. It is a time to take action immediately. Failure to do so is a common mistake, especially with salespeople who are bound to sales presentations rather than using the sales interview approach recommended in Chapter 6. These salespeople tend to ignore the closing signals until their sales presentation is completed. Doing so is being insensitive to the prospect, creates the danger of raising objections the prospect hasn't thought of yet, and is a good way to let a sure sale slip away.

Sales executives must train and persuade salespeople to clearly see that they have everything to gain, and nothing to lose, by pushing for the close. If things go well, they make the sale; if they don't, they get information that moves them closer. Prospects invariably respond with a question or comment that directly or indirectly indicates why they are aren't ready to close. Here are some examples. Notice that each one shows something that must be done before the prospect will be motivated to buy.

- "I need to check with my boss first (B-1)."
- "I don't have that much in my budget (B-1)."
- "I'm not sure I can convince the right people to approve it (B-1)."
- "I'm just not sure I'll get (B-2) the results I want (B-3)."
- "This will cause (B-2) too much change (B-3)."
- "We want flexibility (B-3) and this doesn't have it (B-2)."

Responses often reflect the behavior style of prospects as well as indicate why they aren't ready to buy. Here are statements that touch on both. Again, notice that each statement suggests steps that must be taken before the prospect will feel motivated to buy.

- "So why do you think I can reach (B-2) my objectives (B-3) with this?" (This is a high D who is interested in the bottom line.)
- "How new (B-3) did you say this is?" (This is a high I who likes to buy things that are new and different.)
- "Do you see this fitting into the system we're using now (B-3)?" (This is a high S who wants to maintain stability.)
- "I need to think about it for a while to be sure I make the best decision (B-3)." (This is a high C who wants to make the "perfect" choice.)

Sales executives are aware that anything and everything prospects say following an attempted close can be valuable, maybe even be the key to closing the sale around the next bend in the road. Prospects talk. They give information. When salespeople listen, really listen, they discover exactly what it takes to motivate prospects to buy. The information prospects give, if grasped and used appropriately, moves the salesperson another step nearer to closing the sale. This means an unsuccessful closing attempt is worthwhile. So, sales executives must teach the sales force to go for the close when they pick up a closing signal. There always is something to gain and nothing to lose.

Closing when the Prospect Is Not Ready

Every sales executive who has been on the street is aware that there is another time when salespeople should attempt to close. And they need to be sure their sales force sees it, too. That time is when the salesperson needs to gauge why prospects aren't ready to close. As indicated earlier, when attempting to close, prospects respond with information that suggests what needs to be done before they will be motivated to buy. Attempting to close is an effective method for getting prospects to reveal information needed to eventually close the sale. Even when prospects aren't ready to buy, attempting to close makes sense. So, anytime salespeople feel stumped and don't know how to move ahead, they should be trained to go for the close.

Recognizing that closing has two purposes fills salespeople with a psychological advantage. When closing is seen as having the singular purpose of finalizing the sale, each closing attempt is viewed as either a success or a failure. The fear of rejection and failure continually looms over their head. On the other hand, when it dawns on salespeople that attempting to close has a second important purpose—getting information—every closing attempt truly will be a success. Psychologically, this makes it much easier to repeatedly attempt to close. This is a distinct sales advantage. And sales executives are very much aware that every advantage is another one to grab onto, another one not to let slip away. There is *so* much for salespeople to learn. When sales executives think about it, they may wonder who is teaching their salespeople all these skills, new ones and refined ones, and what are sales managers doing anyway and what more could they do with stronger leadership and direction? What could they do?

So, when should salespeople go for the close? There are three different times: (1) when the B-1, B-2, and B-3 diagnosis says the prospect is motivated to buy, (2) when the prospect gives a closing signal, and (3) when the salesperson needs to know why the prospect isn't ready to buy. Learn more, sell more. Train more.

HOW TO CLOSE

Sales executives do indeed have the nagging feeling that many of their salespeople are not as skilled as they need to be when it comes to closing the sale. This suspicion becomes a stark reality when sales executives take the time to meet with a few salespeople and discuss how they go about closing a sale. Better yet is when they go on sales calls with some of their salespeople. Sales executives get a bird's-eye view and clearly see the need to strengthen closing skills.

How can sales executives get a handle on this kind of equipping? The answer is to provide training that focuses on the three steps in the closing process: (1) choosing and using a closing method, or a combination of them; (2) asking the prospect to buy; and (3) reaching a closing agreement.

There are numerous closing methods. All of them can work. Usually they don't. The key is not in using a closing method in the right way. The secret is in using the right method. All of the methods are easy to understand and easy to use. Success depends on selecting the right one. This means choosing a method of closing that matches the prospect.[3] And it's easy to do. Simply select a method that fits the prospect's behavior style. Let's see how to do this.

Several observations first. First, the closing methods that look and feel right for each of the four behavior styles have a proven track record of success. They match the prospect's primary behavior style and this greatly improves the chances of closing the sale. Second, the closing methods intended for one behavior style may work with another style, particularly if the method matches the prospect's secondary behavior style. Third, when a prospect's primary and secondary behavior styles are equally strong, or nearly so, combining two closing methods will give an even better match. Fourth, remember—it doesn't matter which closing method is used, or how it is used, if the prospect isn't motivated to buy. The closing method is not a substitute for all that must be done to create the prospect's motivation to buy. Fifth, it almost goes without saying, because every sales executive knows, if you want to improve sales results, you want to *really* teach the sales force how to close the sale, not just talk about it.

Closing High D Prospects

Sales executives are firm in recommending the following three closing methods for high D prospects: (1) approach close; (2) direct close; and (3) multiple options close. Each one matches the prospect's behavior style.

Approach Close

The approach close is used early in the sales interview when the prospect is first approached. The idea is to get the prospect to make a commitment to buy on the front end, subject to the salesperson being able to prove certain things to the prospect. Basically, the salesperson is saying up front, "If I can show you such and such, will you buy?" Here are two examples.

- "If I can show you a machine that will increase production by 15 percent, will you make a decision today?"
- "If I can show you a way to save 10 percent on raw materials cost, with no change in quality, are you in a position to decide right now?"

The approach close is a good match with high D prospects because it:

- focuses on their interest in the bottom line;
- gives them an up-front reason to talk with the salesperson; and
- appeals to their preference for directness, brevity, and quick decision making.

Direct Close

The direct close is exactly what the name implies—closing in a very direct way. No beating around the bush. Here are a few ways to say it.

- "Why don't we close this deal right now?"
- "Are you ready to go ahead with this?"
- "If you'll just sign here, we'll wrap this up."

The direct close matches high D prospects because:

- they prefer directness;
- they admire and respect people who get directly to the point (they don't like to buy from wimps);
- they like brevity and not wasting their time; and
- they pride themselves in making fast decisions.

Multiple Options Close

The idea behind the multiple options close is to give prospects some options from which to choose, where all choices are acceptable to the salesperson. Here are some examples.

- "Do you prefer this program or the first one you looked at?"
- "Would you prefer the basic unit, the heavy duty unit, or the deluxe with the extra features?"
- "Do you want this in red, white, or blue?"

This method of closing matches high D prospects because it appeals to their preference for:

- not getting bogged down in details;
- getting to the heart of the matter;
- having clear-cut choices; and
- making fast decisions.

Closing High I Prospects

Four methods of closing are particularly effective with the behavior style of high I prospects, in the view of sales executives: (1) bonus close; (2) "right" person close; (3) urgency close; and (4) "if you were me" close.

Bonus Close

The bonus close offers something extra to entice prospects to close the sale. For this to work, the bonus obviously must be attractive to the prospect. The bonus can come in the form of price discounts, gifts, additional services, and so forth. The bonus close can be stated in various ways.

- "If you buy this now, the delivery charge will be waived."
- "If you order by the end of the day, you'll get a bonus unit free."
- "Buying this today will qualify you for complimentary tickets to the game Saturday."

The bonus close is a good fit for high I prospects because they like:

- rewards;
- recognition;
- being accepted; and
- feeling special.

"Right Person" Close

This method is based on the fact that some prospects will buy largely because others they admire are buyers. Following are some examples of closing statements using this method.

- "This has been very popular with many well known people, such as . . ."
- "Many of your counterparts, like John Smith at Allied International, are switching over to this."
- "Perhaps you know, or are familiar with _____ (a person of high professional or social status) who has one and is very pleased."

The "right person" close matches high I prospects because it appeals to their preference for:

- fitting in and not feeling left out;
- being accepted;
- being part of an "elite" group;
- keeping up with the Joneses; and
- being thought well of.

Urgency Close

The idea behind this closing method is to create a sense of urgency so the prospect will buy now. This can be done in several ways, including the following.

- "I recommend that you decide as soon as possible, since this specially reduced price ends tomorrow (this week or month)."
- "Our price increases go into affect next week (next month)."
- "Our supply is almost gone."

This method is a good match for high I prospects because they:

- don't like to get caught procrastinating;
- don't like to miss out on something good; and
- don't like to lose out on something others have gotten.

"If You Were Me" Close

The idea behind this method of closing is to get prospects involved in the sale from the salesperson's point of view. Following are some ways to do this.

- "If you were me, knowing what a good deal this is, would you take 'no' for an answer?"
- "If you were me, realizing how much this will benefit you, would you walk out of here without an order?"
- "If you were me, being fully aware that this product will meet your objectives better than anything else you can buy, what would you do to close the sale?"

Using the "if you were me" close fits with high I prospects because:

- they like to talk;
- helping others is rewarding to them;
- being asked for advice satisfies their ego need; and
- it appeals to their need to feel important.

Closing High S Prospects

Closings that sales executives feel are a good match for high S prospects include the following four methods: (1) simplifying matters close; (2) minimizing the cost close; (3) relationship close; and (4) summary of benefits close.

Simplifying Matters Close

This method of closing focuses on simplifying everything for the prospect, including matters related to buying the product or service, getting it delivered, having it installed, using it, maintaining it, and so on. The goal of simplifying is to make things easy, rather than hard, to minimize upheavals, problems, changes. Here are some examples of closing statements.

- "The only thing you have to do for us to move forward on this is . . . It's that simple."
- "As we've discussed, once you place the order, we take care of everything to be sure there is a smooth transition. None of the other vendors do this. I need to know how this is to be billed."
- "The best thing about doing business with us is that you don't have to change the way you're doing anything. We take care of everything. It's that simple, okay?"
- "We give more support than anybody else so things don't get complicated for you."

The simplifying matters close matches high S prospects because it appeals to their:

- need for stability and security;
- fear of uncertainty and change;
- preference for the status quo; and
- desire not to increase their time demands.

Minimizing the Cost

The focus with this method of closing is on cost in relation to benefits. Here are some typical closing statements which do this.

- "Considering the price and all of the benefits, this gives you the most value for the dollar."
- "As you can see, this product (service) has many concrete benefits that give lasting results, yet the weekly (monthly, annual) cost of ensuring these benefits is minimal."
- "This really is a good deal. It minimizes your cost and you're not sacrificing quality or service."

The minimizing cost close matches high S prospects because it appeals to their:

- preference for concrete benefits (dollars are concrete);
- tendency to be tight with money; and
- need for security (saving money gives security).

Relationship Close

The central issue with this closing method is the long-term relationship high S prospects want with the salesperson and the selling organization. Here are some closing statements which emphasize this.

- "Relationships are important in our business and we really depend on each other for long-term relationships and stability."
- "You can see, from the way we are involved with design, installation, problem solving, and servicing, that building lasting relationships is the cornerstone of our business."

- "I'm not just a salesperson on this. The favorite part of my job is establishing a close relationship with all of my clients so I can meet their ongoing needs. I plan to be here when others aren't."

Using the relationship method of closing matches high S prospects because it addresses their:

- need for security;
- preference for certainty;
- need for stability; and
- desire for lasting relationships based on trust.

Summary of Benefits Close

As the name suggests, this close summarizes the benefits prospects will receive if they buy. The idea is to put the sales transaction in a positive light and keep any negatives in the background. Here are some straightforward ways of doing this.

- "You will get a long list of benefits. Let me review them quickly. First there is . . . Then . . ."
- "In our first meeting, you told me you were looking for a product that would do four things for you. They were . . . This product will do all of that and more."
- "The main benefit is that you will reach all of your objectives with this. Specifically, you will . . ."

This closing technique matches high S prospects because they like:

- safe, risk-free decisions with lots of positives and no negatives;
- nonthreatening decisions, especially in terms of security, stability, problems, and change; and
- reassurance before making final decisions.

Closing High C Prospects

Three closing methods that sales executives see as putting salespeople in tune with high C prospects are: (1) data balance sheet close; (2) contingency assurance close; and (3) confirmation close. Each one is a strong match for the high C's behavior style.

Data Balance Sheet Close

With this method of closing, all of the data pertinent to the buying decision are arranged into a balance sheet of positive and negative factors. The salesperson should let prospects come up with the two lists, leading them through the process by asking questions and mentioning anything they overlook. The salesperson will want to provide guidance as necessary in coming up with positives, then listen attentively when they come up with negatives. Putting this on paper is a good idea. Following is an example of using this closing method.

> "I know you want to look at all of the relevant factors before making your decision. Let's put everything together to see where we stand. What do we have on the positive side? . . . What else? . . . Anything else? . . . What about . . . ? Okay, that about covers it. Now, can you think of any negatives? . . . Is that it? . . . Let's compare. Seems like there are more positive than negatives . . . Are you ready to move on this?"

This closing method matches high C prospects because it meets their need for:

- analysis;
- completeness;
- looking at all the angles;
- putting things in writing; and
- making the "perfect" decision.

Contingency Assurance Close

The idea of this method of closing is to get the prospect to make a commitment to buy contingent on certain assurances. That is, the salesperson wants to get the prospect to say, "Yes, I'll buy if you will assure me that . . ." Here are some closing statements using this method.

- "So your decision to buy is contingent on my assurance that we can deliver within ten days? Is that right?"
- "Will you buy if I can assure you we will complete the project on schedule?"
- "Your decision is contingent on my assurance that we can have service technicians on site within twenty-four hours. Is that all?"

This method of closing matches high C prospects because it addresses:

- their need for precision, especially the need for salespeople to understand them in a clear, precise way;
- their fear of being pinned down to a decision without having complete and accurate information; and
- their skeptical nature and the accompanying need to be assured of getting everything they want and everything that is promised.

Confirmation Close

With this close, the salesperson wants to get prospects to confirm their agreement on each and every point critical to the buying decision. Following is an example of one way to do it.

"This price is better than you get anywhere else. Do you agree? Would you agree that this product meets all of your technical specifications? The service agreement includes everything you requested, wouldn't you agree? Don't you agree that others in the company, including the operations manager and the CFO, support the decision to buy from us?"

This method of closing matches high C prospects because it addresses their need:

- for detail and thoroughness;
- to weigh all of the factors involved in the decision;
- to confirm the completeness and accuracy of all data; and
- to get confirmation from others before making the final decision.

Combining Closing Methods

In some cases a greater fit is found by combining closing methods. This is true for prospects who have a primary and secondary behavior style where both are of near equal strength. Combining closes that appeal to both styles offers a greater push for wrapping up the deal. This gives salespeople an added advantage, a real opportunity to be successful. Sales executives may want to assess the value to their organization if they were to just go ahead and give their salespeople an edge, an advantage over the buyer, an advantage over the salespeople in competing organizations they go into combat with every day.

Closings That Motivate

Closing the High D, High I Style

Here is an example of a multiple options close (high D) combined with the right person close and the bonus close (high I) to nail the deal down.

"Do you prefer this program or the first one you looked at? Good, John Smith at Allied International made that same decision. If we close this today, I can give you a bonus of _____ like he got."

Closing the High I, High S Style

The following illustrates a combination of the "If you were me" (high I) and relationship close (high S) to close this business.

"If you were me, what would you suggest I do to strengthen our relationship and get our companies working together?"

Closing the High S, High C Style

The minimizing the cost close (high S) is combined with the contingency assurance close (high C) in the example below.

"Considering all of those benefits, this gives you the most value for the dollar, don't you agree? So we can close this contingent on our assurance of the service contract, is that right?"

ASKING PROSPECTS TO BUY

Most sales executives have at one time or another climbed onto the bandwagon and shouted out the importance of asking the prospect to buy. Salespeople don't always hear, or adhere, and when all is said and done it is costly when they don't listen. It is critical, this asking the prospect to buy, and is the second step in how to close. There are many ways to do this. Some are indirect. Here are a few examples.

- "How soon would you require delivery?"
- "Which system (model, style) would you prefer?"
- "When can I expect your affirmative reply?"
- "What terms do you want?"
- "Which of the three plans meets your needs best?"
- "How soon do you want to start these savings?"

- "When would you prefer shipment?"

Asking prospects to buy can be done directly, too. There are a variety of ways. Here are some common ones.

- "Why don't we close this deal right now?"
- "Are you going to buy this or not?"
- "If you'll just sign here, we'll wrap this up."
- "Do I have your go ahead on this?"
- "Can I have your business?"
- "Are you ready to close now?"
- "Can I consider this a firm deal?"
- "Will you place your order now?"
- "Will you authorize this delivery date?"
- "Let's close it now."
- "Let's get it written up now."
- "I have your specs written up. Will you approve them?"
- "Are you ready to sign the sales agreement?"
- "Can I place your order with the production department today?"
- "Shall I schedule it for production next week?"
- "Will you approve this purchase now?"
- "Will you have someone prepare a purchase order now?"
- "I'd like to finalize this now. Do you agree?"

CLOSING AGREEMENTS

Most sales executives, and some salespeople, have become aware the hard way that with every close—whether closing the sale or closing for something else—it is essential for the buyer and seller to reach an agreement on exactly what will happen. Things often fall through, or materialize differently than expected, when such an agreement is not clearly reached. This is a time to solidly nail down the prospect's commitment to buy, or commitment to take steps that eventually will lead to closing the sale. This is not a time for misunderstandings that can be costly and frustrating to both sides. The closing agreement is the third step in how to close.

Agreements when Closing the Sale

The salesperson hears the prospect say, "I'm sold." Now what? What does the salesperson say, "Great," then shake hands and leave feeling good? Nope! That's not the way to hold on to the sale. Instead, this is the time to get out the hammer and nail down the sale so nothing can happen to it. When prospects make a commitment to buy, there always are some issues up in the air. They have to be nailed down, clarified, and agreed upon; otherwise a lot of risk is left laying on the table.

What does a good agreement look, sound, and feel like? What kind of things should be agreed upon? There are quite a few. A checklist is helpful. Here are some of the items related to the product or service to agree upon.

1. *Exactly what will the buyer receive?*
   - product description (make, size, and so on) and number of units
   - type and amount of service

2. *When will it be delivered?*
   - when shipped, when received

3. *What is the exact price?*
   - per unit, total, discounts, and so on

4. *How is the buyer to pay?*
   - when, how much, method of payment, and so on

Failure to have a firm agreement on any one of these issues can cause problems, like delays, wasted time, frustration, hard feelings, and maybe even losing the sale. These problems can be avoided by nailing things down. It pays to concentrate on the closing agreement.

How can agreement be firmed up on these issues? The salesperson needs to go down the checklist, item by item and (1) get confirmation on things already agreed upon with the buyer and (2) clarify agreement on those things where some uncertainty exists.

Salespeople need to take care not to overpromise. It is easy in the excitement of the sale to paint a picture that doesn't represent reality, to throw something in or commit to something that cannot or should not be done. Salespeople must be encouraged to reach an agreement that will satisfy the buyer and at the same time be one that the seller can meet. Effective salespeople often follow this principle: *Underpromise and overdeliver.*

Agreements when Closing for Something

Salespeople sometimes speak up and ask, "If I can't close the sale, what are some other things to close for?" Sales executives are quick to give their view on this and suggest, as mentioned earlier, getting prospects to agree to meet again, review product literature, accept a bid or proposal, attend a product demonstration, use the product or service on a trial basis, talk with other users of the product or service, and arrange a meeting with the decision maker. Salespeople need to be equipped and motivated to close for something, anything, to keep the sales opportunity alive. This means, sales executives, you need to do something, if you want to get better results.

How can salespeople close for these *other* things? Many of the closing methods discussed earlier can be used. Here are the ones recommended with examples of how to use each one.

For High D Prospects

1. Direct Close
   - "Do you want me to give you a one-page proposal?"
   - "Would you like to talk to some of my customers?" (Note: Salespeople should always be cautioned to get customer permission before using them as a reference and never abuse a customer's willingness to help. Then get a commitment to buy if the prospect gets a positive response.)

2. Multiple Options Close
   - "Do you prefer a product demonstration or to use it on trial basis?"
   - "Would you rather meet again or have a short proposal?"

For High I Prospects

1. "Right Person" Close
   - "The sharpest customers I have make their decision to buy after using the product on a trial basis for a couple of weeks. Will you use the product for a while and let me call you in two weeks for a follow-up meeting to see what you think?"

2. Urgency Close
   - "I know you want to talk to some of our clients. Let's set a time you and I can call them. If we do this right away, you can take advantage of the price discount we have through the end of the month."

For High S Prospects

1. Simplifying Close
   - "A product demonstration is simple. I can do it right here. It only takes ten minutes and will not interfere with anything."

2. Minimizing Cost Close
   - "Letting a couple of your people use it on a trial basis gives you the benefit of seeing firsthand how well it fits in with the way you do things now. You'll actually save money doing this because our price for trial materials is less than what you're paying for the supplies you're using now. Will you try it for a week?"

3. Summary of Benefits Close
   - "Visiting our lab before you make a decision has several benefits, including . . . Can we arrange a visit next Thursday?"

For High C Prospects

1. Data Balance Sheet Close
   - "What are the advantages of having your technical people look at this before making your decision? . . . What else? . . . Don't forget . . . Are there any disadvantages? . . . Overall, then, what do you think? Can we set a time for them to examine this?"

2. Contingency Assurance Close
   - "Would you be willing to use this on a trial basis if I assure you it will be available for up to four weeks and not cost you one penny?"

SUMMARIZING FOLLOW-UP ACTIONS

Sales executives are well aware that whether the salesperson has closed the sale, or has closed for something else, there are always next steps to take. Some will be spelled out loud and clear in the closing agreement; other will not. Typical next steps for prospects to take include talking with other customers using the product or service, evaluating a proposal, verifying availability of funds, getting authorization to buy, preparing purchase orders, and so on. Next steps for the salesperson include things like mailing product information to prospects, submitting proposals, answering specific questions, setting the next meeting, getting approval from the sales manager, and so on.

Many prospects and salespeople have a tendency not to follow-up on things that need to be done after the sales interview. This is for good reason. It takes time. Everybody is busy. Many of the next steps are a nuisance. Others demand priority. The result is that good intentions get pushed aside. This easily happens to prospects and salespeople alike.

Sales executives feel that follow-up is essential to the salesperson's success. In business-to-business sales, for example, it typically takes three to six sales calls to close a sale.[4] Selling takes determination and discipline. Persistence is the key. Yet, most salespeople don't have it, typically giving up after one or two sales calls. However, the small percentage of salespeople who continue calling on prospects until they succeed are the highest paid salespeople and are among the highest income earners in the country. Persistence pays off.

Good follow-up is based on more than persistence, however. The starting point is found at the end of the sales interview. Every sales interview should conclude with the salesperson closing for the next step and summarizing who is responsible for doing what and when. A good summary becomes a plan of action that can dramatically increase sales effectiveness. Summarizing follow-up action is the final step in the sales interview.

SUMMARY

- Sales executives find it necessary to stress that the goal is to close. Sometimes the close comes early, so salespeople should always be trying to close. When closing the sale isn't possible, it is important to close for something, anything, to keep the sales process alive.

- Sales executives must teach the sales force when to close. Closing should come when the prospect is motivated to buy, as determined by either: (1) a diagnosis of the prospect's B-1, B-2, and B-3; or (2) closing signals given by the prospect.

- Sales executives also need to make salespeople aware that it is appropriate to attempt to close even when prospects are not ready, if the goal is to find out what is holding back their motivation to buy.

- Sales executives would do well to provide intensive training on how to close. The training should focus on three steps. Choose and use an appropriate closing method. Ask the prospect to buy. Reach a closing agreement.

- Sales executives should teach the sales force the importance of choosing a method of closing that matches the prospect's behavior style and how to make the choice.

- Sales executives need to persuade their salespeople that prospects seldom buy if they are not asked.

- Sales executives want to stress the importance of reaching a closing agreement that nails down everything so the sale will not fall through.

- Sales executives may be wondering about and becoming more aware of the importance of motivating and preparing the sales force and getting closer to deciding to just go ahead and provide training and equip people to get better sales results.

NOTES

1. Joseph P. Vaccaro, "Best Salespeople Know Their ABC's (Always Be Closing)," *Marketing News* (March 28,1988), p. 10.

2. Mack Hannan, "Let the Customer Close for You," *Sales & Marketing Management* (August 1986), pp. 68–70.

3. Alan J. Dubinsky and Thomas N. Ingram, "A Classification of Industrial Buyers: Implications for Sales Training," *Journal of Personal Selling and Sales Management* (Fall–Winter 1981–1982), pp. 46-51.

4. "Sales Tactics Take on a New Look as Corporations Rethink Strategy," *Wall Street Journal* (April 28, 1988), p. 1.

CHAPTER 8

Motivating to Buy Again

Sales executives have a good sense of the importance of follow-up *after* closing the sale. They clearly see the benefits of good follow-up and feel the pain when customers scream in its absence. There is an abundance of research that speaks out and underscores the importance of follow-up. One study shows that dependable, accurate, and consistent follow-up is the single most important factor with about half of all buyers surveyed.[1] Other research provides hard evidence that follow-up allows companies to charge more, grow faster, and gain a competitive edge.[2] Another study makes us aware that about one of every four buyers are dissatisfied enough to switch suppliers and that over 90 percent of these unhappy customers will never buy again from that company and feel strongly enough to tell at least nine other people about their negative experience.[3] Research also presents clear evidence that it cost more than twice as much to sell a new prospect than it does to sell more to an existing customer.[4] As sales executives become aware of and grasp the full meaning of this mounting research evidence, they may want to go ahead and equip and motivate the sales force to provide better follow-up.

A DIFFERENT WAY OF DEFINING FOLLOW-UP

Follow-up is taking steps to be sure buyers *actually* get (B-2) the satisfaction (B-3) they were *expecting* at the time they decided to buy. Remember, buyers want to feel good and they make buying decisions based on this, based on their belief about whether or not they will get (B-2) certain outcomes (B-3). This means that follow-up should focus on being sure—to the greatest extent possible—that buyers are getting their hands on (B-2) the outcomes they want (B-3) and not getting (B-2) outcomes they don't want (B-3). If buyers are looking for exact delivery dates, salespeople must follow up to be sure they get them. If buyers are outspoken about not wanting more than one day of downtime when installing new equipment, salespeople must follow up to be sure their is a smooth transition in getting the equipment up and running quickly. When follow-up efforts focus on being sure buyers are getting, and see they are getting (B-2), what they want (B-3) and avoiding (B-2) what they don't want (B-3), customer satisfaction will be high (B-3). When this happens, sales executives can well imagine that buyers will not only buy again, they will talk about and pass the word and recommend that others buy, too.

Sales executives may want to pass the word as well and impress upon the entire sales force the importance of follow-up and the hard connection between follow-up and resale. Salespeople may be aware of this connection, or so they say, but their behavior often does not appear to logically flow from such an awareness. In light of this, sales executives may want to climb up on the soapbox and sound off, loud and clear, and push salespeople to follow up after the sale.

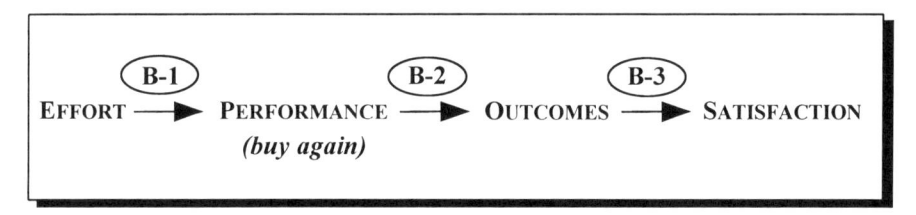

$$\text{Effort} \xrightarrow{\text{B-1}} \text{Performance} \xrightarrow{\text{B-2}} \text{Outcomes} \xrightarrow{\text{B-3}} \text{Satisfaction}$$
(buy again)

PURPOSE AND NECESSITY OF FOLLOW-UP

While there are many reasons to follow up after a sale, sales executives are well aware that the ultimate purpose of follow-up centers on the *motivation to buy again*. Along with this flows a reputation that helps sell to other customers as well. This ultimate purpose is achieved through the accumulated benefits of follow-up. When follow-up is effective, salespeople will:

- build firm, trusting relationships with customers;
- strengthen retention and make it hard for the competition to win over their customers;
- have easy access to their customers;
- have an open door opportunity to show new products or upgrades, which are a primary basis for resale and add-ons;
- be able to get referrals;
- have customers who will talk up the products or services with other prospects; and
- create a feeling of good will, authority, expertise, and service with their customers.

The necessity to follow up flows out of the importance of repeat business and the need to establish and maintain a reputation that will strengthen sales efforts with other customers and prospects. Many things can happen after the sale is made that presses on sales executives to stress the ongoing need for salespeople to follow up. Some of them include:

- shipments are late, incorrect, or damaged;
- products are defective;
- customers have problems installing or using the product;
- services are not provided on time or in the agreed upon way;
- results are different than the customer expected;
- invoices are incomplete, incorrect, or in some way problematic; and
- the follow-up or relationship expectations are not met by the salesperson.

It is easy to see that all customers can experience these problems. And research substantiates the importance of salespeople getting a firm hold on the situation and dealing with problems quickly and effectively. One study shows that up to 70 percent of buyers who complain will buy again if their complaint is resolved to their satisfaction and over 95 percent will buy again if their complaints are resolved promptly.[5] Another study estimates that for every dissatisfied customer that complains, fifty dissatisfied customers will stop buying the product.[6] Sales executives are well aware of the necessity to prepare and motivate the sales force to engage in follow-up and thereby prevent or resolve customer problems; otherwise good customers will be lost and a reputation will be developed that is damaging with other customers and prospects. Just go ahead and do it. Equip and motivate the sales force.

RELUCTANCE TO FOLLOW UP

Although anyone can plainly see the necessity of follow-up, most salespeople find themselves wrapped up in a reluctance that has a strong and tight grip. There are a lot of reasons for this. The following list gives a bird's-eye view of some of the more common ones: (1) "I'm not good at follow-up;" (2) "It's embarrassing when I can't work things out;" (3) "My company doesn't support me if there are problems;" (4) "You don't get much recognition for follow-up;" (5) "Follow-up doesn't guarantee a resale;" (6) "Good follow-up doesn't help with other prospects;" (7) "I'd rather be selling;" (8) "Customers are rude and critical;" (9) "I'm blamed for everything;" (10) "I know I've overpromised;" and (11) "I'm not sure my product (service) is of the quality expected." When any of these reasons exist, there is reluctance to follow up. When several of them take hold, the reluctance factor can be very difficult to overcome.

Overcoming Reluctance to Follow Up

The best way for sales executives to get a handle on this reluctance is to view it in the context of motivation. When all is said and done, reluctance to do anything boils down to a lack of motivation. Viewing reluctance within this framework makes it easy to notice that its causes clearly fall into and touch on one of three categories.

The first category has a hard connection to the belief about effort leading to performance (B-1), where performance is defined as "effective follow-up" and the salesperson may conclude, "I can't do it." This sounds like a B-1 problem. That is, the "I can't do it" belief strips the salesperson's motivation to put out the necessary effort to perform well on follow-up activities. This is summarized on the following page.

The second category of reasons for reluctance to follow up speaks to the belief about performance leading to outcomes (B-2). Here, the salesperson may conclude, "I won't get (B-2) what I want (B-3) even if I do follow-up." This causes a pronounced drag on salespeople, it holds back their motivation, and makes it rough for them to follow up. This is summarized on the following page.

The third category touches on the belief about outcomes leading to satisfaction (B-3), where the salesperson may conclude, "I will get (B-2) outcomes I don't want (B-3)." This has the clear ring of a B-3 problem. It is a third and powerful reason that gets a grip on salespeople and keeps them from being motivated to follow up. This is summarized shortly.

B-1 Rating Is Low
"I can't follow up effectively."

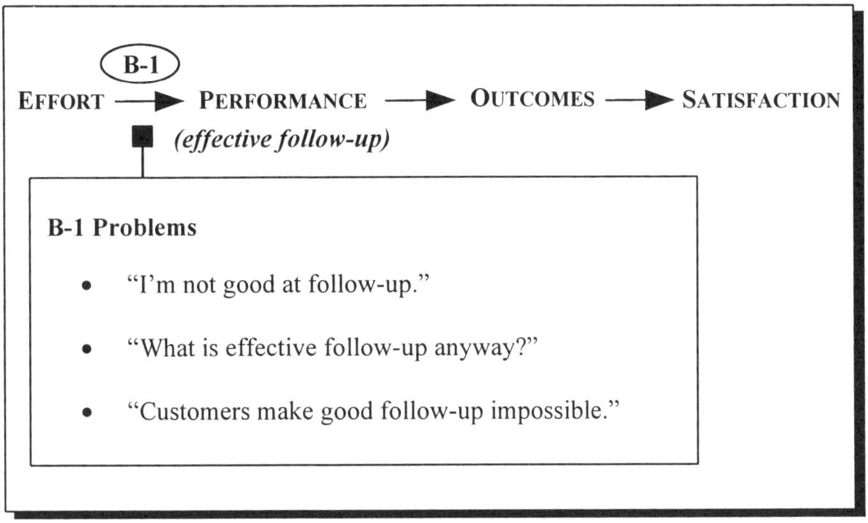

EFFORT ⟶ PERFORMANCE (B-1) ⟶ OUTCOMES ⟶ SATISFACTION
(effective follow-up)

B-1 Problems

- "I'm not good at follow-up."
- "What is effective follow-up anyway?"
- "Customers make good follow-up impossible."

B-2 Rating Is Low
"I will not get the outcomes."

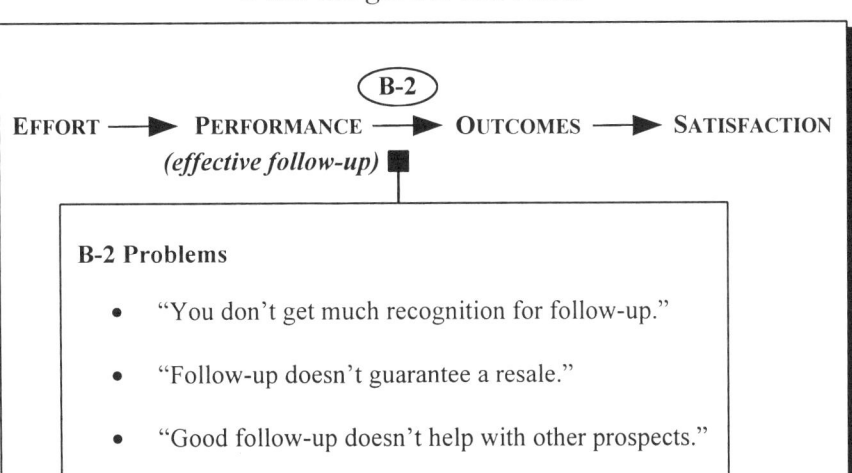

EFFORT ⟶ PERFORMANCE ⟶ (B-2) OUTCOMES ⟶ SATISFACTION
(effective follow-up)

B-2 Problems

- "You don't get much recognition for follow-up."
- "Follow-up doesn't guarantee a resale."
- "Good follow-up doesn't help with other prospects."

Overall B-3 Rating Is Negative

"I don't want these outcomes."

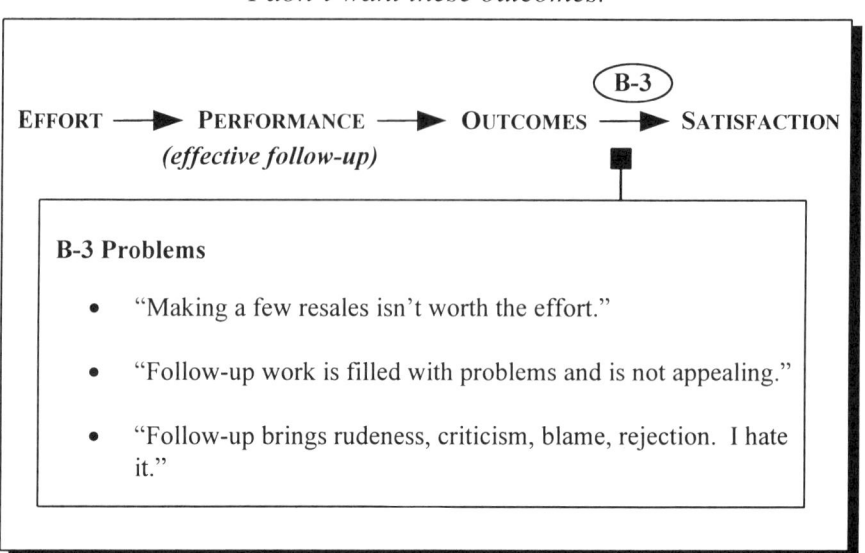

EFFORT ⟶ PERFORMANCE ⟶ OUTCOMES ⟶ SATISFACTION
(effective follow-up)   (B-3)

B-3 Problems

- "Making a few resales isn't worth the effort."
- "Follow-up work is filled with problems and is not appealing."
- "Follow-up brings rudeness, criticism, blame, rejection. I hate it."

What solutions are available to sales executives who want to tackle these B-1, B-2, and B-3 problems? That is, when salespeople are reluctant (not motivated) to follow up after the sale, what can be done? Here are some solutions that sales executives have observed will work when salespeople are not motivated because they don't believe they can provide effective follow-up. This is a B-1 problem, "I can't do it."

B-1 SOLUTIONS

1. Be sure salespeople get in tune with what customers want and expect in terms of follow-up.

2. Provide training to give the sales force a solid handle on the skills they need for effective follow-up, skills like handling conflict and dealing with irate customers.

3. Stress the importance of sales managers setting realistic follow-up goals with salespeople, goals that define percentage of follow-up problems handled effectively and percentage of customers that buy again.

Motivating to Buy Again 165

B-1 Solutions
(Continued)

> 4. Press sales managers to work with salespeople to develop follow-up plans and stick to them.
>
> 5. Call on sales managers to create opportunities for salespeople to have small successes. In other words, have sales managers work with their salespeople and guide them to provide follow-up to customers that are most likely to respond positively. This allows salespeople to see that they *can* do it.
>
> 6. Be sure salespeople hear words of support and encouragement that will build self-confidence in their ability to provide effective follow-up.

Here are some solutions that appear effective for sales executives to use when salespeople are not motivated to follow up after the sale because they don't believe outcomes are tied to performance, where performance is defined as providing effective follow-up. That is, they do not believe they will get (B-2) outcomes they want (B-3) even if they do effective follow-up.

B-2 Solutions

> 1. Get salespeople to apply logic and realize that good follow-up is hard to come by and that when they give it, they will stand out and customers will stay with them and they will sell more.
>
> 2. Encourage salespeople to talk with a couple of top producing salespersons and find out the extent to which follow-up contributes to their success.
>
> 3. Help salespeople get a true feel for the value of their own follow-up experiences. Get them to determine their success rate in getting repeat business with satisfied customers compared with those who were not satisfied.
>
> 4. Document success throughout the sales organization that flows from effective follow-up. Then share the results with the entire sales force.

Salespeople often are not motivated to do follow-up because they believe they will get (B-2) outcomes they do not want (B-3) and they believe the unwanted outcomes will outweigh the desired outcomes they expect to get. Here are some solutions that sales executives can make work and will give them a good handle on the situation.

B-3 Solutions

1. Help salespeople become fully aware of the value of the outcomes they can expect to receive if they provide effective follow-up:

    a. referrals, introduction to new prospects, and maybe even tips on how to sell a tough prospect;

    b. loyal customers that can be used as references with prospects;

    c. discovering new ways to apply products and services to satisfy new demands resulting from business trends, problems, and needs;

    d. industry knowledge that can be used to help sell more effectively; and

    e. information about competitors that can provide a selling edge.

2. Get salespeople to view follow-up as a challenge rather than something simply to be dreaded.

3. Encourage salespeople to get a feel for the methods of follow-up and choose those that are the easiest, most effective, and most rewarding to them personally.

4. Call on salespeople to look at follow-up as the beginning of the next sale rather than a requirement of the last one. Then have them make a comparison of (a) the time and effort it takes to follow up with a customer and get a resale versus (b) the time and effort required to find several new prospects, prepare to meet with them, conduct sales interviews with them, make repeat visits, and close the sale with one of them. This helps salespeople to get a feel for how good of an investment follow-up can be.

Motivating to Buy Again

B-3 SOLUTIONS
(CONTINUED)

5. Get salespeople to notice how much easier their job would be if most of their sales calls were with satisfied customers.

6. Get salespeople to calculate and get in tune with how much their sales would increase if they never lost a customer (100 percent customer retention).

Sales executives will observe that while all of these solutions may not apply to every salesperson, some of them will touch and aptly fit everybody. Collectively these solutions come through loud and clear as being more than adequate to quickly turn around the reluctance to follow up that most salespeople experience. This is a powerful, smooth way for sales executives to get a handle on providing the kind of follow-up that customers want and need. Maybe now is the time for sales executives to step up to the problem, do something about it, deal with reluctance to follow up, and get the results customers want. Maybe now is the time to do it.

WAYS TO FOLLOW UP

Sales executives will remember that follow-up should focus on being sure, to the extent possible, that buyers are getting (B-2) outcomes they want (B-3) and not getting (B-2) those they don't want (B-3). This means salespeople need to get and stay in tune with their customers. There are three ways to do this, namely: (1) servicing the sale; (2) combating buyer remorse; and (3) developing a relationship with the buyer.

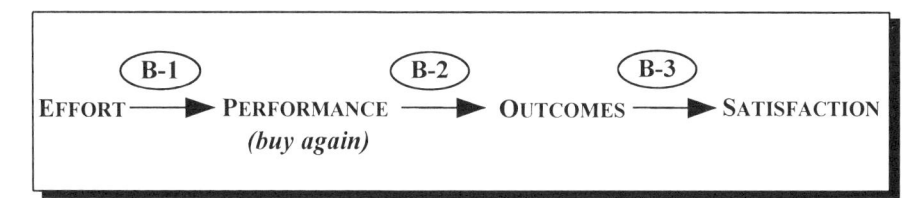

```
         (B-1)              (B-2)            (B-3)
EFFORT ──▶ PERFORMANCE ──▶ OUTCOMES ──▶ SATISFACTION
              (buy again)
```

Servicing the Sale

Sales executives know that buyers expect to see and hear from salespeople after the sale. They expect salespeople to rush forward and do certain things once the sale is made. Here are some ways salespeople can follow up and service the sale.

- Make the buyer aware of what is being done to get shipments delivered on time.
- Check immediately with the buyer to see if the shipment arrived on time and if it was correct with no damage. Take swift action to handle any problems.
- Call on or visit the buyer to hear if everything is going well with the installation and/or utilization of the product. Provide help as needed.
- Talk with buyers to get a feel for whether or not services are being provided in a timely, satisfactory way. Step in and correct things if necessary.
- Discuss results or benefits with the buyer to see if things are working as expected. If they aren't, get them fixed quickly.
- Call or visit the buyer and simply ask, "Is everything going okay?" or "How do you like the product?" or "Is there anything I can do to help?" When problems appear, deal with them promptly.
- Talk with the buyer and give helpful reminders about easy-to-overlook benefits that can flow out of discounts from early payments, rebates when deadlines are met, warranty agreements sent in on time, increases in insurance coverage, developing a schedule of preventive maintenance, and so on.

Servicing the sale often appears to be, and frequently is, onerous and it takes time. That's the problem. Servicing the sale just doesn't feel good to many salespeople. But it's part of the bargain, too. When salespeople make the sale, they are agreeing to service the sale. Many salespeople quickly forget this. Buyers don't. Sales executives may need to remind salespeople that their responsibility doesn't end when they close the sale. Professional salespeople take servicing the sale seriously and they reap the benefits through buyer loyalty. Buyers are motivated to buy again and again when their service expectations are met. Sales executives will do well to drill this into the sales force, over and over, that follow-up pays off.

Combating Buyer Remorse

Sales executives have heard it time and again, felt the sting of it, have seen buyers start questioning the wisdom of their buying decision soon after the purchase is finalized. They get that gnawing feeling, those second thoughts, the questioning about what they have done. Here are some ways they talk to themselves.

- "I might have paid too much."
- "I should have bought the other model."
- "I got conned by a great salesperson."
- "Is this really what I needed to buy?"
- "Maybe I should have held off on this until next year."
- "Maybe this will not give the results I need."
- "What will everybody think when they see what I've done?"
- "This may upset things too much."
- "Did I check everything out like I should have?"

Consequences of Buyer Remorse

Some buyers worry themselves sick about buying decisions. Sales executives have time and again caught a glimpse that this can be a problem. A big problem. Here are some of the things that can happen. This is not a new list to sales executives, but it may make sense to use the list as a reminder for the sales force, too.

- Buyers often blame the salesperson for a buying decision that no longer feels right. This is a natural tendency for many buyers. As a result, their relationship with the salesperson may be strained. They may not want to see the salesperson again, at least not for a while, and may even decide never to buy again.

- Buyers may be unable to relax, may want to cancel the order before it is delivered or return it after it has arrived. Buyers do this all the time.

- People around buyers can sense buyer displeasure and regret about the purchase and may cause them, as users, not to give the product or service a chance. The prophecy of a "bad decision" is fulfilled.

- Buyers not only may be unwilling to give referrals, in addition they actually may talk negatively to others who may be considering buying the product or service.

Handling Buyer Remorse

Sales executives are quite sure that salespeople can avoid these consequences by staying in contact and in tune with the buyer. This makes it possible to become more aware of possible buyer remorse and enables salespeople to take steps to prevent it, or at least minimize the effect it can have. How can sales executives equip salespeople to deal with buyer remorse? There are three things that salespeople can be trained to do.

1. Tell the buyer the right decision was made. Soon after the purchase is made, the salesperson can talk to the buyer and say, "You made the right decision and here's why . . ." Here are two examples.

    - "Buying now definitely was the right decision. Price increases have just been announced."

    - "I've reviewed everything again that you wanted to accomplish, and I'm still convinced you made the right decision by going with this."

2. Give the buyer evidence the right decision was made. Follow up with the buyer after the product or service has been used for a short while, gather evidence that shows things are going well, then tell the buyer she made the right decision, and give supporting evidence.

3. Get others to tell the buyer the right decision was made. Encourage others to reinforce that the buying decision was a good one. Anyone whose opinion is valued by the buyer will be reassuring.

Developing the Relationship

Sales executives feel comfortable in their knowledge that relationships of any kind do not last unless both sides are making equal contributions to it. In the buyer-seller relationship, the buyer gives the seller the business. What do salespeople give in return? Servicing the sale is one thing. Giving reassurance that the right decision was made is another. But there has to be more—much more, for buyers to be motivated to buy again. What else can salespeople do to contribute to the relationship? There are many possibilities. Sales executives should encourage salespeople to choose several that will have value to each customer, remembering that different people prefer different things and that salespeople have to stay in tune with their buyers to know what their preferences are. Salespeople need to be reminded of the simple things, like those listed here, they can do that go a long way in developing relationships with customers.

1. Send thank-you cards. Customers feel good when thanked for effective meetings, recommendations and referrals, placing orders, and so on. Keeping the four Ps in mind can help:

    - promptness—get it out within a week;

Motivating to Buy Again

- personalized—use the customers name and say thanks in specific terms;
- perfection—make sure spelling (particularly the customer's name), grammar, and so on are perfect; and
- a P.S. adds punch—it's the most-often read part of the letter.

2. Send news articles relevant to the customer. Watch for articles written about the customer and the customer's family, organization, industry, and anything else relevant to the customer. Cut them out and send them along with a brief note. It shows an interest in the customer's business.

3. Send news articles about the seller. Let customers know the good things that are going on with the salesperson and the selling organization.

4. Send new product/service announcements. Create customer awareness that may open the door to sales calls and a sale. Announcements of upgrades and modifications are good, too.

5. Send new product literature. Always send new and revised brochures and other literature that may be relevant to the customer.

6. Send holiday and birthday cards. Holidays and birthdays provide the opportunity to thank customers for their business.

7. Send personal notes or cards. A good time to do this is during holidays, when on vacation, and when traveling to interesting places on business. Most people enjoy a break from routine business mail.

8. Offer congratulations. Make phone calls or send notes congratulating customers on promotions, awards, and special events and achievements. Everybody likes recognition. And it shows awareness and interest in customers.

9. Give small gifts. Send customers small gifts pertaining to their interests or hobbies.

10. Send newsletters. Write a newsletter and send it monthly or quarterly to let customers know what's going on in the business and how they can benefit from a continuing relationship.

11. Have social events. Organizing get-togethers with customers may be well received. This can be done around a customer appreciation picnic, an open house, or an anniversary party, for example.

Salespeople are not expected to use all of these suggestions, but every salesperson should use at least two or three to stay in contact with customers and develop an ongoing relationship with them. With the exception of planning a party or event, none of the suggestions are particularly costly or time intensive. The only thing that is needed is the desire of the salesperson to be a professional, showing courtesy and concern for the customer. Sales executives may want to consider and just go ahead and press salespeople to focus on relationships.

FOLLOW-UP THAT CUSTOMERS LIKE AND DISLIKE

Research published in *Harvard Business Review* shows that customers generally have certain likes and dislikes when it comes to follow-up by salespeople.[7] The postsale actions and behaviors that customers tend to view as positive include initiating positive phone calls, making recommendations, using candid language, using the telephone, showing appreciation, making service suggestions, using "we" problem-solving language, anticipating problems, using their jargon or concise language, airing personality problems, talking of "our future together," routinizing responses, accepting responsibility, and planning the future.[8] Corresponding postsale actions and behaviors that customers view as negative include making only callbacks, making justifications, using accommodative language, using correspondence, waiting for misunderstandings, waiting for service requests, using "owe us" legal language, responding only to problems, using long-winded communications, hiding personality problems, talking about making good on the past, shifting blame, and rehashing the past.[9] Sales executives may want to encourage their salespeople to develop lists similar to this that are tailored to each of their key customers.

FOLLOW-UP AND THE SALES MODEL

Sales executives may want to hear what follow-up has to do with the sales model. Up to the point of making the sale, the sales model is used to: (1) understand how prospects decide to buy and (2) show how to influence their buying decisions. The sales model points out that buyers will not buy unless they: (1) believe they can buy (B-1), (2) believe they will get certain outcomes if they do (B-2), and (3) believe the outcomes will be satisfying (B-3).

How does the sales model apply *after* the sale is made? At this point it is used to be sure customers *actually* get (B-2) the satisfaction (B-3) they were *expecting* at the time they decided to buy. Doing this simultaneously lays the foundation for the motivation to buy again and for building a reputation that will help sell other prospects.

All aspects of the follow-up described earlier focus on being sure the buyer actually gets (B-2) the outcomes (B-3) expected at the time the buying decision was made. First, follow-up that focuses on servicing the sale addresses B-2 and B-3. Steps are taken to be sure things turn out as promised and as perceived by the buyer.

Second, follow-up to handle buyer remorse also deals with B-2 and B-3. Remorse comes when buyers change their mind and conclude that they will *not,* after all, get (B-2) the outcomes they want (B-3), or that they do not want (B-3) the outcomes they expect to get (B-2). The salesperson's objective in dealing with buyer remorse should be to take buyers back to their original position so they once again believe "I will get (B-2) the outcomes I want (B-3) and avoid (B-2) those I don't want (B-3)." Follow-up like this clearly focuses on the sales model.

Third, follow-up that develops a relationship with the buyer stresses the sales model. This shows buyers they will get (B-2) certain outcomes they want (B-3), such as someone available to help when assistance is needed (high D), a friend to socialize with from time to time (high I), a trusted companion (high S), or a person who stands behind what they sell (high C).

FOLLOW-UP AND BUYER BEHAVIOR STYLE

Sales executives are confident in their observation that all buyers do not want the same kind of follow-up. They have different preferences. This is determined largely by buyer behavior style, as can be seen in the following discussion. The key for salespeople to get in tune with individual buyer preferences is to know behavior style. So again we see the push for sales executives to decide to equip their salespeople with the tools needed to effectively sell to the behavior style, the unique behavior style, of each and every buyer as one of the principal ways to for each salesperson to sell more, for the entire sales organization to make a leap forward in sales results, and for everyone to feel themselves get a step closer to reaching their potential.

Follow-up with High D Buyers

High D buyers prefer follow-up that focuses on the bottom line results they want. They like to know someone is available to help, but they don't want follow-up that requires a lot of their time.

Follow-up with High I Buyers

High I buyers prefer follow-up that reinforces their decision to buy and brings them the recognition they want from their purchase. They also like follow-up that involves social interaction. They are thinking, "Hey, we had fun while I was buying. Let's have some fun now, too."

This means phone calls, visits, golf, tennis, joking, laughing, and generally having fun as part of the follow-up process.

Follow-up with High S Buyers

High S buyers look for follow-up that shows the salesperson is a steady, reliable person they can depend on day in, day out to help them use the product or service while keeping things running smoothly. Follow-up that slowly evolves into a trusting, long-term relationship is what touches the high S. Follow-up that is regular, systematic, predictable, and steady is preferred over follow-up that is infrequent but intense.

Follow-up with High C Buyers

High C buyers want to feel that follow-up includes everything promised to them, and they want it when it was promised. They prefer that the salesperson plan the follow-up, and follow up with the plan. Perfection will be expected in everything. Getting more than was bargained for is one of their goals. The more they get, the more they expect to get.

FOLLOW-UP AND SALESPERSON BEHAVIOR STYLE

All salespeople do not provide the same kind of follow-up. That is easy to see. It is clear that each has their own unique preferences regarding follow-up. And they have things they do not like to do, ways that don't feel right. What they do, and how they do it, depends largely on their own behavior style. Let's take a look at the follow-up tendencies of each style.

Follow-up by High D Salespersons

High D salespersons focus on results, and that means making the sale. Once the sale is made, they will do whatever is necessary to keep it from falling through, but their main interest is pressing on and making another sale elsewhere. However, high Ds can and will give good short-term follow-up if it can quickly lead to a second sale of considerable magnitude. When they do follow up, it is likely to be infrequent, but intense, and come during periods when the buyer is ready to buy again. Long-term follow-up is not the strong suit of the high D.

This means that high D salespeople tend to: (1) neglect developing an ongoing relationship with buyers, (2) handle buyer remorse well if they are around to notice it, and (3) overlook the necessity and details of servicing the sale.

Follow-up by High I Salespersons

Salespeople with the high I style tend to see follow-up as an opportunity to have more friends, to visit and talk, and to have fun. They like the sound of follow-up that has a social focus, emphasizing dinner, drinks, and gatherings with groups. Their follow-up is more likely to be spontaneous than well planned. If something is overlooked, they will scramble hard and fast to smooth it over. High I salespeople tend to focus their follow-up efforts on the bigger issues rather than on the smaller more detailed matters. All of this means that high I salespeople tend to: (1) be strong at developing friendships with buyers, (2) do a pretty good job of handling buyer remorse, and (3) focus only on the major issues when servicing the sale.

Follow-up by High S Salespersons

The follow-up of high S salespeople tends to stress the development of ongoing relationships with buyers. They will call or come around on a fairly regular basis. High Ss are good listeners and buyers tend to open up and talk with them. This enables the high S to identify and deal with problems and concerns buyers have about products or services purchased. High Ss steadily plug away at follow-up. They prefer follow-up activities that deal with relationship matters and they may overlook other kinds of follow-up. In view of this, it is fair to say that the high S salesperson tends to: (1) excel in developing relationships with buyers, (2) be adept at handling buyer remorse, and (3) place moderate emphasis of servicing the sale.

Follow-up by High C Salespersons

High C salespeople tend to have a hard set of follow-up rules, procedures, guidelines, and so on, and stick with them. For example, their plans may call for checking with the buyer the day after delivery of products, visiting two weeks after product delivery, reminding the buyer of the early payment discount option the day the invoice is mailed, sending a card on the buyer's birthday, and checking on equipment maintenance six months after installation. Once established, the follow-up plan will be carried out to the letter with every buyer in a mechanical rather than interpersonal way. The high C tends to: (1) focus on developing working relationships rather than interpersonal relationships with buyers, (2) not always recognize and effectively handle buyer remorse, and (3) be very strong in servicing the sale.

SUMMARY

- Sales executives may want to encourage salespeople to view follow-up as being sure customers *actually* get (B-2) the satisfaction (B-3) they were *expecting* when they decided to buy.

- Sales executives will find it advantageous to stress the two ultimate purposes of follow-up: (1) to lay the foundation for a resale with each buyer and (2) to build a reputation that will help sell other prospects.

- Salespeople will do well to get the message loud and clear from sales executives that follow-up requires staying in tune with buyers after the sale is made.

- Many salespeople are reluctant to follow up. Sales executives can readily overcome this by viewing reluctance in the context of motivation and applying principles of motivation to get a handle on it.

- Sales executives would do well to equip the sales force with the skills required for each of the three primary ways to follow up, namely: (1) servicing the sale, (2) combating buyer remorse, and (3) developing a relationship with the buyer.

- Salespeople are more effective when sales executives help them see that follow-up is an application of the sales model in the sense that it focuses on being sure customers actually get (B-2) the satisfaction (B-3) they were expecting when they decided to buy.

- Sales executives will want to press salespeople to understand that the kind and amount of follow-up that should be given to each buyer depends on the buyer's behavior style—high D, high I, high S, high C.

- Salespeople can strengthen the follow-up they give by understanding their own behavior style and their resulting follow-up tendencies.

- Sales executives can help salespeople give follow-up the attention it deserves by giving them a sense for the solid connection between follow-up and sales performance in both the short term and long term.

NOTES

1. Leonard L. Berry, A. Parasuraman, and Valarie A. Zeithaml, "The Service-Quality Puzzle," *Business Horizons* (September–October 1998), pp. 35-43.
2. Eric R. Blume, "Customer Service: Giving Companies the Competitive Edge," *Training & Development Journal* (September 1988), p. 25.
3. Joan C. Szabo, "Service = Survival," *Nation's Business* (March 1989), pp. 43-45.
4. Thomas P. Reilly, "Sales Force Plays Critical Role in Value-Added Marketing," *Marketing News* (July 5, 1989), p. 8.
5. Ibid.
6. "Don't Complain About Complaints," *Sales & Marketing Management* (September 13, 1982), p. 158.
7. Theodore Levitt, "After the Sale Is Over," *Harvard Business Review* (September–October 1983), pp. 87-93.
8. Ibid.
9. Ibid.

CHAPTER 9

Self-Management Is Motivating

Sales executives are very much aware that successful salespeople are good at managing themselves. They have to be. The freedom and independence of the sales profession speaks for the necessity of self-management. This means salespeople must have a self-management philosophy. That's right. An approach, a theory, a framework, a model to follow. One that's been tried and tested. One that fits and works for them. One that will move them from the kind of salesperson they are to the kind they want to be. Very few salespeople have a practical and effective approach for managing themselves successfully. Sales executives sense this and can only imagine what their salespeople would say if asked, "What is your approach to self-management?"

Now may be the time for sales executives to start expecting salespeople to get a better handle on managing themselves more effectively. It is simple. Announce the new expectation, then equip the sales force to meet it. Equip them. The intent is not to reduce the responsibility managers have for managing the sales force. Rather, self-management should be viewed as a way of strengthening the ability to meet that responsibility. What better way to manage the sales force than to have salespeople shoulder more of the responsibility? The vehicle for doing this is a practical self-management approach that allows salespeople to manage themselves more effectively.

Okay, so how can sales executives get a firm grip on equipping salespeople to do a better job of self-management? Here is a way— a proven way. It is based on the expectancy theory of motivation developed in the 1960s by Victor H. Vroom,[1] then refined in the 1970s, tested in the 1980s, and presented in the 1990s by this author as The Belief System of Motivation and Performance™.[2] This model appears here for the first time as a practical method of successful self-management. It is not a theory; instead, it is a set of simple, specific things salespeople can do. The "set of things" is organized into a *model* way for salespeople to manage themselves. It works, and salespeople can make it work for them.

THE SELF-MANAGEMENT MODEL

The self-management model will ring a bell with sales executives because it has the same theoretical foundation as the sales model presented on Chapter 1. Both are based on the effort-performance-outcomes-satisfaction chain of events and the concept of B-1, B-2, and B-3. Whereas the sales model looks at the prospect's motivation to buy (perform), the self-management model focuses on salesperson's motivation to sell (perform). Let's take a closer look and get a better feel for this.

The first step sales executives must take in equipping salespeople to use the self-management model is to help them become aware of the chain of events that occurs when they go to work each day. Salespeople put out a certain amount of effort, which results in some level of performance, which leads to certain outcomes, which results in some level of satisfaction, or dissatisfaction, for them. For example, working hard (effort) results in doing a good job (performance) which leads to substantial income, good benefits, recognition, and so on (outcomes) which please the salesperson (satisfaction). This is a simple, but very important chain of events for salespeople to understand.

EFFORT ⟶ PERFORMANCE ⟶ OUTCOMES ⟶ SATISFACTION

The second step sales executives must take to prepare salespeople to use the model is to give them a feel for how their motivation to perform is determined. Specifically, their motivation is based on what they sense and believe will happen in their jobs. They are motivated to put out the most effort when three conditions are met: (1) when they believe their effort will lead to performance, (2) when they believe their performance will lead to certain outcomes, and (3) when they believe the outcomes will be satisfying to them. These three beliefs (B-1, B-2, and B-3) are shown as follows to emphasize that the first belief (B-1) refers to the relationship between effort and performance, the second (B-2) deals with the performance-outcomes relationship, and the third (B-3) focuses on the outcomes-satisfaction relationship.

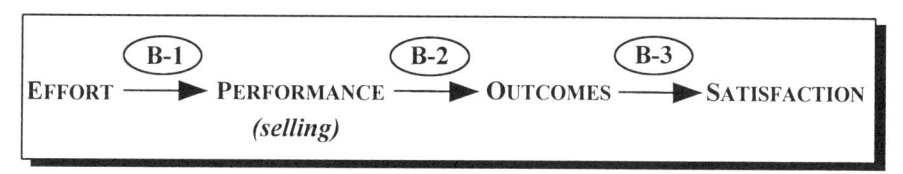

$$\text{EFFORT} \xrightarrow{\text{B-1}} \text{PERFORMANCE} \xrightarrow{\text{B-2}} \text{OUTCOMES} \xrightarrow{\text{B-3}} \text{SATISFACTION}$$
(selling)

The key point sales executives must stress is that all three of these *conditions* must be met for salespeople to be motivated to perform. Let's see why. Suppose a $10,000 bonus is offered a struggling salesperson if he is at 200 percent of quota for the year. The $10,000 sounds great, but the salesperson likely would say, "I'd love to have the bonus (B-3). And I believe they'd give it to me if I produced (B-2). The only problem is that there is no way I can be at 200 percent of quota this year. It's impossible (B-1)."

Does the $10,000 bonus motivate this salesperson to perform at the 200 percent level? No. Even though two of the three conditions are met (B-2 and B-3), the salesperson will not be motivated as long as he believes "I can't do it" (B-1).

Suppose another salesperson is offered the same $10,000 bonus if she makes 110 percent of quota for the year. She says to herself, "I'd love to have the bonus (B-3) and I believe making 110 percent of quota is possible this year (B-1), if I really work hard. But look, I'm not stupid. They've been promising me and everybody else better territories, bigger commissions, and bonuses ever since I started working here, and they never came through. There is no reason to believe them now" (B-2).

Does the $10,000 bonus motivate this salesperson to perform at the 110 percent level? Not really. Even though two of the three conditions are met (B-1 and B-3), she will not be motivated as long as she believes "There is no way I'll get that bonus no matter how well I perform" (B-2).

Suppose still another salesperson hears from his boss that if he makes 120 percent of quota this year, he will get a $100 bonus. He might say to himself, "I'm sure they would give me the bonus (B-2) because $100 is nothing to them. And I believe I have a good chance of making 120 percent of quota (B-1). But I'd have to work day and night seven days a week, stay on the road all of the time, never see my family, do a lot of things I don't enjoy, work with people I don't like, be under a lot of pressure, and risk having another heart attack. It's just not worth it for a $100 bonus" (B-3).

Does the $100 motivate this salesperson to perform at the 120 percent level? No. Even though two of the three conditions are met (B-1 and B-2), he will not be motivated to be at 120 percent of quota as long as he believes "It's not worth it" (B-3).

Sales executives can see that the self-management model is simple and paints a clear picture that explains the motivation to perform. Salespeople who hear about the model find it easy to understand, view it as a good fit for explaining the way they are motivated, and feel comfortable and excited about applying it to themselves. The role of the sales executive is to take the first step and help the sales force understand the model. When this happens, salespeople clearly see a brighter future for managing themselves more effectively and engineering the circumstances so they can meet the three conditions essential for the motivation to perform, namely: (1) believing their effort will lead to performance, (2) believing their performance will lead to certain outcomes, and (3) believing the outcomes will be satisfying to them. Sales executives may be wondering whether this can really make a difference in sales results. And whether or not to go ahead and give it a try.

DIAGNOSING ONE'S OWN PROBLEMS

Sales executives can plainly see and feel secure in being aware that it is only when all three conditions are met that salespeople are truly motivated to perform. The importance of these conditions can be seen more clearly with some additional concrete examples.

Let's look at B-1 first, where motivation drops, effort declines, and performance goes down when salespeople have doubts about effort leading to performance (B-1). This happens when salespeople can't get a hold on good leads, when telephone prospecting isn't paying off, when they run into a brick wall on cold calls, when they can't tie down the big sale, and when verbal commitments fall through on them. Sales executives can picture in their minds, can recall the faces of specific salespeople whose motivation fell short in the past because they didn't really believe they could get the job done (B-1).

What about B-2, where motivation sags, effort lags, and performance suffers when salespeople don't hear the praise they deserve, when the promise of a bright, new, colorful company car never materializes, and when raises are based on seniority rather than performance. Sales executives can hear voices from the past, salespeople complaining because they didn't get certain outcomes that were promised to them (B-2). And sales executives can recall the negative impact this had on the performance of those salespeople.

Self-Management Is Motivating

Finally, there is B-3, where motivation is low and effort and performance suffer, when salespeople don't believe the outcomes will be satisfying to them (B-3). Salespeople aren't motivated to work hard when the boss complains no matter how good their results are, when high-performing salespeople are "rewarded" with all of the hard-to-sell accounts, and when getting a better sales territory requires moving some place the salesperson doesn't want to live. Sales executives can sense it when salespeople are unhappy and unmotivated because they are not getting outcomes that are satisfying to them (B-3).

Sales executives can listen for, but will never hear, the way salespeople talk to themselves about matters that affect their motivation. If sales executives could get inside the minds of their salespeople, they would hear an endless flow of self-talk like "I can't do it" (B-1), "I never get what my performance deserves" (B-2), and "All things considered, this is not a very satisfying job" (B-3).

It isn't easy to step inside a salesperson's head, to hear what is going on in there, to see the impact it is having on their motivation to perform. That's why it makes sense for sales executives to focus more on teaching the sales force the principles of self-management. Salespeople are aware of what they are seeing, hearing, feeling, and believing. They know what their problems are. They know the causes. They know the solutions. This puts them in a good position to manage themselves. A better position than anyone else. They just need a little training, guidance, and support to manage their own issues, to manage all those things that are floating around in their heads and having a negative impact on their motivation to perform.

Sales executives can imagine how effective this can be. Just take a look at some of the common self-talk among salespeople and see how easy it is for them to get a handle on interpreting what they are saying to themselves. Using a 10-point rating scale makes it even easier. For B-1, a 10 means the salesperson believes "I can do it" and 0 means "I can't."

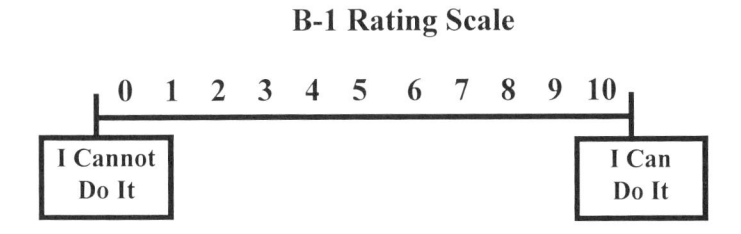

B-1 Rating Scale

0 1 2 3 4 5 6 7 8 9 10

| I Cannot Do It | | I Can Do It |

Self-talk like the following sounds like "I can do it" and B-1 ratings of 10 would be appropriate.

- "I can sell swampland in Florida. This will be a piece of cake."
- "I know what it's like to make fifty phone calls in a day. Making only twenty will be nothing."
- "Based on the sales call today, I'm certain I'll close him on the next visit."

Self-talk like the following suggests the salesperson is saying and feeling, "I can't do it," and B-1 ratings of 0 are appropriate.

- "There's no way I can make quota with my territory cut in half."
- "I'll never be able to take on a new product line and maintain my current sales level during the next few months."
- "Sell twice as much as last year with the economy like it is now? That's impossible."

Some self-talk is not clearly "I can" or "I can't." Here are a few examples.

- "There's a 50-50 chance I'll sell this new account." (This means "The odds are even that I can do it." This would have a rating of 5.)
- "I've got about 1 chance in 10 of exceeding my sales quotas by 20 percent." (This means "It's possible, but not likely." A B-1 rating of 1 would fit.)
- "I've got a pretty fair chance of closing this sale by the end of the month." (This means "The odds are in my favor." The B-1 rating probably would be in the 6 to 8 range.)

Let's look at some self-talk related to B-2 and how to interpret it. The 10-point rating scale can be used again, with a B-2 rating of 10 meaning "I will get the outcome(s)" and a 0 rating meaning "I will not get the outcome(s)."

B-2 Rating Scale

0 1 2 3 4 5 6 7 8 9 10

| I Will Not Get the Outcome(s) | | I Will Get the Outcome(s) |

Self-Management Is Motivating

Some self-talk has a definite ring of "I will get the outcome(s)" and B-2 ratings of 10 are appropriate. Here are some examples that deserve such ratings.

- "Sure, they always give us our sales commission."
- "I'm certain I'll get a company car if I reach the required sales level."
- "Everything is based on sales performance here and you always get what you deserve."

It is very common for salespeople to engage in self-talk that has the sound of "I will not get the outcome(s)" and B-2 ratings of 0 would fit. Here are several examples.

- "There is absolutely no way I'll get that promotion to sales manager."
- "I'm totally convinced there will be no sales bonuses this year."
- "Promises, promises. That's all we ever get here."

Salespeople often are uncertain about whether or not they will get particular outcomes. Here is some self-talk that shows feelings of uncertainty.

- "There's a 50-50 chance I'll finally get that company car this year." (A "50-50 chance" yields a B-2 rating of 5.)
- "The odds are 9 to 1 that I'll get some kind of special recognition for my sales performance this year." (This means "I'm almost certain I'll get it." A B-2 rating of 9 is appropriate here.)
- "You seldom get rewarded around here even when you do a good job." (This means "There is only a slim chance." The B-2 rating probably is in the 1 to 3 range.)

The final self-talk to look at and interpret deals with B-3. This is the self-talk that relates to the satisfaction or dissatisfaction salespeople find in the outcomes they are receiving, or believe they will find in outcomes they expect to receive. The rating scale used to interpret B-3 self-talk is considerably different from the scales used for B-1 and B-2. The B-3 scale actually is the combination of two separate rating scales, one a satisfaction rating scale, the other a dissatisfaction scale. When combined into one scale, it ranges from –10 to +10. A rating of +10 matches an outcome that gives maximum satisfaction, with a +1 indicating some, but not much satisfaction. A rating of –1 would indicate the outcome would be slightly dissatisfying, while a rating of –10 sends a loud and clear message of maximum dissatisfaction.

B-3 Rating Scale

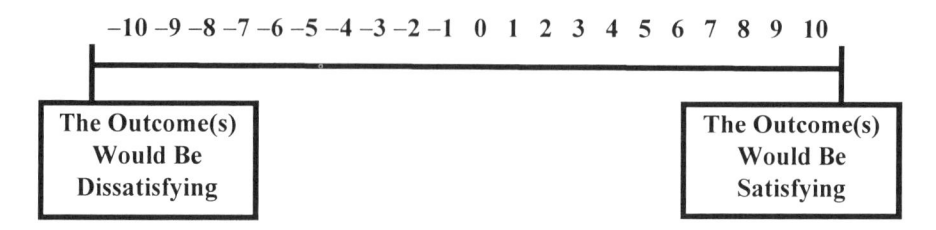

−10 −9 −8 −7 −6 −5 −4 −3 −2 −1 0 1 2 3 4 5 6 7 8 9 10

The Outcome(s) Would Be Dissatisfying	The Outcome(s) Would Be Satisfying

Here are some examples of using the rating scale to give a feel for interpreting self-talk that is related for B-3.

- "Being assigned a new territory would be the worst thing that could ever happen to me." (A B-3 rating of −10 would properly indicate the extreme dissatisfaction of this strong, outspoken comment.)
- "Getting that promotion to sales manager means more to me than anything else in the world." (The extreme satisfaction would be best shown with a B-3 rating of +10.)
- "If he keeps complaining about everything I do, I may start looking for a new job." (The B-3 rating probably would be somewhere in the −7 to −9 range.)

Rating the level of B-1, B-2, and B-3, as shown above, contributes to successful self-management. If salespeople can sense why they are not performing as well as they would like, they can do something about it. If they don't know why, the odds are stacked against them and it's hard to get back on track. However, when they are consciously aware of their beliefs (B-1, B-2, and B-3), and the impact they have, salespeople can turn to specific, proven, hands-on ways to manage themselves more effectively and strengthen their motivation and performance. It raises the question: Are sales executives aware how much this will improve sales results?

COMING UP WITH ONE'S OWN SOLUTIONS

How can salespeople get a handle on using the self-management model to solve their own problems and get better sales results? Sales executives need to teach salespeople how to follow three fundamental steps:

- constantly evaluate their self-talk to diagnose any B-1, B-2, and B-3 problems they might be having;

Self-Management Is Motivating

- identify the cause(s) of the B-1, B-2, and B-3 problems; and
- come up with solutions that match the causes.

Most B-1 problems that salespeople experience are caused by:

- not having the selling skills required to do the job;
- not having sufficient product knowledge;
- not being given adequate sales support;
- not being sure what to do or how to do it;
- being expected to accomplish too much; and
- a history of failure.

The main causes of B-2 problems are:

- outcomes not being given based on performance;
- a history of not getting what performance deserves; and
- inequity of outcomes relative to others. ("I was satisfied with my bonus until I heard what everybody else got.")

The most common causes of B-3 problems are:

- not getting desired outcomes;
- getting outcomes not wanted; and
- the work itself is not rewarding.

Sales executives need to stress two points with salespeople regarding these causes. First, since the main causes of B-1, B-2, and B-3 problems are few in number and relatively simple to recognize, salespeople will find it easy to notice and pinpoint the causes of any B-1, B-2, and B-3 problems they may be experiencing. Second, since solutions are based on causes, properly identifying each cause tends to make solutions fairly obvious. For example, suppose a salesperson says to himself, "I can't meet my sales quota." This is a B-1 problem—"I can't do it." Furthermore, suppose the salesperson is fully aware that the problem is caused by not having adequate closing skills. That is, the salesperson does a great job on everything until it's time to close the sale, and then it slips through his fingers. What is the solution? It's clear that some form of skill building is required to strengthen his closing skills. This solution becomes obvious once the salesperson identifies what is causing the problem. This is the way it usually works. It all boils down to having an accurate perception of the problem, and getting a good feel for what is causing it, then workable solutions usually flow easily.

There are some typical solutions to B-1, B-2, and B-3 problems. And causes and solutions always go hand-in-hand. The solution that fits depends on what is causing the problem. Salespeople who understand this have a real edge in solving their own problems. Sales executives may want to go ahead and equip the sales force with this knowledge. Training is the answer. Preparing salespeople to manage and solve their own problems takes much of the burden off the shoulders of sales managers and places it where it more appropriately belongs. Sales executives can go a long way in helping salespeople help themselves. The issue is whether or not to decide to make things better. Sales executives, this is your choice. It is in your hands, just one more decision, one that can have a positive impact on every person in the sales organization. All it takes is a decision to go ahead and do some training, some training that will make a difference. Just help salespeople understand the causes and matching solutions summarized as follows.

SOLUTIONS TO B-1 PROBLEMS

B-1 Causes	B-1 Solutions
1. inadequate skills	skill building (training, coaching, experience)
2. inadequate product knowledge	acquire the necessary product knowledge and learn how to explain it in the context of value to the buyer
3. inadequate sales support	get the sales support that is needed
4. unsure what to do	clarify performance expectations
5. unsure how to do it	find out how to do it
6. expectations too high	ask for changes in expectations, or change the ways to accomplish them
7. history of failure	confidence building (see the section Solution to a Special Problem), creating opportunities for small successes

SOLUTIONS TO B-2 PROBLEMS

B-2 Causes	B-2 Solutions
1. outcomes not tied to performance	ask that outcomes be tied closer to performance, focus more on desired outcomes that are tied to performance
2. history of outcomes not being tied to performance	find out if the present and future really are like the past
3. inequity of outcomes	ask for treatment that is more equitable

SOLUTIONS TO B-3 PROBLEMS

B-3 Causes	B-3 Solutions
1. not getting desired outcomes	ask for the outcomes wanted but not getting, ask for substitutes
2. getting outcomes not wanted	ask not to receive the unwanted outcomes, ask for less of them, ask for offsets
3. the work itself is not rewarding	change the way of doing things so the work is more rewarding (like selling a different way, selling a different product or service, or even changing jobs)

SOLUTION TO A SPECIAL PROBLEM

Sales executives are very much aware that one of the most common barriers to effective selling is lack of confidence. Yet it is a problem that is easy to go unnoticed. People normally don't share feelings of self-doubt. But all salespeople are faced with it. It holds them back. It keeps they from performing as well as they want to, as well as they could. And unfortunately, only they can solve it and most are ill-equipped to do so. This is where sales executives should get excited because, while they cannot personally erase nagging self-doubts every time they crop up and get a grip on their salespeople, they can prepare salespeople to respond appropriately when they start questioning themselves, when self-doubt starts to creep in, when self-confidence plummets.

Lack of confidence flows out of many circumstances during one's lifetime, including: (1) failure in school, sports, jobs, marriages, and other relationships; (2) abuse by parents; (3) criticism at home, school, and work; and (4) rejection by family and friends. Everybody comes eye to eye with some of these circumstances at one time or another. It is entirely unavoidable, and it takes a toll on confidence levels.

It is easy to see that organizations often compound the problem. Good salespeople are given weak territories. Prices of products and services are too high, quality too low. The competition is two steps ahead. Sales support is weak. There is no opportunity for skill development. Sales managers are demanding and critical. Any one of these can cause people to feel less confident; in combination, they can create real confidence problems.

Failure is viewed as one of the major contributors. It happens to everyone. All salespeople are faced with failure. Maybe it's not having a good handle on prospecting. Or not sensing how to close a sale. It could be letting a valued customer slip away to the competition. Or not making quota. Failures are unavoidable. When they occur, a rush of events, a chain reaction, begins. Salespeople get discouraged. Get down on themselves. Maybe even get depressed. This is stressful. It robs their energy and takes away their incentive to work. Effort declines and performance suffers even more.

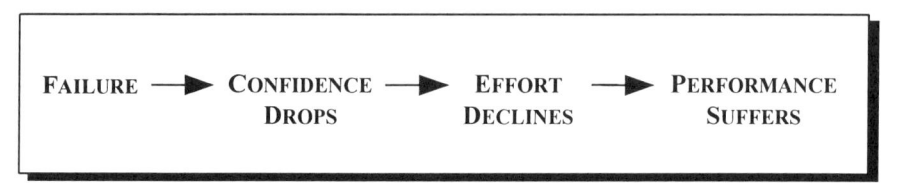

FAILURE ➤ **CONFIDENCE DROPS** ➤ **EFFORT DECLINES** ➤ **PERFORMANCE SUFFERS**

Sales executives can help salespeople get a hold on this situation by making them aware of certain safeguards that can prevent this chain of events from occurring. Salespeople should be made aware that they can guard against failure by: (1) getting into sales positions they are best qualified to handle; (2) being sure their job matches their interests and behavior style; (3) finding out exactly what is expected of them; and (4) getting the kind of training they need.

Even with this focus, salespeople obviously cannot prevent all failure. In view of this, it becomes doubly important to prepare salespeople to prevent this chain of events from becoming a problem when they do fail. This means teaching the sales force how to recognize when failure is causing feelings of self-doubt and how to take immediate action to minimize the damaging effects it can have on their effort and performance. Okay, so what can sales executives do to help? It all boils down to education and preparation and sales executives may want to step up and go ahead and start training salespeople how to deal with self-doubt.

Salespeople need to become aware that most people respond to failure by engaging in *negative self-talk*. People say negative things to themselves. Here is some typical self-talk about a failure.

- "I can't do anything right."
- "I screw up everything."
- "I can't cut it."
- "I'm stupid."
- "I'm worthless."
- "I'm a failure."

Salespeople take it a step further as they tie negative self-talk specifically to their job. Here are some things commonly said after failure.

- "I'm terrible at prospecting."
- "Cold calls scare me to death."
- "I'll never learn how to close a sale."
- "Fear of rejection will always hold me back."
- "There are certain kinds of prospects I just can't sell."

When negative self-talk sets in, the chain of events is acted out quickly. Self-confidence sags, and effort and performance decline dramatically. That is, when salespeople conclude, "I can't do it," it is natural for them to get down on themselves, at least temporarily, and not to try as hard, or maybe even give up and stop trying at all, and the result is a drop in performance.

Positive Self-Talk

Sales executives would do well to show salespeople effective ways to respond when faced with failure. Rather than being negative, putting themselves down, creating self-doubting, and feeling bad, salespeople can learn how to be positive, lift themselves up, build self-confidence, and feel good. There is a special, proven way to do this called *positive self-talk*.[3] It is a simple and effective method of building self-confidence that salespeople can easily grasp, if someone will only give them the chance to learn it. Six straightforward steps make it easy to use. Here are the steps, with examples to demonstrate each.

1. *Objectively state the failure.* "I didn't make the sale yesterday."
2. *Objectively interpret what the failure does not mean.* "This doesn't mean I can't sell."
3. *Objectively state what the failure does mean.* "It simply means I didn't make that particular sale."
4. *Objectively identify the cause of the failure.* "The problem was never getting in tune with the prospect. I wasn't sure of his behavior style and when I didn't understand his objectives, I knew I was losing him, but I couldn't recover."
5. *Identify positive steps to prevent another failure.* "I need to do two things. One is to improve my ability to recognize behavior style more quickly. Another is to become more skillful when it comes to identifying prospect objectives."
6. *Make positive statements about yourself.* "I'm a hard worker and I know my job. I'm not the type to give up, either. I'll keep developing my skills until I can sell as well as anybody."

Sales executives can see that positive self-talk accomplishes several important things: (1) it keeps salespeople from feeling failures are worse than they really are (Steps 1, 2, and 3); (2) it identifies the specific causes of the failure (Step 4) and ways to eliminate them (Step 5); and (3) it helps salespeople feel good about themselves (all steps, especially Step 6). The net effect is that positive self-talk prevents a damaging, long-term decline in self-confidence and a corresponding drop in effort and performance.

Confidence Building and Behavior Style

Confidence building is more effective when salespeople have a firm understanding of their own behavior style. There are three considerations to notice. The first deals with the inherent confidence level of the individual. High Ds tend to be naturally self-confident, tending to believe their dominating style will enable them to control their sales environment enough to perform well. Salespeople with the high I style also tend to have a lot of self-confidence, seeing their influencing style as sufficient to sell effectively. Individuals with the high S style typically are not as self-confident. They tend to have trouble saying "no" and often take on more work than they can handle, and the result is that

Self-Management Is Motivating 193

they often can't do it all or can't do all of it well. This has a negative impact on their confidence level. High Cs tend to want everything (every prospecting effort, every sales call, and so on) to work out exactly the right way all of the time. When things aren't perfect—as usually is the case for everyone—they realize they don't have complete control over the situation and tend to lose confidence in their ability to perform.

The second consideration involves the extent to which salespeople feel a need for confidence building in individual situations. This varies with behavior style and depends on the nature of the failure and the way the salesperson interprets it. High Ds tend to see the need for confidence building most when then are faced with bottom line failures. ("I lost the sale and that keeps me from getting the big bonus.") The need for confidence building tends to be highest for high I salespeople when they are faced with failures that people who are important to them will hear about. ("Everybody will know I didn't reach my sales goals.") Salespersons with the high S style tend to feel the need confidence building more when they experience failures that threaten their need for security and predictability. ("If I lose another customer to the competition, they're going to pull me from this territory and give me a new one I don't know anything about.") The need for confidence building tends to be highest for high C salespersons when failures are viewed as a threat to their job security. ("I'll lose my job if I don't reach my sales goals.").

The third consideration deals with where salespeople should stress emphasis in the confidence building process. That is, some of the six steps in positive self-talk deserve special attention and the right touch. This varies with behavior style. High Ds want to focus on the bottom line; what caused the failure (Step 4) and how to prevent it from happening again (Step 5). High Is want to be aware that others still like and accept them in spite of the failure (Steps 3 and 6). High Ss want to feel assurance that the failure will not affect the security and predictability of the job (Step 3). High Cs want to see every cause of the failure identified (Step 4) and a step-by-step outline of conventional ways to prevent the failure in the future (Step 5).

Confidence Building and the Self-Management Model

As shown earlier in this chapter, salespeople are motivated to put out the most effort and perform best when three conditions are met: (1) when they believe their effort will lead to performance (B-1); (2) when they believe their performance will lead to certain outcomes (B-2); and (3) when they believe the outcomes will be satisfying (B-3). When salespeople see they have failed, they tend to lose confidence in themselves and question their ability to sell. They start feeling insecure and having doubts about their effort leading to performance (selling). In the language of the self-management model, this is a B-1 problem. There are several causes of B-1 problems, as articulated earlier in the chapter, and one that comes down hard is failure. When failure shakes confidence levels and causes self-doubt, salespeople need something to get themselves back up, to strengthen their self-confidence, to renew their belief in themselves. Positive self-talk will do all this, but the patient doesn't know what medicine to take unless the doctor prescribes it.

Sales executives may want to get in touch with the value of salespeople seeing their self-doubt disappear and gaining confident feelings about themselves and their ability to get the job done. Self-doubt is the biggest threat to effective sales performance, especially in sales environments that are increasingly competitive and organizational environments where performance expectations continue to soar. Sales executives may want to, when all is said and done, minimize self-doubt in the sales force, show everyone how to maintain strong, solid levels of self-confidence, and go ahead and teach salespeople to use positive self-talk.

EQUIPPING PEOPLE TO MANAGE THEMSELVES

Sales executives need to be very outspoken about three things when instituting better self-management throughout the sales force. First, sales executives will want to be loud and clear when setting the expectation that salespeople are to be held accountable for managing themselves more effectively. Second, sales executives will want to make it crystal clear that successfully completing a short, well-structured training program is essential for giving everyone the knowledge and skills they need to meet this new expectation. Third, sales executives will want to prepare sales managers not only to provide support but also to hold each member of their sales team accountable for better self-management. When sales executives imagine the positive impact of these three steps on sales results, they may decide this approach looks, sounds, and feels right. And they may decide to just go ahead and do it.

SUMMARY

- Sales executives are aware that all successful salespeople hold on to a self-management model that guides the way they manage themselves.
- Sales executives may be wondering how much better sales results would be if all of their salespeople were equipped to manage themselves more effectively.

- The self-management model discussed here is a simple, practical approach and salespeople can use it and make it work for them.

- This model recognizes that motivation is highest and performance is best when salespeople: (1) believe their effort will lead to performance, (2) believe their performance will lead to certain outcomes, and (3) believe the outcomes will be satisfying.

- This is a self-management model that has a ring of success and looks, sounds, and feels right when placed in the hands of salespeople.

- Sales executives can improve sales results by equipping their salespeople with the self-management model shown here.

NOTES

1. Victor H. Vroom, *Work and Motivation* (New York: John Wiley & Sons, 1964).

2. Thad B. Green, *Performance and Motivation Strategies for Today's Workforce: A Guide to Expectancy Theory Applications* (Westport, Connecticut: Quorum Books, 1992); Thad Green and Merwyn Hayes, *The Belief System: The Secret to Motivation and Improved Performance* (Winston-Salem, North Carolina: Beechwood Press, 1993); and Thad Green and Bill Barkley, *Manage to the Individual: If You Want to Know How, ASK!* (Atlanta, Georgia: The Belief System Institute, 1995).

3. Thad B. Green, *Performance and Motivation Strategies for Today's Workforce: A Guide to Expectancy Theory Applications* (Westport, Connecticut: Quorum Books, 1992), pp. 80–85.

CHAPTER 10

Making Goals Motivating

Sales executives have a very clear picture of the importance of goals at every level in the sales organization, yet they often feel stumped when sales goals are not fully embraced, and maybe even rejected, by the sales force. It is not easy to get a handle on setting goals in a way that has a positive impact on the motivation and performance of salespeople. Whether the goals focus on sales performance (quota), servicing the customer, growth and development, or personal goals salespeople might have, sales executives feel a kind of oppressive frustration when they see that others do not share an appreciation for goals and resist the workings of a goal-oriented environment. Could it be that salespeople are not in tune with goals simply because they do not have the experience and knowledge base that sales executives have? Could it be that fortifying skill levels and insights of salespeople around goals would make a difference? And could it be that sales executives might, when they think about it, learn more about how to make goals more motivating?

A starting point in making goals more motivating is for sales executives to help salespeople see, hear, feel, and ultimately grasp the relationship between goals and their own individual success. There is a strong relationship and several noteworthy observations scream out loud and clear about it. First, most people, even those who are intelligent and well educated, do not have goals. Second, people with goals accomplish more than people without goals. Third, people with written goals accomplish far more than both people without goals and people with specific but unwritten goals. Fourth, people who really want to get ahead of the pack can do so by setting specific goals and writing them down.

Why do goals clearly make such a big difference in how much people accomplish? Here's why. Goals, particularly written goals, provide purpose and direction, give something to work toward, and make it easier to concentrate and harder to procrastinate. Goals cause people to focus their thinking, energy, abilities, and resources in a direction they want to go. Goals build the enthusiasm people need to feel to get there. Goals help people keep a perspective on what is really important, keep them from wasting time on things that *seem* important, help them say "no" to low priority activities, and provide a standard for measuring progress and performance. Goals not only increase performance, they also make people feel better and this provides the motivation to achieve even more. Goals get people committed, clarify their priorities, prevent them from wandering around aimlessly, and serve as a reminder about how they can best spend their time, effort, money, and other resources.

So, why are goals important? The bottom line is that goals help people accomplish more, help them get more of what they want. In short, goals help people become more successful. And when salespeople are more successful, sales organizations are, too. Sales executives may want to consider whether or not to just go ahead and step up the pace toward results, yes, step forward and persuade salespeople to focus more on goals, both personal and work related, and equip them with the skills they need around goals, goal setting, and goal attainment.

OVERCOMING RESISTANCE TO GOALS

Even though goals clearly contribute to individual success, sales executives are very much aware that many salespeople have a strong sense of reluctance to jump onto the bandwagon when it comes to goals, and for good reason. Salespeople can be outspoken and sound off about the variety of reasons for resisting goals and goal attainment.

- "It's not worth the effort."
- "I don't have the skills to do this."
- "They don't pay me enough."
- "Even when I reach my goals, nobody seems to notice."

Making Goals Motivating

- "I won't have any balance in my life."
- "If I exceed my quota, they'll just increase it again next year."
- "My track record isn't very good."
- "I'd like more recognition for my accomplishments."
- "Nothing happens when people fail."
- "The hours are too long and there is too much pressure."
- "These goals are impossible to reach."

The best way for sales executives to get a handle on resistance to goals is to view it in the context of motivation. When doing so, it is easy to see that the reasons for reluctance fall into three categories.

The first category of reasons for resisting goals and goal attainment that salespeople speak out loud and clear about involves the belief about effort leading to performance (B-1), where performance is defined as goal attainment. Salespeople often conclude, "I can't do it." This clearly is a B-1 problem. The "I can't do it" belief strips the salesperson of the motivation to strive toward goal attainment. It leaves salespeople unmotivated and unwilling to put out the effort needed to perform well (attain the goals). This is summarized as follows.

B-1 Rating Is Low

"I can't do it."

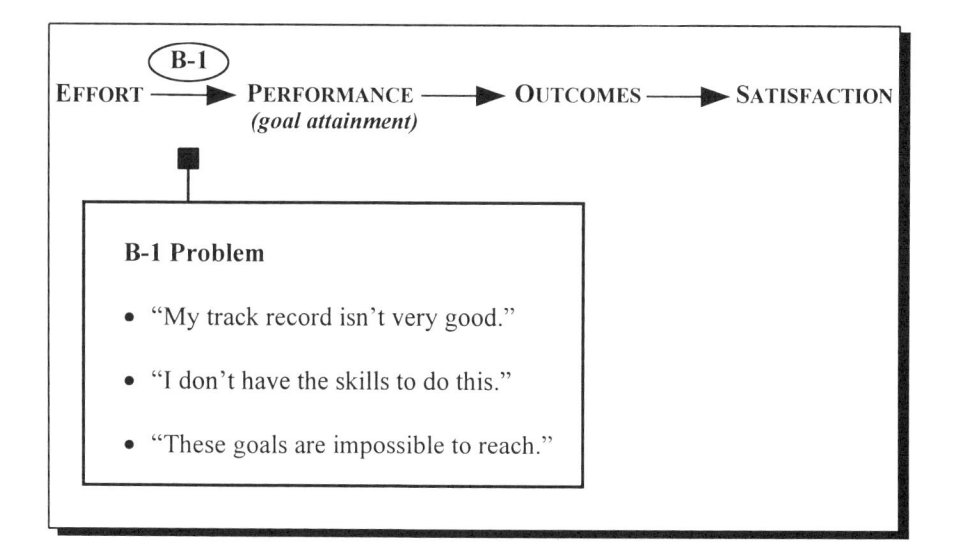

Effort —(B-1)→ Performance *(goal attainment)* → Outcomes → Satisfaction

B-1 Problem

- "My track record isn't very good."
- "I don't have the skills to do this."
- "These goals are impossible to reach."

The second category of reasons for resistance to goals and goal attainment that salespeople talk about involves the belief about performance leading to outcomes (B-2). In some sales organizations, salespeople often conclude, "Outcomes are not tied to performance. People who reach their goals aren't treated much differently from those who fail to reach their goals." This happens in sales organizations where the corporate culture is based on the belief that everybody should be treated the same. It also occurs in organizations when reward systems are not performance based, but instead are based on seniority, loyalty, and other measures unrelated to performance. The belief that "Even when I perform, nothing much happens" (B-2) holds salespeople back and leaves them reluctant to support sales goals. It just doesn't make sense to expect salespeople to be motivated when outcomes are not based on their performance. While in most organizations compensation is based in part on performance, the part tied to performance may be too small to motivate many of the salespeople. Outcomes other than compensation typically are not closely tied to performance in most sales organizations. This problem is summarized as follows.

B-2 Rating Is Low
"I won't get the outcomes."

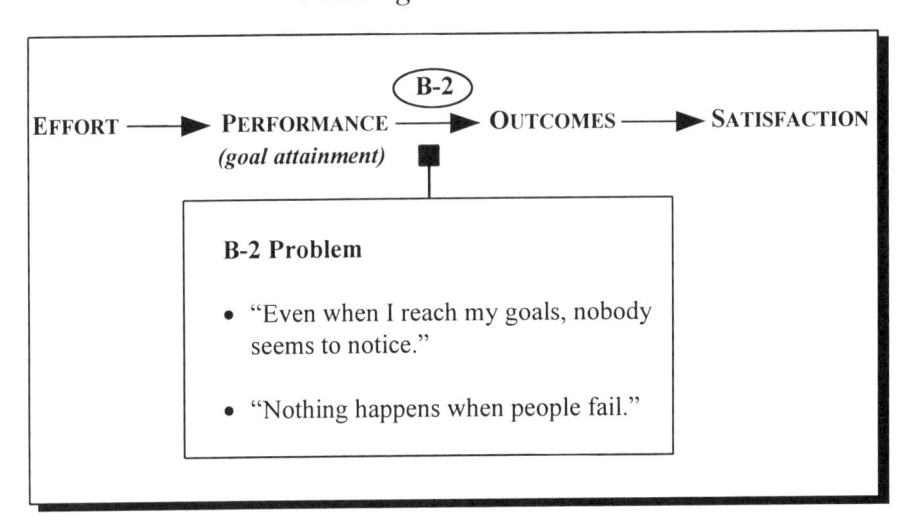

EFFORT ⟶ PERFORMANCE *(goal attainment)* ⟶ (B-2) OUTCOMES ⟶ SATISFACTION

B-2 Problem

- "Even when I reach my goals, nobody seems to notice."
- "Nothing happens when people fail."

The third category of reasons sales executives might hear that explain resistance to goals and goal attainment involves the belief about outcomes leading to satisfaction (B-3). While some salespeople find satisfaction in the outcomes related to goals and goal attainment, many see these outcomes as dissatisfying and this causes resistance. This is summarized as follows.

B-3 Rating Is Low

"The outcomes aren't satisfying."

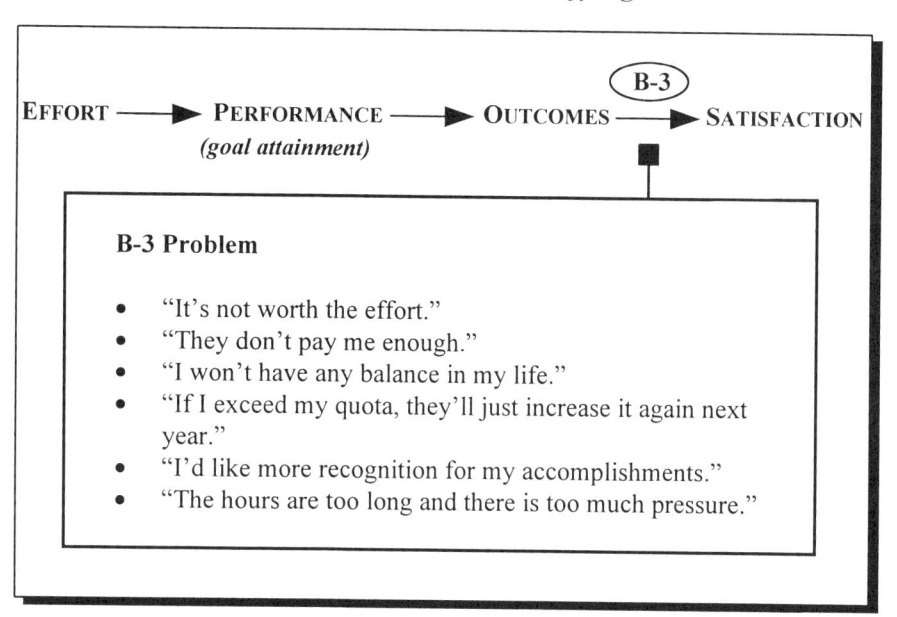

EFFORT ⟶ PERFORMANCE ⟶ OUTCOMES ⟶ SATISFACTION
(goal attainment)   (B-3)

B-3 Problem

- "It's not worth the effort."
- "They don't pay me enough."
- "I won't have any balance in my life."
- "If I exceed my quota, they'll just increase it again next year."
- "I'd like more recognition for my accomplishments."
- "The hours are too long and there is too much pressure."

Sales executives may be wondering what they can do to overcome the resistance to goals and goal attainment that has a firm grip on many salespeople. Viewing resistance in the context of motivation, and defining the problems within the framework of B-1, B-2, and B-3, provides a new depth of understanding and opens the door for solutions that will work. Sales executives can, if they wish, review the solutions that follow and pick out the ones that fit, the ones that look, sound, and feel right. Then do something with them. Do something. A handful of options may be enough to turn the corner and overcome much of the resistance that has been holding people back. Do something. Give it a try. And sit back and wait for a pleasant surprise.

B-1 SOLUTIONS

1. Make salespeople aware of the relationship between goals and personal success.

2. Stress to salespeople the importance of having a firm grasp of exactly what has to be done, step by step, for successful goal attainment.

B-1 Solutions
(Continued)

3. Develop in each salesperson the skills needed to reach their goals. In other words, provide training.

4. Make available the resources salespeople need for goal attainment.

5. Have sales managers work with salespeople and agree on realistic goals, ones salespeople are confident they can accomplish.

6. Have sales managers work with salespeople to develop and implement plans to reach their goals.

7. Create opportunities for small successes. Have sales managers work with each salesperson to assist and to provide coaching and feedback that will ensure success and allow salespeople to see that they *can do it*.

8. Provide support and encouragement that will build self-confidence in the salesperson's ability to reach their goals.

B-2 Solutions

1. Set up compensation plans where money clearly is tied to goal attainment. In other words, reward people who perform and withhold rewards from people who don't.

2. Establish incentive programs where nonfinancial as well as financial incentives flow directly from goal attainment, including nonfinancial outcomes like promotions, growth and development opportunities, and trips and clubs for elite performers.

3. Design sales contests where outcomes are tied to performance *levels*, not performance *rankings*. In other words, use a design where everyone who reaches certain *levels* can win, not just a predetermined, specified number of top performers.

B-2 Solutions
(Continued)

4. Help sales managers become fully aware of the importance of tying outcomes to performance and the impact this has on the motivation and performance of each member of their sales team.

5. Equip sales managers with the insight and skills they need to give people what their performance deserves. For example, sales managers could assign territories and customers to salespeople based on performance (goal attainment), not politics and favoritism.

6. Insist that sales managers take swift and firm action with salespeople who are not meeting quota. When sales managers let salespeople get by with poor performance, the wrong message is sent to everyone, yes, everyone, that outcomes are not tied to performance, that it doesn't matter whether people perform.

B-3 Solutions

1. Be aware that a prerequisite for overcoming resistance to goals and goal attainment is giving salespeople a solid opportunity to get outcomes they want and avoid those they don't want.

2. Notice that satisfaction and dissatisfaction for outcomes is an individual matter and varies from one salesperson to another. An outcome that gives a sense of satisfaction to one person may be dissatisfying to another.

3. Hear salespeople when they say money is very important, and listen when they talk about how they also value many other outcomes.

4. Get a sense for the limited number of outcomes that can be made available to salespeople through decisions at the sales executive level, like money, growth and development opportunities, and career advancement, versus the majority of outcomes that are primarily in the hands of the sales manager, like management style, coaching, feedback, respect, relationships, trust, and so forth.

B-3 Solutions
(Continued)

5. Equip and motivate sales managers to manage to the individuality of each salesperson. In other words, prepare and encourage sales managers to communicate with each salesperson and find out which outcomes they want and which they want to avoid.

GOOD GOALS ARE NOT WHAT THEY USED TO BE

Sales executives have long had a firm grasp on creating well-formed goals and recently have come to see that this is not enough. Well-formed goals that are stated in specific, measurable terms are essential but hardly matter if salespeople do not believe the goals are attainable. This is a B-1 issue. Even when goals are well stated, salespeople are not motivated to achieve them unless they can look at the goals and say to themselves, "If I put out the effort, I believe *I can do it.*"

Competition has caused a greater focus on performance and sales organizations have translated this into sales goals that are very tough to attain and often simply out of reach. Unprecedented levels of turnover, *churn* in the language of sales executives, have flowed out of this with a rush of salespeople packing their bags and leaving impossible jobs behind with others being terminated for not meeting quota. This is bringing a shift in emphasis from the traditional criteria of good goals, namely that they be specific and measurable, to a greater focus on *attainability*. Sales executives may want to zero in on the real issue and take a close look at, and get a feel for, how attainable goals are *from the salesperson's perspective.*

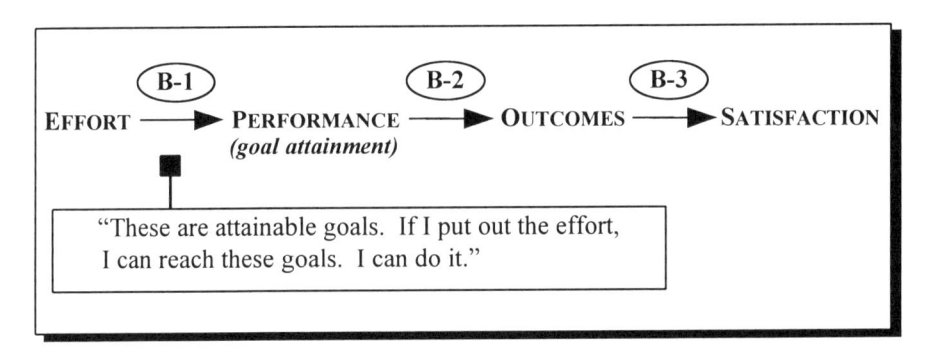

Effort → Performance (B-1) → Outcomes (B-2) → Satisfaction (B-3)
(goal attainment)

"These are attainable goals. If I put out the effort, I can reach these goals. I can do it."

Sales executives have seen, time and again, that people have goals like "get a good education," or "make a lot of money," or "be successful," or "be the best salesperson in my group," or "have a nice house." In one sense, all of these are worthy goals, yet they are not good goals because they are filled with problems that make them difficult, if not impossible, to reach. Why? Each of these goals is ambiguous, hard to measure, and, for some people, not attainable. Sales executives, sales managers, and salespeople can sidestep these problems when setting goals simply by focusing on making each and every goal specific, measurable, *and* attainable, with the latter being the most difficult of the three. This means that sales executives who have a vision of achieving better results may want to, after due consideration, pull a few strings and spread some solid wisdom about goals throughout the sales organization.

Making Goals Specific

Sales executives hear over and over that one of the common problems in setting goals is the failure to be *specific*. People often construct goals using vague terms like "improve income," "reach my potential," "more time with family," "get an education," and "reduce hours at work." These goals sound good, but they are filled with so much ambiguity that they lose their meaning. The same vagueness is seen in other common goals like the following, and may cause sales executives to want to examine the goals that are the foundation for their success, and that of each individual salesperson, and determine if it would be prudent to make them more specific.

VAGUE GOALS

Goal	Vagueness
1. Get a raise.	How much money? By when?
2. Increase sales.	How much increase? By when?
3. Find more prospects.	How many more? By when?
4. Advance career.	How? By when?
5. Own a nice house.	What kind? Where? By when?

It is difficult to get a handle on goals that are filled with unanswered questions. When goals are not specific, it is hard for salespeople to focus on the right things, like deciding exactly what to do and how to do it. This indecision leads to procrastination and eventually to losing sight of what the goals actually were. It is easy to see that nothing much happens when goals are vague. Specific goals, on the other hand, encourage action. Compare the following specific and vague goals. Notice that coming up with specific goals means focusing on end points.

SPECIFIC GOALS

Vague Goal	Specific Goal
1. Get a raise.	Get a 10 percent raise by October 31.
2. Increase sales.	Sell $20,000 more next year than this year.
3. Find more prospects.	Identify two new prospects per week.
4. Advance career.	Become a sales manager by August 1.
5. Own a nice house.	Own a 2,500-square-foot house similar to John and Mary's in Hillcrest Acres by May 1.

With specific goals, salespeople know what they are going after, they can figure out what they are up against, and they can move ahead to make things happen. What a difference being specific can make! Sales executives can picture the difference when all goals, not just goals around quota, are stated in specific terms.

Making Goals Measurable

One of the biggest problems that easily can be observed in corporate America today is that executives and managers at all levels can be negligent when it comes to holding people *accountable* for accomplishing goals. Sales organizations feel the impact of this, too, as everyone from sales executives right on down to sales managers sometimes get caught up in focusing on setting goals and then become remiss at following up and holding people accountable to accomplish them. One of the reasons for this, and there are many, is that goals often are stated in a way that goal attainment, and progress toward attainment, cannot be easily measured and this makes accountability difficult, if not impossible. Trying to hold people accountable does not have any teeth when goals are not measurable.

It is imperative that sales executives take a hard look at goals at all levels and shore up any deficiencies around the measurability of goals. Deficiencies are less likely to appear with goals dealing with sales quota because, by their very nature, they tend to be measurable, but other goals are particularly vulnerable to measurability problems.

It is easier to measure goal attainment when goals have single-event end points with completion dates, such as getting a 10 percent raise by October 31, identifying two new prospects per week, becoming a sales manager by August 1, or owning a 2,500-square-foot house similar to John and Mary's in Hillcrest Acres by May 1. It can be harder to get a handle on measurability when specific goals are stated in a comparative format, like selling $20,000 more than last year, finding 10 percent more new prospects than last year, and reducing monthly expenses by 5 percent. Comparative goals require the availability of information on past as well as present performance. Some organizations have a clear-cut way of gathering and processing such needed information, but others do not. This likely is a problem in many sales organizations.

Sales executives like the sound of having measurable goals to make it easier to hold salespeople accountable for goal attainment, and at the same time they sense the value of measurable goals in tracking *progress* toward goal attainment. Tracking allows sales executives to monitor progress, to see if things are on course or not. Clearly this is important. Getting off course is not a problem if early detection sounds an alarm that allows time to take corrective action and get things back on course. That's what tracking does, it gives a second chance, and works best when goals are *measurable*.

Tracking progress means focusing on and checking to be sure each step toward the goal is being completed correctly and on time. Some sales executives say this sounds too much like micromanaging and prefer not to do it, at least not with all goals. However, good sales executives have a sense for knowing when goals are important enough to track progress and be sure goal attainment stays on course. When this is the case, it means extending the measurability idea to encompass not only the end result but also the intermediate points toward goal attainment. With this in mind, sales executives will want to clarify key intermediate points and establish specific, measurable goals for each point, including completion dates. That is, tracking progress simply calls for applying the same principles to the subgoals, the intermediate points, as well as the end points. When each step is stated in specific, measurable terms, including completion dates, tracking is the simple task of checking for two things. Was the step completed? Was it completed on time? This gives a clear picture about progress toward goals.

The importance of attaching competition dates to goals, as one component of measurability, cannot be stressed enough. The absence of such dates for each and every goal, and holding people accountable for meeting them, is viewed as a pervasive and serious problem in sales organizations. Goals like, "Get out there and find some new prospects" and "Everybody has to sell more" and "Get those sales reports completed" simply don't cut it. "Find two new prospects each week beginning next week" and "Get signed contracts for $300,000 by the end of this quarter" and "Complete all of your sales reports by 5:00 P.M. Friday" are examples of goals salespeople can sink their teeth into. Completion dates make goals real. They bring goals down to earth and signal the need to roll up some sleeves and get to work. They are the basis for motivation and performance for the individual and the foundation for getting results for the organization. Without completion dates, goals are slippery, they offer an open invitation to procrastination, and salespeople are coaxed into the mire and muck rather than nudged forward toward goal attainment.

Sales executives know the sting of completion dates that don't work. To finish something "by summer" is not good enough. To get it done "by June" isn't either. Stating the month and day always are called for, and sometimes even time of day may be appropriate. Being clear and specific pushes salespeople into action. The best completion dates exert some, but not too much, pressure on salespeople. Dates that give too much leeway cause delays in goal attainment, while dates that are impossible to meet cause salespeople to get discouraged (a B-1 problem). Sales executives also want to really get tuned in to setting completion dates that are attainable and make sense to salespeople. Salespeople are not likely to rush to meet completion dates that they see as either impossible or arbitrary. Generally, it is important to stick with completion dates once they are set, but it makes sense to be flexible when necessary. It may be foolish to abandon a worthwhile goal because it can't be accomplished on time or to pressure salespeople with completion dates that are so unrealistic as to be laughable. Sales executives will want to use their wisdom and revise completion dates when it makes sense to do so. It is important to be aware that revising dates too often, especially as a matter of convenience, causes deadlines to lose their meaning. But revising completion dates, for good reason, such as to enhance the likelihood of reaching goals, certainly can be appropriate.

Sales executives can brighten the day for every salesperson by focusing on and taking steps to ensure that goals are measurable. Good salespeople don't mind being held accountable, but they do want to know what the measures are. Tell them the rules of the game and they will play. The absence of measurable goals is like binding their hands behind their back, restricting their ability to get the job done, and holding back their motivation to perform. When it comes to measurability, the guideline is to quantify as much as possible, without going overboard with ridiculous, meaningless measures. It simply is easier to get a solid handle on goals and goal attainment when goals are measurable.

Making Goals Attainable

Sales executives who have a good sense for the pressure that salespeople feel, especially when it comes to meeting quota, always get better results. The idea is to take advantage of the positive impact pressure can have and avoid the negative consequences. Smart sales executives are aware that the right amount of pressure can improve sales results, while too little pressure may hold people back, and too much can cause them to throw their hands up in the air and give up. Setting good goals is one of the best tools available for sales executives to get a handle on using pressure in an effective way. Sales executives seldom err in the direction of setting goals that create too little pressure. Increasingly, the problem is one of setting goals that impose so much pressure that salespeople give up and conclude, "No matter how hard I try, I can't do it" (a B-1 problem), and with this comes a going through the motions that is self-defeating rather than aggressively trying to make quota.

Clearly A B-1 Problem

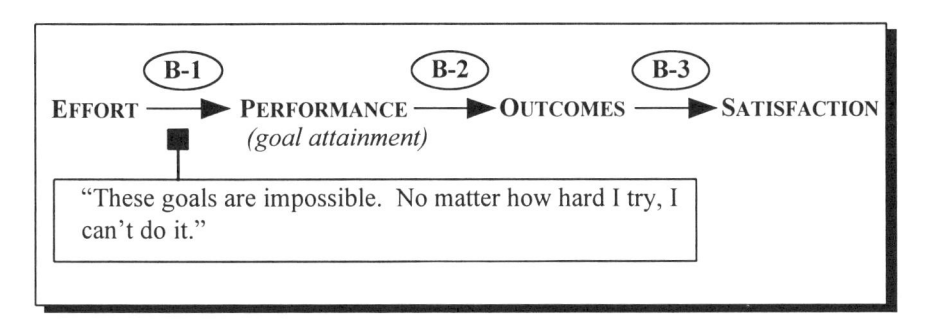

EFFORT —(B-1)→ PERFORMANCE —(B-2)→ OUTCOMES —(B-3)→ SATISFACTION
(goal attainment)

"These goals are impossible. No matter how hard I try, I can't do it."

Prudent sales executives are sensitive to setting goals that salespeople will view as attainable. This is a two-part process. The first part involves setting the goals and centers on creating a smooth-flowing process whereby goals are thoughtfully established with attainability in mind. Though sales executives will not see the advice that follows in a positive way, getting input from sales managers and salespeople can be invaluable. Also, thinking and talking through all that must take place for goals to be successfully met is helpful. This comes best when sales executives get in the shoes of the sales force and find an accurate perspective, first, on what it looks, sounds, and feels like out there on the street everyday and, second, on how much time salespeople are required to spend on activities that pull and tug them away from selling. Goals will be more effective and better accepted, fewer salespeople will walk away from the job, fewer will be fired for poor performance, and overall sales results will be stronger when sales executives stress the importance of creating goals that are attainable.

The second part of helping salespeople view goals as attainable comes after the goals have been established. The first reaction often is an emotional one with many salespeople feeling, "These new goals are unreasonable. There is no way I can do this." The key is to get them to go beyond the emotion of their initial reaction, to think through, to clearly hear and see what lies ahead, and to make a more objective assessment of the likelihood of achieving the goals. The burden for this lies principally with sales managers who can best accomplish this with individual meetings with each salesperson. The idea is to help each salesperson. Here are the steps a sales manager and salesperson can use together to help.

1. Identify the obstacles and roadblocks to meeting the goals.
2. Decide which ones are real.
3. Determine if they can be overcome and how.
4. Decide which ones they are willing to overcome.
5. Determine if the goal is attainable.

How can the steps be applied? Consider the goal of selling $20,000 more next year. That doesn't sound like much. Or does it? Let's see what one salesperson has to say about it with the help of her sales manager. Notice how the five steps are applied. "I had $96,000 is sales last year. Is doing $20,000 more this year realistic? I'm not sure. There are several obstacles (Step 1). First, they've changed my territory. It doesn't have as much potential and hasn't been worked well. My biggest client last year—$18,000—is in another territory now. This is a bigger territory geographically and will require a lot of travel time. Other obstacles include price increases, stiffer competition, and the general condition of the economy. All of the obstacles are real (Step 2). And I don't have much control over any of them, so it isn't likely I can overcome them (Step 3). I'm willing but unable to deal with the obstacles related to my territory (Step 4). All things considered, increasing sales by $20,000 over last year doesn't seem attainable (Step 5)."

Sometimes the analysis leads the salesperson to feel that goals are not attainable. And that's okay. Not just okay, but good. Very good, in fact. It is far better for the salesperson to see this on the front end and in the presence of her sales manager. Now something can be done to get a handle on the problem and prevent the salesperson from giving up at the very beginning or, equally as bad, to blindly hope that the goals will be met, only to later be faced with nothing but frustration, disappointment, and failure. There is no hard and fast prescription for solutions, but the problem has surfaced and action can be taken. Sales executives are pretty clear on this point: Identifying the problem on the front end gives a fighting chance to do something about it.

Sales manager and salesperson can work hand in hand to rough out a plan to deal with the belief that goals are not attainable. When obstacles can't be overcome, changing the goals may be appropriate, changes that recognize and take the obstacles into account. This could mean revising goals downward until they become attainable. This may be hard advice for sales executives to swallow, although after thinking about it for a while, they may just conclude that it makes sense to, sometimes, go ahead and change the goals. Goals that are not attainable are not good goals and only lead to trouble. However, before revising goals downward, obstacles should be carefully assessed to be sure they are real, not just imaginary. Sometimes by understanding obstacles better, they do not seem as imposing. For example, lack of sales support is a common barrier in achieving goals. Support sometimes is available, if the sales manager and salesperson work through the situation together. It pays off to force salespeople to analyze the obstacles carefully. They should get opinions from others, too. This will help them see things more clearly. It will enable them to better determine if the obstacles truly will prevent the attainment of the goal.

The bottom line is that salespeople must believe their goals are attainable. Otherwise the deck is stacked against them. When they conclude, "No matter how hard I try, I can't do it," it is easy to observe a decline in their motivation and just as easy to grasp the likelihood that performance will not, can not, be where they want it to be. Sales executives may want to just make up their minds and take every possible step, when all things are considered, and go ahead and focus on making goals attainable, and increase overall sales results by doing so, because when salespeople believe their goals are unattainable, nothing else matters.

GOOD GOALS, GOOD INTENTIONS, BIG PROBLEMS

Sales executives who have good intentions and focus on formulating goals that meet the criteria of good goals (specific, measurable, attainable), and then move ahead in other ways to short shrift the attainability criterion, have a rough time getting the results they want. The importance of creating goals that salespeople view as attainable can not be stressed enough. Goals that are viewed by salespeople as unattainable cause them to conclude, "I can't do it" and this strips away their motivation to try. This B-1 problem, summarized below, clearly is a serious problem in sales organizations today and sales executives may want to become more aware of the negative impact it has on the overall results of the organization. The problem flows across the thinking and actions of many sales executives in a variety of ways, especially in their use of stretch goals, sales contests, and multiple goals.

A B-1 Problem
"I can't do it."

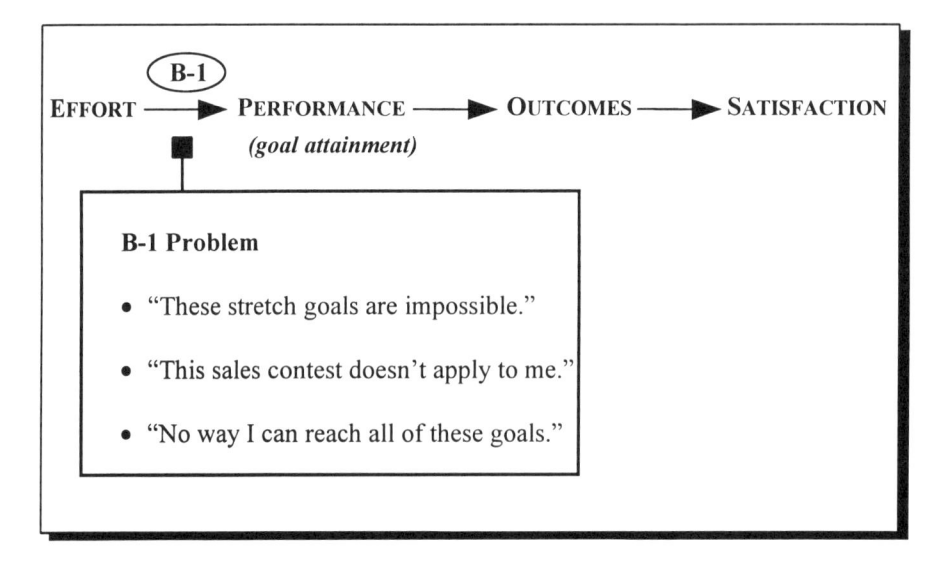

Effort ⟶ Performance ⟶ Outcomes ⟶ Satisfaction
  (B-1)   *(goal attainment)*

B-1 Problem

- "These stretch goals are impossible."
- "This sales contest doesn't apply to me."
- "No way I can reach all of these goals."

Stretch Goals

It is easy for sales executives to have good intentions and start the march toward good goals, and maybe even get there, then the idea of stretch goals sounds too attractive to resist. Well-intentioned people can get heavy-handed, or just overly persuasive with stretch goals, and they become a diversion from the direction of setting good goals, and maybe even a diversion from good goals that already have been created, and all the work that went into them gets put on the shelf. It is hard to ignore stretch goals because they are seen as a way of getting salespeople to extend themselves, to put out that extra bit of effort, to go the extra mile. Stretch goals do have the potential to touch salespeople in

Making Goals Motivating   213

this way, but it seldom happens. In fact the opposite is far more likely. All too often salespeople view stretch goals as unattainable, like a yearly quota that simply is stretched too far, and this can lead to a damaging chain of events. Salespeople say to themselves, "I can't do it." Many of them lose hope, feel helpless, question their self-worth, and simply give up. Their lives change. Many look to leave the organization, some go, some stay. Those who stay are enveloped with feelings of anxiety, fear of failure, uncertainty, and dissatisfaction. They go through the motions, giving the appearance that everything is fine, but their effort is halfhearted at best; they do not seek help, and, naturally, they end up falling short of goal attainment, just as they expected. And sales managers are left to deal with all of the issues around poor performance. This is not a pretty picture, though an accurate one, and it all stems from stretch goals that stretch people too far.

Sales executives may not be aware of the negative impact that stretch goals can have. After all, some salespeople do rise to the occasion and reach their stretch goals, and this can create the illusion that stretch goals are working better than they really are. The unknown is how much greater sales would have been overall if the stretch goals had not left a goodly number, maybe even the majority, of salespeople believing "I can't do it" and consequently not motivated to try. The benefits of stretch goals that work are easy for sales executives to see but less clear is the negative impact of increased turnover, lack of motivation, and poor performance that also may result when salespeople view stretch goals as unattainable. Stretch goals *can* be used effectively, and sales executives may want to think about it, assess how they are doing, and take steps to use stretch goals wisely.

Sales Contests

Many sales executives are committed to sales contests even though they can be very deceptive, appearing to have far greater benefit than actually accrues. This is a function of design, not an inherent lack of potential, and stems from ignoring sound principles around setting good goals (specific, measurable, attainable). An examination of sales contests typically shows they are structured in a way that the vast majority of salespeople do not enter the game and play at all. Here is an actual example that clearly shows the point. A sales organization with 700 salespeople announces, with a lot of talk and flash, a sales contest in which the top eight producers over a specified time period will win new automobiles. When the sales executive who designed the contest was asked to estimate how many of the 700 salespeople believed they had a chance of being one of the eight winners, his response, loud and clear and without hesitation, was, "Probably about twenty." When asked what the other 680 salespeople thought about the contest, the lights came on and he simply said, "Good point." The message screamed out at him that when salespeople conclude, "I can't do it, I can't win, this sales contest doesn't apply to me," as approximately 97 percent of his sales force had done, it was time for him to stop, dead in his tracks, and look hard at the whole business of sales contests and come up with some bright new ideas for sales contests that would motivate the other 680 salespeople.

Some sales executives are outspoken and quick to rebut by claiming that sales contests typically accomplish what they were designed to do, namely take the organization over some desired level in overall sales performance. While this often is an undeniable truth that rings out loud and clear, and certainly is a praiseworthy accomplishment, there is a question sales executives may want to consider just to see what potentially is within their grasp: What would the results be if all of their salespeople (like the other 680) had been equally as motivated as the few who took them over the top (like the 20)? In other words, what is the opportunity cost of motivating only the few, and not the many? Just how much is slipping through the cracks?

Multiple Goals

Sales executives who create a performance culture tend to articulate performance in the form of multiple goals. This approach looks, sounds, and feels right, especially when each of the goals is specific, measurable, and attainable. A problem, however, flows out of the reaction that often cuts through the sales force when multiple goals are aggregated. Even when salespeople perceive each of the multiple goals as individually attainable, they often view the goals collectively as unattainable. At that point, it becomes a question of priorities from the salesperson's point of view. When this happens, when salespeople don't believe they can reach *all* of the goals, they want to know which ones to focus on. The message salespeople usually hear from sales executives is a terse and firm mandate that all of the goals, yes, all of them, are important and must be met, a response that keeps salespeople in the dark as to priorities. They hear the message loud and clear, but having a good sense about the dangers of spreading themselves too thin, they place on their own shoulders the burden of deciding the relative importance of the multiple goals. Sometimes they make good decisions, sometimes they don't, but in both cases *they* set their own priorities. In view of this, sales executives may want to become more thoughtful when formulating and communicating multiple goals.

When salespeople say to themselves, "I can't do it," whether in relation to multiple goals or anything else, they usually feel more comfortable turning within themselves for answers, especially after being rebuffed the first time they ask for help, and they struggle in their own way, in their own time, to overcome the obstacles they face. Sometimes they are successful, though usually they fail because "I can't do it" is not the kind of problem easily overcome alone.

Sales executives may want to, by now, realize they are fully aware that people are motivated to attain goals only when they believe the goals are attainable. When stretch goals stretch them too much, they see the goals as unattainable and their motivation to perform is diminished. When sales contests have only a few winners, the majority of the salespeople see winning as unattainable and become passive bystanders rather than active participants. When multiple goals call for more time and effort than they are either willing or able to give, salespeople view the multiple goals collectively as unattainable and establish their own priorities, rightly or wrongly. Sales executive can avoid the problems created by setting goals if they will stop and reconsider, move ahead with an eye firmly fixed on the real target, and set goals that motivate. This highlights the need to focus on goal setting, to get a handle on it, to realize how much damage unattainable goals can have, and step up to the challenge of setting goals that truly motivate.

GOOD GOALS ARE NOT ENOUGH TO MOTIVATE

Sales executives, by now, are very much aware that the absence of good goals (specific, measurable, attainable) prevents motivation, but good goals alone do not ensure that salespeople will be motivated. Borrowing from the language of mathematics and problem solving, good goals are seen as a "necessary but insufficient condition" for motivation. In short, good goals are not enough to motivate, and sales executives have a strong sense for this. What else is required? Sales executives will readily see the answer by recalling the self-management model discussed in Chapter 9 which indicates that people are motivated to put out the most effort when three conditions are met: (1) when they believe their effort will lead to performance (B-1); (2) when they believe their performance will lead to certain outcomes (B-2); and (3) when they believe the outcomes will be satisfying to them (B-3). These three beliefs are shown in the figure that follows to stress that the first belief (B-1) refers to the relationship between effort and performance (where performance is defined here as goal attainment), the second belief (B-2) deals with the performance-outcomes relationship, and the third (B-3) focuses on the outcomes-satisfaction relationship. How do goals fit into the self-management model and how does the model explain that good goals are not enough to motivate? Let's take a look at these two questions.

```
         B-1              B-2              B-3
EFFORT ──▶ PERFORMANCE ──▶ OUTCOMES ──▶ SATISFACTION
            (goal attainment)
```

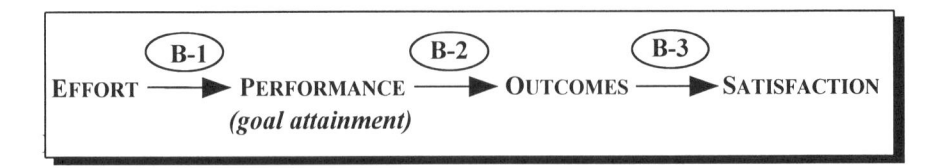

Relation of Goals to B-1

Sales executives will readily see that goals fit squarely into the self-management model in two ways. First, goal attainment is synonymous with performance. That is, goals can be viewed as a way of defining performance and spelling out performance expectations. Second, the extent to which salespeople feel the goals are attainable is equivalent to B-1. As mentioned frequently, salespeople must see and believe that goals are attainable; otherwise they will not be motivated to achieve them. In other words, when salespeople assess their belief about effort leading to performance (B-1), they must conclude and say to themselves, "I believe that if I put out the effort, I can performance. I believe my effort will lead to goal attainment." Salespeople must view goals as attainable, but that alone is not enough to motivate them to goal attainment.

Relation of Goals to B-2

Believing that goals are attainable (B-1) is only one of the three conditions that must be met for salespeople to be motivated. Good goals (specific, measurable, and attainable) are not enough to motivate. Salespeople must also believe that performance (goal attainment) will lead to certain outcomes (B-2). It must be very clear, indeed, that goal attainment will lead to outcomes. Salespeople must feel, must sense deep down inside, that they will get the outcomes promised if they meet the performance expectations. They must trust the sales organization, and their sales manager, to honor promises made in exchange for goal attainment. Problems rush in and come down hard when promises made are not promises kept. This happens when the sales manager clearly states that a promotion will be forthcoming if all goals are achieved again this year, then reneges on the promise. It happens when a bonus is guaranteed for exceeding quota, then doesn't materialize. And it happens when the sales contest rules are changed at the end because someone found a loophole in meeting the criteria for winning.

The bottom line for sales executives to firmly grasp is this: Salespeople must believe performance (goal attainment) will lead to outcomes; otherwise they will not be motivated nearly as much as they could be, and maybe not at all. They can want the outcomes (B-3) and believe they can reach the goals (B-1), but when they do not believe goal attainment will lead to the outcomes (B-2), motivation suffers. Good goals are not enough. Salespeople must believe outcomes are tied to their performance. And sales executives will want to get a handle on this important issue and provide the leadership needed to help salespeople believe that performance will lead to outcomes.

Relation of Goals to B-3

Sales executives can see that the picture is complete when salespeople also believe the outcomes will be satisfying (B-3). This is the third and final condition that must fit for salespeople to be motivated. Salespeople not only must believe that effort leads to performance (B-1) *and* that performance (goal attainment) leads to certain outcomes (B-2), they *also* must believe that the outcomes will lead to satisfaction (B-3).

Consider a typical incentive plan designed by sales executives, the all-expenses-paid vacation for two, say to Hawaii, for any anyone who exceeds quota by 25 percent. This will be a very satisfying outcome to some people but not to the person who has a fear of flying or the person who prefers cash for a down payment on a new house. Sales executives will be smart not to rush into decisions about outcomes to offer salespeople as incentives for goal attainment, but instead to slow down, stop and think, and make careful decisions so salespeople will say, "If I get that, it definitely will be satisfying."

This means sales executives will want to reconsider the use of blanket approaches where everybody gets the same reward. On the surface this may look more difficult, trying to figure out how to please everybody, because, after all, sameness, giving everybody the same thing, seems simple. But sales executives may be wondering what value simplicity has if it does not motivate.

It Takes More Than Good Goals

The continual challenge that rings out loud and clear for sales executives is how to motivate the sales force. Having good goals (specific, measurable, attainable) is a necessary part of it, but this alone clearly is not enough. Salespeople have to believe and feel strongly that the goals are attainable, but there is more. Sales executives also must get in tune with their salespeople and engineer the circumstances so each and every one of them believes, without a doubt, that if they perform well (accomplish their goals), they will get (B-2) outcomes they want (B-3) and will avoid (B-2) those they don't want (B-3).

SUMMARY

- The best way for sales executives to get a handle on resistance to goals is to view it in the context of motivation.

- Well-formed goals that are stated in specific, measurable terms are essential but hardly matter if salespeople do not believe the goals are attainable.

- Sales executives may want to rethink the way they use stretch goals, sales contests, and multiple goals to be sure salespeople view the goals as attainable.

- Sales executives will want to have a crystal clear understanding about why good goals alone are not enough to motivate salespeople.

- Salespeople are motivated best when they believe they can perform (attain the goals) and believe, without a doubt, that if they perform, they will get the outcomes they want and avoid those they don't want.

- Sales executives, when all is said and done, will find big dividends when they take a different perspective on goals and make goals motivating.

CHAPTER 11

The Motivation to Sell

One of the most constant, nagging issues sales executives plainly see and face day in and day out is motivating salespeople to sell. Motivation spurs salespeople onward and upward, and lack of motivation holds them back. Even when motivation is high, and seems solid and firm, sales executives are aware that downturns always are on the horizon, just around the corner from hearing the next rejection, finally getting the picture that the customer is switching to the competition, feeling the pressure of an increase in quota, grappling with the latest change in territory, or reeling from the new compensation plan. Then there is the dry spell when nobody feels like buying, the sting of introducing a new product and no time to fully learn about it, the noisy demand for more paperwork that further reduces time with customers, the rush of customer complaints that eat into selling time, and on and on and on.

    It is easy to see that all of these, and more, can cause the motivation to sell to take frequent and rapid downward plunges. Sales managers who are not equipped to recognize and resolve these issues will be saddled with a sales team that is short on motivation and long on excuses. Everyone looks to the sales executive to take action to prevent downturns in motivation and performance and to keep the dips shallow when they do occur, as they will. Sales executives can get a firm grasp of the issues around motivating people to sell by focusing on doing a better and better job of *preparing* salespeople to sell and creating an organization culture for *motivating* them to sell.

PREPARING PEOPLE TO SELL

Feeling prepared is fundamental to the motivation to sell, as any salesperson will sound off about when given the opportunity. Salespeople must believe "I can do it" and see preparation as essential to building a kind of unshakable self-confidence that wards off self-doubt and shortens those bitter periods of feeling inadequate to get the job done. Salespeople send the message, loud and clear, about the importance of preparation, yet the right people do not always hear it or sense the import and urgency of it. Sales executives may want to put an ear to the rail, listen up to the calls for help, and do something about it.

Barriers to Preparation

Sales executives who feel the voice of logic tugging them in the direction of better preparing salespeople are, more often than not, able to resist the pull. They typically experience a moment of panic when they get tuned in to all of the barriers they face. Finding a clear picture of the obstacles is an essential first step to get a firm hold on them and make the right decision.

One barrier is not having a full and accurate view of the need for more and better preparation of the sales force. Sales executives typically underestimate the need, grossly, and for good reason. It is natural not to see the need because, let's face it, sales executives are, simply by the nature of their jobs, removed from the action. It also is natural not to hear about the need because of all the usual reasons upward communication tends to be flawed, including fear, dishonesty, and lack of access, to mention a few. Hence, sales managers don't always rush to tell the truth, nor do salespeople race to confess their shortcomings. Sales executives would be wise roll up their sleeves and get in touch with how well their salespeople really are prepared to sell in today's environment.

Another barrier boils down to faulty thinking. It is easy to dismiss and push aside the need to prepare salespeople by adopting, without thinking, platitudes like "the cream will rise to the top" and "the fit will survive." These statements no doubt have a ring of truth, but believing them, without imagining the consequences of believing, can result in not seeing a need that is clearly in view. Another example of faulty thinking is believing that sales results flow primarily from putting pressure on salespeople. This appears to work, in part because some people do perform well when the pressure is on. There are two questions that should be heard on this. First, does putting pressure on salespeople work better than other options, or is it just the easier solution? Second, what is the cost, over the long haul, of repeatedly using pressure to get people to perform? Faulty thinking also shows up with the pronouncement that a poorly prepared sales force can be traced back to a hiring problem. In other words, hire the right people and they already will be prepared to sell. There is some truth in this, but believing it too much is a way to rationalize the need to prepare the sales force better. Faulty thinking, oddly enough, can be observed in *not* recognizing that poor preparation is a hiring problem because stronger salespeople do need less preparation to get the job done.

A third barrier is not knowing the cost of not preparing salespeople better. How many prospects go unnoticed because salespeople are not adequately prepared for prospecting? How many salespeople can't out-tough the competition because they are poorly prepared to overcome objections? How many buyers are never heard from again, except to complain, because salespeople are ill prepared for giving good customer service? When sales executives are not clear about the opportunity cost associated with not preparing the sales force better, the need for better preparation simply isn't felt. Not being aware of how much better results could be is a real barrier to preparing people to sell. When sales executives think about it, they may want to just go ahead and do it and get the ball rolling toward more thorough, more effective preparation.

Another common barrier is the often-heard belief that preparing people to sell takes too much time and money. Everybody knows that time and money are just excuses, excuses used when the real reasons for resistance are not clearly seen. Sales executives will want to rethink this barrier and take a closer look at it in view of opportunity cost associated with not preparing salespeople well.

A fifth barrier to preparing salespeople to sell is having a false sense of security about, and relying too heavily on, training. Training can be a good solution, but more often than not training is too much talk and too little action and does not prepare salespeople with solid, effective ways of dealing with the issues they face. Training, as a rule, simply is neither equal nor even roughly equivalent to effective preparation, as most sales executives probably have observed time and again. In other words, sales executives can get a better handle on preparing the sales force if they do not turn to training departments for effectively preparing their own salespeople to sell.

The final barrier mentioned here, but by no means the final one, is being unaware of exactly how to proceed. Sales executives who sense the need to strengthen and lift up the preparation of salespeople often find themselves in the uncomfortable position of being uncertain about what to do, not knowing roughly or precisely what steps to take. Out of this uncertainty flows hesitancy, a holding back, procrastination, maybe even believing things can't change, and the end result is inaction, when clearly they need to be proactive.

In the final analysis, these barriers add up to a mounting pressure in favor of the status quo. Sales executives may want to get a grip on the situation and do what is right. Make a decision, let people hear about it, and prepare people to sell. If salespeople need better prospecting skills, prepare them. When they need to ask more questions and listen to customers better, prepare them. Get a handle on the development needs of salespeople, and develop them. It would be sound advice to just go ahead and get everyone prepared.

Prepared for What?

Experience talks, speaking loud and clear, saying what every sales executive can sense, that salespeople perform best when they are well prepared to sell. Sales executives see this need to prepare salespeople better and will go ahead and decide to do something about it, and make good decisions about the kind of preparation to offer. They are aware, as are sales managers and salespeople themselves, that the right kind of preparation pays off with the stronger sales results, and it makes sense to take steps to prepare the sales force with the essentials summarized as follows.

PREPARE SALESPEOPLE TO

- Gather information about the prospect's *motivation to buy*. Do this by getting the answer to six questions. "Do you have the: (1) need; (2) authority or influence; and (3) money to buy? If you buy from me, what do you believe you will: (4) get and want; (5) get, but not want; and (6) want, but not get?"

- Build their sales approach around what prospects believe they will get and not get, and want and don't want, if they buy.

- Move away from the tendency to sell everyone the same way.

PREPARE SALESPEOPLE TO (CONTINUED)

- Sell prospects the way they want to be sold. Determine prospect behavior style (dominant, influencing, steady, conforming). Sell in a way that matches behavioral preferences.

- Overcome reluctance to prospect.

- View prospecting as the starting point for motivating people to buy.

- Apply the set of *skills* needed for successful prospecting.

- Anticipate questions, objections, stalls, "no," the need to ask, and the need to listen.

- Prepare in advance for all that can be foreseen.

- Recognize interviews as more effective than presentations.

- Apply the set of *skills* needed to conduct effective sales interviews.

- Overcome reluctance to close the sale.

- Recognize that the goal is to close.

- Choose and use a close that matches the prospect's behavior style.

- Overcome reluctance to follow up.

- Be sure buyers get what they want and not what they don't want.

- Understand that self-management leads to sales success.

- Use the self-management model to diagnose and solve their own motivation and performance problems.

- Overcome resistance to goals.

- Recognize the link between goals and sales success.

- Set, and accept, only goals that are specific, measurable, and attainable.

The starting point in the preparation clearly should focus on *the two most important pieces of the puzzle when motivating people to buy*. One is the use of the sales model (Chapters 1 and 2). The model allows salespeople to get a solid handle on the prospect's motivation to buy. This is important because it gives salespeople a firm grasp on the information needed to overcome any resistance prospects may have to buying. The motivation to buy flows to the surface quickly and easily when salespeople get the answer to three questions, namely, "If you buy from me, what do you believe you will: (1) get and want; (2) get but don't want; and (3) not get but want?" These three questions allow salespeople to get a good feel, actually a complete and accurate sense, about the prospect's beliefs about performance (buying) leading to outcomes (B-2) and outcomes leading to satisfaction (B-3). "If you buy from me" (the performance part of the sales model), what do you believe you will "get or not get" (B-2 in the model) that you "want and don't want" (B-3 in the model). This is shown as follows.

Foundation for Motivating Prospects to Buy

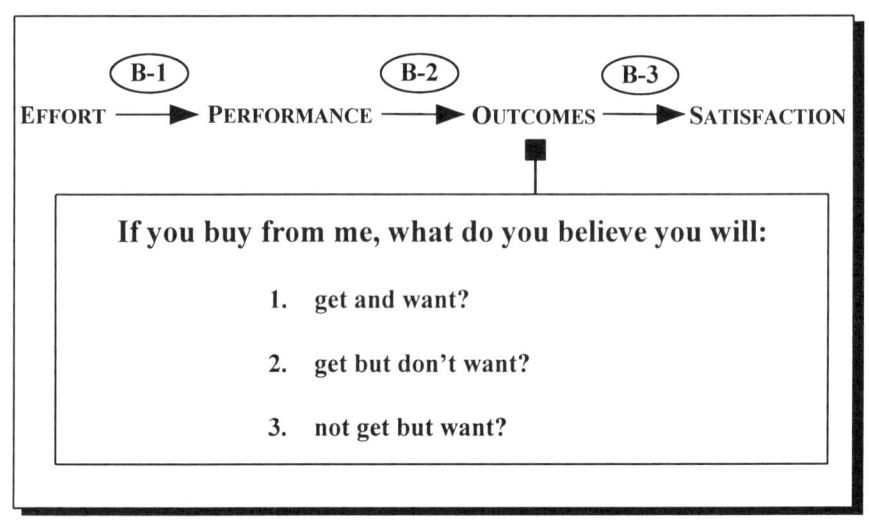

Effort → Performance (B-1) → Outcomes (B-2) → Satisfaction (B-3)

If you buy from me, what do you believe you will:

1. get and want?
2. get but don't want?
3. not get but want?

Sales executives can readily see that the answers to these three questions provide the *foundation for motivating people to buy*. The questions paint a crystal-clear picture of what prospects believe they will get and not get, and what they want and don't want. This, in essence, is perfect information, the key to making the sale. The value of this information cannot be stressed enough. It gives salespeople a laserlike focus, allowing them to show prospects how buying will give them more of what they want and less of what they don't want. And every sales executive knows this is the secret to successful selling.

The second of the two most important pieces of the puzzle is behavior style (Chapter 3). The behavior style of prospects shows how they prefer to be sold. Sales executives are aware of the importance of this, of selling people the way they want to be sold, not selling the way the salesperson likes to sell. The starting point is getting an accurate sense of the prospect's behavior style, a task that can throw salespeople into a moment of panic, unless sales executives prepare them. The preparation that gives salespeople a smooth way to do this simply is to teach them how to quickly read anyone's behavior style, shown as follows.

Behavior Style Quick Read

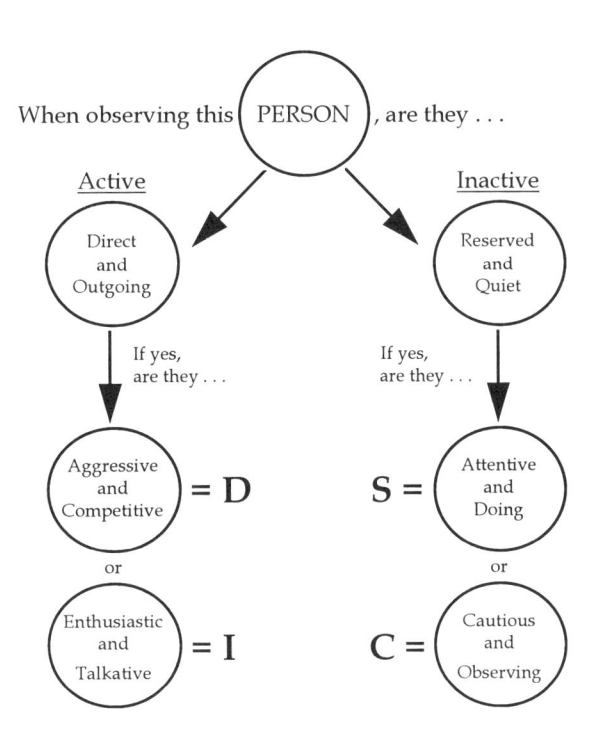

When observing this (PERSON), are they . . .

Active — Direct and Outgoing
Inactive — Reserved and Quiet

If yes, are they . . . Aggressive and Competitive = D
or Enthusiastic and Talkative = I

If yes, are they . . . S = Attentive and Doing
or C = Cautious and Observing

How to Prepare Salespeople

Sales executives are aware that sales training has little impact on sales results, little in an absolute sense, and it is even less relative to what is needed. When most training sessions are over, salespeople are outspoken, stressing how little they learned that really can be applied. When training is good, salespeople freely admit that any good intentions of using what was learned typically do not materialize because circumstances work against them and they quickly drift back into their same old way of selling. These shortcomings do not always hold true for product training but are common for sales training that is *supposed* to focus on developing selling skills.

Sales training doesn't rush to the heart of the matter. Training usually is mostly talk. Talking and giving information do not develop skills, and salespeople speak out loud and clear about being left empty-handed for the time they have been taken out of the field. They sense, correctly so, that the training really is not equipping them to sell differently and better and consequently they are not motivated to do so. Some sales training goes beyond talk to include exercises and games, and this can be grand, expensive fun, but it rarely develops skills.

The failure of training to have an impact on sales results boils down to the absence of the motivation to do something different. Salespeople can hear about new ways of selling, but hearing alone does not equip them to use what they heard, nor does it motivate them to do so. The hard fact is that salespeople are left unwilling and unable to apply what they heard during the training. Even when training clearly develops new skills, resistance to change holds salespeople back. Nothing happens during the training, or afterward, that motivates salespeople to apply any new skills they may have learned. In other words, training that focuses on skill development may leave salespeople able, but unwilling, to apply what they have learned.

The practical side of sales executives leaves them with a clear understanding that training without application has little value, but they also are left with the pressing unanswered question about what to do. The only solution that fits is one that equips salespeople with the skills they need and, hear this, at the same time requires, in some form or fashion, that they apply those skills in actual sales situations. Training with 100 percent application is the answer. Holding people accountable for applying what was learned is the key. Sales executives may be curious if it is really possible to have 100 percent of the salespeople apply the training they receive. They also may be wondering how much time and money is wasted if they don't get 100 percent application of the training.

Sales executives will say it sounds like rough going to get a grip on and implement the notion of training with 100 percent application. Here is the flow of things, for those sales executives who want to go ahead and be open and consider this, a flow that shows, clearly and without question, that 100 percent application is both possible and practical. The first step is to shorten training, narrow the focus, and make the decision to do so now. Whittle the training down and hold salespeople accountable to apply it. It doesn't make sense to teach something and not have them use it. Simply *expecting* salespeople to use what they learn is entirely different from making the decision to get a firm hold on the situation and take action, decide to have people apply what they learn, and hold them accountable for doing so. The second step is to hold sales managers accountable, in their normal course of accompanying salespeople on sales calls, for observing the hands-on application of the new learning, and for providing feedback and coaching to the salesperson afterward. Sales executives can sense how effective this can be and how easy it is to have sales training with 100 percent application. All it takes is to decide to do it, hold people accountable, and step back and see the positive impact on sales results.

Sales Training with 100 Percent Application

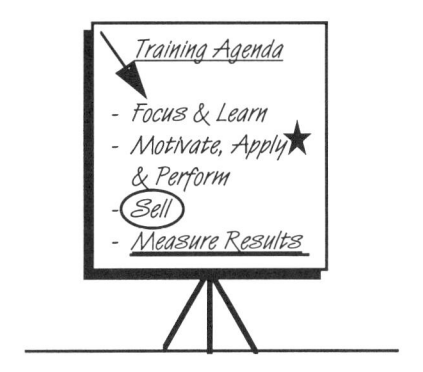

Training Agenda
- *Focus & Learn*
- *Motivate, Apply ★*
  & Perform
- (*Sell*)
- *Measure Results*

Belief System Selling™

Recent success in sales organizations clearly shows that an effective solution to prepare salespeople to sell places the responsibility squarely on the shoulders of both the sales manager and salesperson. The approach follows the recommendation outlined above and has a solid foundation that focuses on training with 100 percent application. Sales managers have a tight grip on the success of this approach because they are charged with holding their salespeople accountable to apply what was learned until skills are developed to an acceptable level. Sales executives will recognize how important it is that while sales managers are holding their salespeople accountable, sales managers likewise must be held accountable for ensuring that their salespeople are learning, applying, and developing the skills they need to meet or exceed quota. Sales executives can clearly see that accountability is the key to successful preparation of the sales force.

One solution, called Belief System Selling™, is a way of preparing salespeople to sell to the individual. This solution has a solid theoretical foundation and has been described in detail in the first eight chapters of this book. The focus in on two essential ingredients: (1)

motivating people to buy, introduced in Chapters 1 and 2; and (2) selling the way buyers want to be sold, introduced in Chapter 3.

The implementation model takes a firm hold on preparing salespeople to sell by incorporating three main components. The first is a 1-Day Learning Session for the entire sales team, including the sales manager. The second is a 3-Month Application Period during which sales managers hold their salespeople accountable by going on sales calls with them and observing them apply what they learned in the 1-Day Learning Session. Sales managers observe each salesperson on enough sales calls for each to say, with conviction, "I can do it." The implementation model concludes with the third component, a 1-Day Accountability Session in which every salesperson in the group shares their application experiences, specifically the learnings they applied, what worked, what didn't, and, most important, the sales they made because of the new skills they used. Although learning is a byproduct of this sharing, the primary purpose and focus of the session is on holding everyone accountable for becoming better prepared to sell.

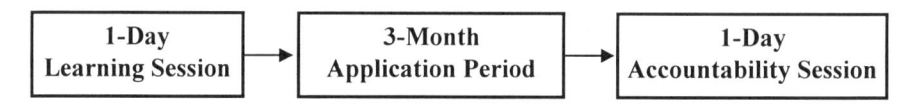

| 1-Day Learning Session | → | 3-Month Application Period | → | 1-Day Accountability Session |

Sales executives will see that this implementation model of 1-Day Learning Session, 3-Month Application Period, and 1-Day Accountability Session can be repeated as often as needed, with each cycle stressing a well-defined and limited number of skills, until the sales force truly is prepared to sell, and knows it, feels it deep down inside, and believes "I can do it." This moves away from the traditional model of preparing the sales force by holding training sessions where some expert talks and gives information, and salespeople sit irritated and frustrated because they don't feel it is helpful and know they will not be held accountable for using it. Sales executives know it does not have to be this way because they can decide to change it. Sales executives can, if they will, prepare the sales force and, in doing so, take sales results to a new level. Where there is a will, there is a way and it only takes one sales executive who can decide to do it.

MOTIVATING PEOPLE TO SELL

Sales executives may want to, by now, be outspoken and say that the only way to motivate salespeople is to help them: (1) believe they can meet performance expectations; (2) believe that outcomes are tied to their performance; and (3) believe that they will get outcomes they want and avoid those they don't want. In other words, three firmly held beliefs must clearly flow through salespeople for them to truly feel motivated to sell, namely "I can meet my sales quota if I really try (B-1), and if I do I will get certain outcomes (B-2), and those outcomes, overall, considering the good and the bad, will be satisfying (B-3)." Preparing salespeople to sell is one essential way to shine the spotlight brightly on the first of these three conditions to motivate people to sell. Sales executives, however, must go beyond B-1 and take other solid steps to motivate people to sell.

Manage to the Individual

In light of the importance of individual motivation to sales success, sales executives will want to take a hard look at the notion, and pass along the skills, to manage to the individual throughout the sales organization. Managing to the individual is based on the notion that one size doesn't fit all, that blanket approaches don't work, and stresses the merits of managing to the individuality of each salesperson. Sales managers can see that fundamental to managing to the individual is the principle, "If you want to know, ask." If you want to know what the motivation or performance problem is, ask the person with the problem. If you want to know the cause of the problem, ask the person struggling with it. If you want to find a solution, ask the person who must make it work. Some managers at first feel intimidated with this approach, not being fully aware about how to manage to the individual and fearing that it will take too much time. Sales executives can relax because there are at least three simple tools for managing to the individual, tools that sales executives may want to decide to pass them along to managers throughout the sales organization.

Ten-Step Formula

Managers can get a firm grip on motivating people to sell by applying a simple ten-step formula for managing to the individuality of each salesperson. It stresses the "If you want to know, ask" principle and calls on managers to ask questions that allow salespeople to identify problems, causes, and solutions when their own motivation and performance are not up to desired levels. The ten-step formula, shown shortly, only requires that managers ask questions and listen to what salespeople have to say. It gives salespeople hands-on involvement is solving their own motivation and performance problems. Sales executives can decide to adopt this structured approach and go ahead and prepare managers to use it.

Managers use the ten-step formula when it dawns on them that salespeople are experiencing motivation and performance problems.

The ten-step formula fits, for example, when a salesperson is feeling the pressure of not meeting quota, when a salesperson is having difficulty closing the sale with prospects who have a certain behavior style, when the number of sales calls falls short, or when salespeople are not secure in prospecting for new customers.

Use of the ten-step formula begins by asking the salesperson what the problem is. Managers don't expect to hear good problem statements, but this gets the conversation going, gives it direction, and puts the discussion in perspective. Step 2 calls on the salesperson to define the performance that is not measuring up. The importance of this can be sensed because all of the problem solving that follows revolves around the performance that is in question. The focus of Step 3 is on B-1 as the salesperson is asked about the kind of effort it would take to reach the performance expectations articulated in Step 2. Getting the salesperson to think through and get a rough gauge on all that is required to perform as expected sets the stage for the salesperson to diagnose B-1 later in Step 8.

Step 4 calls for the manager to get in tune with the salesperson's B-2 and is accomplished best by hearing about the outcomes the salesperson would expect to get, and not get, if the performance goals were achieved. The best way to get a good handle on this is for the salesperson to discuss three categories of outcomes, those wanted and expected, those not wanted but expected, and those wanted but not expected. Step 5 calls for the salesperson to talk about how satisfying or dissatisfying each of these outcomes would be.

Steps 1 through 5 lay the foundation and prepare the salesperson to plainly see and diagnose any B-1, B-2, and B-3 problems that may exist. In Step 6 the salesperson is asked to indicate overall how satisfying or dissatisfying the full set of outcomes would be. It is helpful to get the salesperson to express this overall satisfaction as a point on the satisfaction rating scale. This rating clearly shows the salesperson's B-3 diagnosis. Step 7 follows in the same light by asking the salesperson if the outcomes are viewed as being tied to performance. Getting the salesperson to place this belief on the B-2 rating scale makes it a firm diagnosis. Step 8 refers back to Step 3, the kind of effort required to perform as defined, as the salesperson is asked to give a sense for whether or not the effort will lead to performance. This belief can be expressed on a rating scale to give a clear B-1 diagnosis.

The diagnosis of B-1, B-2, and B-3 shows which of the three are problems and sets the stage for salespeople to get a handle on solutions that will work for them. Step 9 calls on salespeople to identify and talk about what is causing each of the problems that show up in the diagnosis. Becoming aware of the causes helps salespeople flow naturally into Step 10 and get a firm grasp on solutions they believe will solve their problem.

A Person's Motivation and Performance Will Be Strengthened If the Person Answers These Ten Questions (in the sequence indicated)

1. What is the problem?

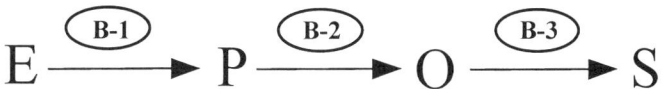

E —(B-1)→ P —(B-2)→ O —(B-3)→ S

3. What kind of effort would it take for *you* to perform as defined?	**2.** How do *you* define performance?	**4.** If you performed as defined, what outcomes would *you* get? **a.** Outcomes you want and expect to get? **b.** Outcomes you don't want but expect to get? **c.** Outcomes you want but don't expect to get?	**5.** How satisfying or dissatisfying would *each* of these outcomes be to *you*?
B-1 Diagnosis **8.** Can *you* perform as defined? (B-1) 0 5 10 ├────┼────┤ ***B-1 Cause*** **9.** What do *you* think is causing the problem? ***B-1 Solution*** **10.** What solution would work for *you*?		***B-2 Diagnosis*** **7.** Would these outcomes be tied to *your* performance? (B-2) 0 5 10 ├────┼────┤ ***B-2 Cause*** **9.** What do *you* think is causing the problem? ***B-2 Solution*** **10.** What solution would work for *you*?	***B-3 Diagnosis*** **6.** Overall, would these outcomes be satisfying or dissatisfying to *you*? (B-3) -10 0 +10 ├────┼────┤ ***B-3 Cause*** **9.** What do *you* think is causing the problem? ***B-3 Solution*** **10.** What solution would work for *you*?

The role of the sales manager, then, is not to solve motivation and performance problems their salespeople are experiencing, but instead to be sure they get solved by leading their salespeople through the problem-solving process of identifying problems, causes, and solutions that fit and will work for them. The idea is not for the sales manager to feel responsible for solving the motivation and performance problems of every salesperson, but rather to view salespeople as a resource for solving their own problems.

Behavior Style

Sales executives can well imagine the value of behavior style when managing to the individual. Just as being aware of behavior style helps salespeople motivate prospects to buy, the same awareness gives managers the same sharp edge when motivating salespeople to sell. A summary of behavior style and how to use it, based on the discussion in Chapter 3, follows.

Responding to Behavior Styles

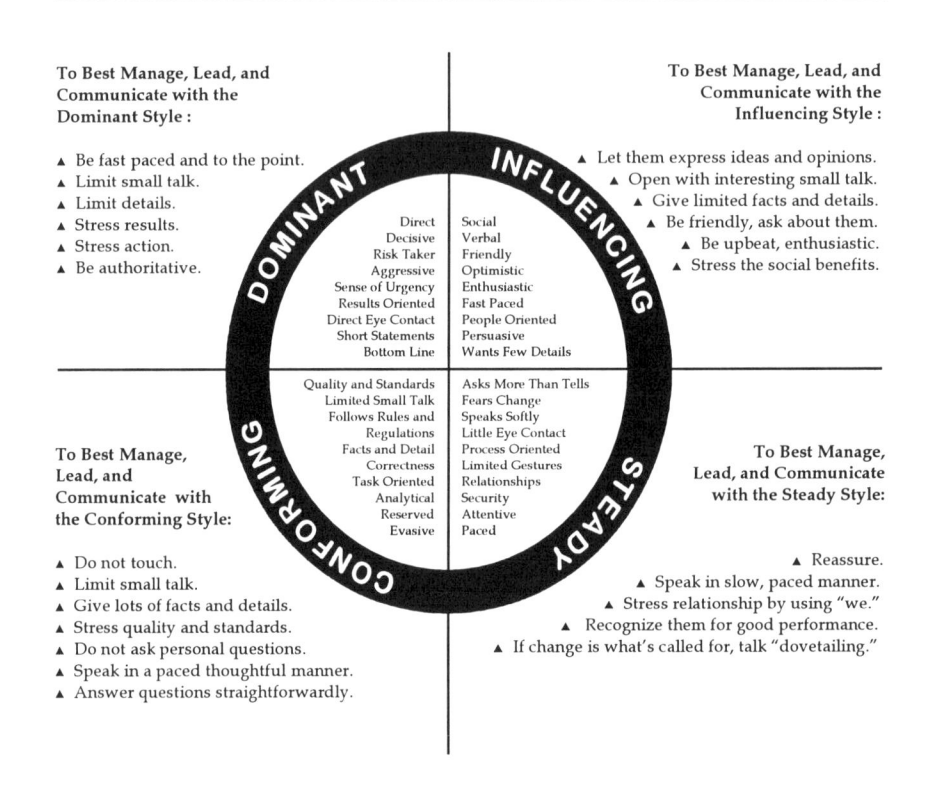

To Best Manage, Lead, and Communicate with the Dominant Style:

- Be fast paced and to the point.
- Limit small talk.
- Limit details.
- Stress results.
- Stress action.
- Be authoritative.

To Best Manage, Lead, and Communicate with the Influencing Style:

- Let them express ideas and opinions.
- Open with interesting small talk.
- Give limited facts and details.
- Be friendly, ask about them.
- Be upbeat, enthusiastic.
- Stress the social benefits.

To Best Manage, Lead, and Communicate with the Conforming Style:

- Do not touch.
- Limit small talk.
- Give lots of facts and details.
- Stress quality and standards.
- Do not ask personal questions.
- Speak in a paced thoughtful manner.
- Answer questions straightforwardly.

To Best Manage, Lead, and Communicate with the Steady Style:

- Reassure.
- Speak in slow, paced manner.
- Stress relationship by using "we."
- Recognize them for good performance.
- If change is what's called for, talk "dovetailing."

Dominant: Direct, Decisive, Risk Taker, Aggressive, Sense of Urgency, Results Oriented, Direct Eye Contact, Short Statements, Bottom Line

Influencing: Social, Verbal, Friendly, Optimistic, Enthusiastic, Fast Paced, People Oriented, Persuasive, Wants Few Details

Conforming: Quality and Standards, Limited Small Talk, Follows Rules and Regulations, Facts and Detail, Correctness, Task Oriented, Analytical, Reserved, Evasive

Steady: Asks More Than Tells, Fears Change, Speaks Softly, Little Eye Contact, Process Oriented, Limited Gestures, Relationships, Security, Attentive, Paced

Sales executives may choose to, by now, decide to incorporate behavior style into the leadership of the sales organization. Two steps. Go ahead and decide to do it and then prepare sales managers and the sales force to use it.

The Belief System of Motivation and Performance™

A recent track record of success in sales organizations shows that the most effective approach to motivate salespeople to sell calls for the sales manager and salesperson to share the responsibility. This takes the full burden off the sales manager, relieves some of the pressure, and makes the task easier and more effective. Look at it this way. Motivating salespeople is a big and complex job, too big and complicated for a sales manager to do alone. Sales executives get the picture. They are very much aware that sales managers sense and feel the enormity of this part of their job. Sales executives are in touch with the fact that every salesperson is different and motivational preferences and roadblocks vary from one person to another. Motivating salespeople to sell means getting inside their hearts and minds and getting a glimpse of what they are thinking, feeling, and believing. Short of this, sales managers are left to play a guessing game, a game they can't win. The odds are stacked against the sales manager when it comes to deciding what to say, and what to do, to unleash the motivational potential in each salesperson. Sales executives will feel good, maybe even euphoric, and can relax knowing it doesn't have to be this way.

There is a solid solution to this problem, tried and tested in major corporations since 1991, that clearly makes it possible for sales managers to quickly get in tune with each and every salesperson and paint a complete and accurate picture for how to truly motivate each salesperson to sell. The solution sounds too good to be true, but empirical data, to be presented shortly, clearly demonstrate its soundness and give a sense for the powerful results that are just a grasp away, if decision makers choose to use it. The solution, called The Belief System of Motivation and Performance™, is a way of managing to the individual that finds its soundness in the combination of its theoretical underpinnings,[1] application model,[2] and implementation methodology.[3] The theoretical and application models were shown in Chapters 1 and 2 in the context of motivating people to sell and in Chapters 9 and 10 as applied to self-management. The implementation model is presented as follows.

The implementation model is designed so salespeople will feel comfortable enough to come to the sales manager and share the information needed for the sales manager and salesperson to work together to maximize the salesperson's *motivation to sell*. The implementation model is a hands-on approach with four major components: (1) 2-Day Learning Session with the full sales team, including the sales manager; (2) One-on-One Session between manager, salesperson, and a trained facilitator; (3) Team Meeting after all one-on-ones are completed; and (4) Follow-up One-on-Ones.

The 2-Day Learning Session takes the view that changing behavior and improving performance requires both learning and persuasion. The learning element is intended to give the sales team a clear picture of basic principles of motivation and performance and a good sense for how they relate to them personally. Essentially they hear about and get a feel for: (1) B-1, B-2, and B-3; and (2) how to diagnose their own motivation and performance problems, recognize the causes, and come up with solutions that will work for them. The persuasion element takes two directions. It focuses first on convincing salespeople to be willing to share information about themselves with their manager so together they can get a handle on how to best create an environment that will remove barriers, build bridges, and strengthen the salesperson's motivation and performance as much as possible. Just as salespeople have to be persuaded to open up and talk to their sales manager, managers must be convinced to be open and hear what their salespeople have to say. The learning and persuasion sets the stage to flow smoothly into the next stop in the implementation model, the One-on-One Session.

It should be stressed that in the weeks that follow, the most important step in the implementation model takes place as the sales manager meets individually in One-on-One Sessions with each salesperson, along with a trained facilitator, to talk and share as they were persuaded to do, and apply what they learned, in the 2-Day Learning Session. This coming together follows thoughtful preparation on the part of both parties, much of which is put on paper and exchanged at the beginning of the discussion for each to see. The view that both take during the preparation focuses on motivating the salesperson to sell. During the actual discussion, the salesperson talks about, and the manager listens for, what motivates the salesperson and what can be done to strengthen the motivation to sell and improve sales performance. The role of the facilitator, who also led the 2-Day Learning Session, boils down to promoting open and honest communication, keeping the discussion on track, and, in general, leading the interaction toward decisions and solutions that will motivate the salesperson to sell and perform better.

At the end of the several week period when all One-on-One Sessions have been completed, a team meeting is conducted to bring closure to, and get a feel for, all that has taken place to date in the process.

Implementation Model for The Belief System of Motivation and Performance™

1. **2-Day Learning Session**

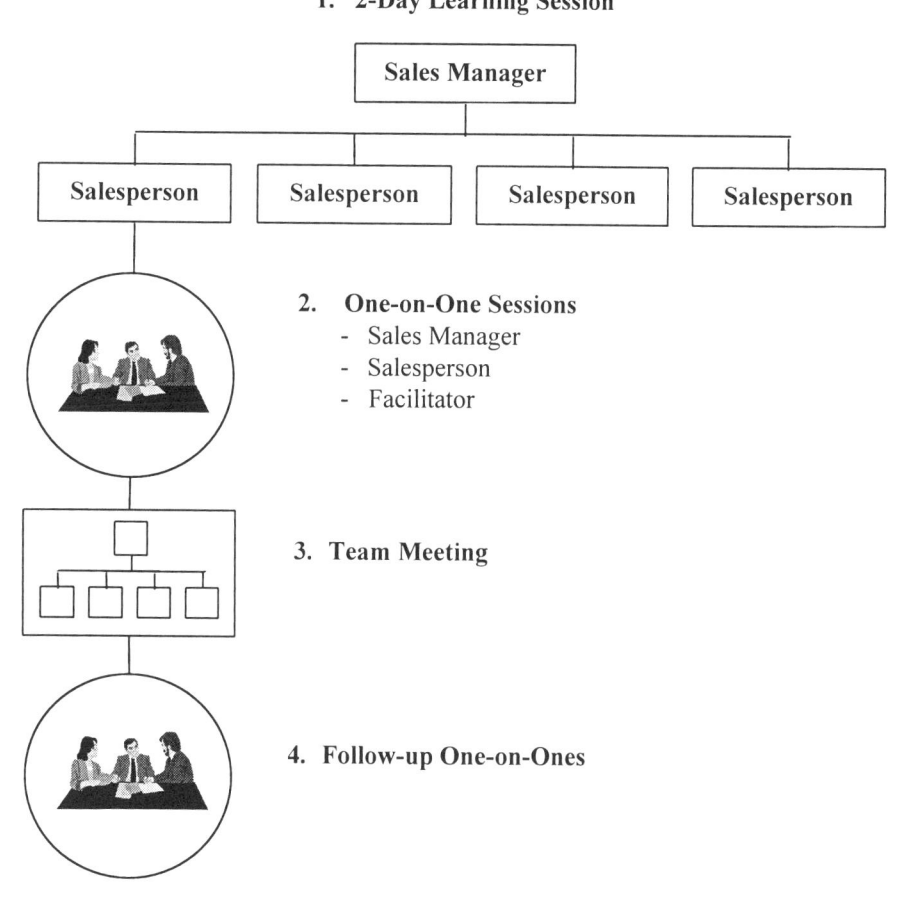

   Sales Manager
   - Salesperson
   - Salesperson
   - Salesperson
   - Salesperson

2. **One-on-One Sessions**
   - Sales Manager
   - Salesperson
   - Facilitator

3. **Team Meeting**

4. **Follow-up One-on-Ones**

Several things happen in the team meeting: (1) the facilitator talks about common themes heard in the One-on-Ones; (2) the team hears the facilitator make recommendations for changes and improvements to both the sales manager and the salespeople; (3) all team members and the sales manager are called upon to share what they are working on as a result of their One-on-One, actions they have taken, and results they are seeing; (4) the salespeople give feedback to the sales manager regarding progress they see on commitments made during the One-on-One, and the sales manager makes the team aware of noticeable progress the salespeople have made on their commitments; and (5) decisions are made about next steps each person will take to ensure a solid continuation of forward progress in managing to the individuality of each salesperson.

Four to six months later, Follow-up One-on-One Sessions are conducted primarily as a forum to stress and focus on accountability. This is an opportunity to hear about progress both manager and salesperson have made on commitments flowing out of the previous One-on-One Sessions. Decisions are made for getting back on track whenever progress falls short on hard and firm commitments and expectations. The session also is used to focus on any new issues that either manager or salesperson wants to talk about. Sales teams often feel a need and find it helpful to periodically schedule additional Follow-up One-on-One Sessions.

This implementation model for managing to the individual has been tested in numerous sales organizations. The results clearly point out the positive impact that managing to the individual has on sales performance. The bottom line is that approximately 81 percent say that, as a result of this approach, they are performing better, and their managers confirm it. Any intervention that improves sales performance in eight of every ten salespeople is enough to cause any sales executive to stand up and take notice, and maybe even send out a call for help to this way of managing to the individual and decide to do it because it works and improves sales results. Sales executives, this is in your hands. Decision making is the name of the game and the question is whether or not this is a decision you want to make.

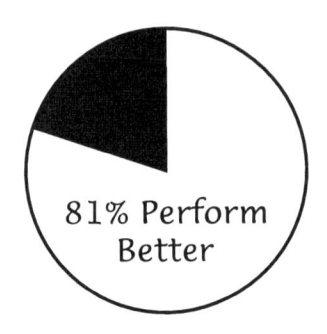

81% Perform Better

WHAT LIES AHEAD?

Sales executives, you can see that you hold the future firmly in your hands and you are left to, if you want to, choose the right course of action. The right course is to call on the resources available to you, the resources you know will help, and make the future what you want it to be. You can, if you will, decide what lies ahead. You may be wondering if you are ready to, by now, go ahead and decide to take the next step and turn performance up a few notches in your organization. You have thought about it and probably can imagine that you are ready to make the right decision. If you will, just imagine the benefits you will receive. Think about it. With the right decision, see what you will see, hear what you will hear, feel what you will feel, and use that impetus to go ahead and call on whatever or whomever you need to do it.

Getting Unstuck

If your sales organization is like most, it is in the grip of rapid and constant change, but you also are aware that in some respects it is stuck with the same old thinking and same old way of doing certain very important things, like holding a hard line on training and keeping it at the bare minimum to reduce cost and keep salespeople in the field, assuming salespeople have a sense for figuring things out on their own (they usually can't) and that they can and will get on with the work to be done (they usually don't), firmly believing that the cream will rise to the top (it sometimes does) and ignoring the needs of everyone because of this belief (not a good decision), overlooking (a major mistake) how much help people need to strengthen their skills and bolster their motivation to sell, and the list goes on. As a sales executive, you may feel like this is the right time to get some things unstuck and do something about it.

Do Something Different

Can you feel the competition getting tougher? Do you want to see your sales managers lead and solve problems more effectively? Would you like to hear that your salespeople were more focused, more goal oriented, and managing themselves better? Would you like to see better results? If so, then you need to do something different. Continuing to do things the same way will continue to produce the same results. The message is clear. If you are not getting the results you want, you need to do something different, and perhaps you are ready to, by now, just do something different.

You Can Do It

Just do it, because you can. You already see that you can prepare salespeople to motivate prospects to buy. You have a good feel for how to prepare sales managers to motivate salespeople to sell. Prepare your people. Equip them. Motivate them. Because, when you think about it, you know you can. Reap the benefits. You can. Make it work. Decide to do something different, because you can, because you will make it work, because you want to, because it is the right thing to do. You are ready to, by now, get the results and benefits you want. Anything is possible when you call on the resources available to you, if you will.

SUMMARY

- There is a need for sales executives to get a clear and firm focus on and prepare and motivate salespeople to sell.

- Sales executives will find it helpful to get a close and conscious look at the many barriers they face in preparing salespeople to sell and not be swayed in the wrong direction by them, and instead just go ahead and prepare the sales force to sell.

- Sales executives need to get a good sense for the kind of preparation salespeople need, and how to provide it, and decide to move in the right direction so it will pay off.

- Managing to the individual is viewed as the most effective approach for discovering how to motivate salespeople to sell.

- Empirical data show that the best way to get a handle on managing to the individual is to use a structured implementation model.

- Sales executives, you are ready to, by now, get the results and benefits you want. Anything is possible when you call on the resources available to you, if you will.

NOTES

1. Thad B. Green, *Performance and Motivation Strategies for Today's Workforce: A Guide to Expectancy Theory Applications* (Westport, Connecticut: Quorum Books, 1992); and Victor H. Vroom, *Work and Motivation* (New York: John Wiley & Sons, 1964).

2. Thad B. Green, *Performance and Motivation Strategies for Today's Workforce: A Guide to Expectancy Theory Applications* (Westport, Connecticut: Quorum Books, 1992); and Thad Green and Merwyn Hayes, *The Belief System:*

The Secret to Motivation and Improved Performance (Winston-Salem, North Carolina: Beechwood Press, 1993).

3. Thad Green and Bill Barkley, *Manage to the Individual: If You Want to Know How, ASK!* (Atlanta, Georgia: The Belief System Institute, 1995).

Index

Active listening techniques: paraphrasing, 97-98; responding to feelings, 101-102; responding to nonverbal messages, 99-101; restating, 99; summarizing, 98-99
Anticipating questions, 72-75
Attainable goals, 209-211

Behavior style: anticipating questions by behavior style, 72-75; behavioral tendencies of each style, 30-35; and closing the sale, 141-151; comparing behavior styles, 28-29; and confidence building, 192-193; determining behavior style, 30; and follow-up, 173-176; four styles defined, 26-28; and motivating people to sell, 232-233; and "no," 90-91; and prospecting, 65-68; and the sales interview process, 117-125; the sales model and behavior style, 37-39; selling to behavior style, 35-37; and stalls, 87-88

Behavioral tendencies, 30-35
Belief-1 defined, 7
Belief-2 defined, 7-8
Belief-3 defined, 8
Belief System of Motivation and Performance, implementation model, 233-236
Belief System Selling™: the model, 5-7; the process, 227-228
Buyer remorse, combating, 168-170

Clarifying questions, 95-96
Close, defined, 130
Closing: agreements, 152-155; asking prospects to buy, 151-152; dealing with reluctance, 132-138; defined, 130; how, 141-151; techniques by behavior style, 142-151; when, 138-141
Confidence building: and behavior style, 192-193; and self-management, 193-194

Diagnosing buyer beliefs, 14-20
Direct questions, 94

Follow-up: and buyer behavior style, 173-174; that customers like, 172; defined, 160; necessity, 160-162; overcoming reluctance, 162-167; purpose, 160-162; reluctance, 162-167; and the sales model, 172-173; and salesperson behavior style, 174-176; summarizing actions, 155-156; ways to, 167-171

Goals: attainable, 209-211; measurable, 206-209; motivation, 215-216; multiple, 214-215; overcoming resistance, 198-204; problems, 211-215; sales contests, 213-214; specific, 205-206; stretch, 212-213

Listening: active listening techniques, 97-102; anticipating the need, 97

Manage to the individual, 229
Measurable goals, 206-209
Motivating people to sell: behavior style, 232-233; the Belief System of Motivation and Performance™, 233-236; manage to the individual, 229; ten-step formula, 229-232
Multiple goals, 214-215

"No": and behavior style, 90-91; handling, 89-90; meaning of, 89

Objections, anticipating, 75-84
Open questions, 92-94

Paraphrasing, 97-98
Preparing people to sell: barriers, 220-222; how to prepare them, 225-227; what to prepare them for, 222-225

Prospecting: and behavior style, 65-68; overcoming reluctance, 43-48; reluctance, 43-48; and the sales model, 64; and the sales process, 49; steps, 51-64

Questions: anticipating by behavior style, 72-75; clarifying, 95-96; direct, 94; open, 92-94

Reluctance: to close, 132-138; to follow up, 162-167, to prospect, 43-48
Responding to feelings, 101-102
Responding to nonverbal messages, 99-101
Restating, 95

Sales contests, 213-214
Sales interview process: and behavior style, 117-125; and the sales model, 125-127; steps, 105-117
Sales model: and follow-up, 172-173; the model, 5-7; and prospecting, 64; and the sales interview process, 125-127; and the sales process, 50-51
Sales process: and behavior style, 51; steps, 49
Self-management: and confidence building, 193; equipping people, 194; model, 180-182; and positive self-talk, 191-192; problems, 182-186; solutions, 186-189; special problem, 189-194
Self-talk, positive, 191-192
Selling to behavior style, 35-37
Solving B-1, B-2, B-3 problems, 21-24
Specific goals, 205-206
Stalls: and behavior style, 87-88; handling, 86-87; interpreting, 85-86; recognizing, 84-85
Summarizing, 98-99

About the Author

THAD B. GREEN is the founder and principal of The Belief System Institute, a Center for the Advancement of Motivation and Performance in Atlanta, Georgia. Considered the foremost authority on motivation and performance in the United States, many corporations, such as AT&T, Lucent Technologies, Delta Air Lines, and Metropolitan Life Insurance, seek his expertise.